Reading and Writing Pathways through Children's and Young Adult Literature

This thought-provoking book will provide student teachers, teachers and researchers with a toolkit and theoretical framework for teaching literacy through children's and young adult literature. It features innovative ideas for developing student and teacher experiences with literature and popular culture texts in the classroom, providing practical examples and teaching aids throughout.

Taking a collaborative approach, Curtin explores how teachers and learners can engage with literature and its authors for the development of literacy in classroom practice. Connecting reader and writer identities and worlds through interviews with and suggested classroom activities from authors themselves, this text combines author, teacher and learner perspectives in the development of creative pedagogies that extend understandings of literacy beyond reading, writing and text.

Exploring fairy-tales, comic books and graphic novels; children living in literature (i.e., texts which portray children, their lives and experiences); popular culture; young adult fiction and non-fiction and digital texts such as blogs etc., this text develops a sociocultural understanding of literacy as a lived and contextually dependent practice where meaning is derived through relationships between people, settings and culture. Different contexts for literacy are explored, including reading and writing strategically (to learn about literacy and literature), widely (for personal purposes) and deeply (to transform understanding) (Short, 2011).

This text is an invaluable resource for teachers, researchers or anyone interested in reading and writing stories. The author interviews will also be of particular interest to older learners as a way to develop their understanding of their own reading and writing practices. Pedagogies can be adapted to any age group, ranging from the early years to young adult.

Alicia Curtin is a Lecturer and Programme Director of Education Gaeilge at the School of Education, University College Cork, Ireland, and researches and writes in the areas of learning, identity, assessment, neuroscientific perspectives on literacy, creative approaches to pedagogical design and innovative pedagogical research methods. Her work employs sociocultural theories to problematise and explore these central aspects of learning in ways highly relevant to education, teaching and our understanding of learning itself in all of its forms, inside the classroom and beyond.

Reading and Writing Pathways through Children's and Young Adult Literature

Exploring literacy, identity and story with authors and readers

Alicia Curtin

LONDON AND NEW YORK

Cover image: Getty images

First edition published 2023
by Routledge
4 Park Square, Milton Park, Abingdon, Oxon, OX14 4RN

and by Routledge
605 Third Avenue, New York, NY 10158

Routledge is an imprint of the Taylor & Francis Group, an informa business

© 2023 Alicia Curtin

The right of Alicia Curtin to be identified as author of this work has been asserted in accordance with sections 77 and 78 of the Copyright, Designs and Patents Act 1988.

All rights reserved. No part of this book may be reprinted or reproduced or utilised in any form or by any electronic, mechanical, or other means, now known or hereafter invented, including photocopying and recording, or in any information storage or retrieval system, without permission in writing from the publishers.

Trademark notice: Product or corporate names may be trademarks or registered trademarks, and are used only for identification and explanation without intent to infringe.

British Library Cataloguing-in-Publication Data
A catalogue record for this book is available from the British Library

Library of Congress Cataloging-in-Publication Data
A catalog record has been requested for this book

ISBN: 978-0-367-82100-5 (hbk)
ISBN: 978-0-367-82101-2 (pbk)
ISBN: 978-1-003-01354-9 (ebk)

DOI: 10.4324/9781003013549

Typeset in Bembo and Helvetica Neue LT Std
by KnowledgeWorks Global Ltd.

Acknowledgements

I would like to thank sincerely and deeply the contributing children's and young adult literature authors for sharing so openly and honestly their reading and writing stories, experiences, practices and ideas. To Cethan, Deborah, Joan, Judi, Kevin, KJ, Máire, Margaret, Marita, Michelle, Neal, Patricia, Paul, Roddy, Shaun and Todd: thank you for your time, interest and engagement with this text and the potential reading and writing identities, experiences and worlds of its readers.

I would like to thank Kathy and Mary for sitting me down and telling me that I should write this text. Thank you Kathy also for helping me understand literacy and learning as I now come to explore it in this text. Thank you to everyone in the School of Education at University College Cork for your constant and heartfelt encouragement, support and stories about literacy and learning. Understanding literacy as a sociocultural practice you will no doubt recognise yourselves in various spaces and places within this text.

Finally thank you to Willie John, Joan, April and Barry for making this journey with me.

Contents

List of interviews xiii
List of boxes xv

Introduction 1

Going with the tiger: Reading and writing strategically, widely and deeply

PART I
Reading and writing strategically to learn about literacy and literature

1 Understanding reading and writing as multimodal literacies: Mapping literary and literacy pathways through text 13

About this chapter 13
About the authors 14
Introduction 15
Multimodal pathways through the intuitions of childhood and young adulthood: Understanding text as a visual object, multimodal event and sociocultural artefact 18
From breadcrumbs to story fragments: Mapping the worlds of Shaun Tan through an understanding of reading, writing and mode as strategic personal tools for thinking and meaning making 24

*Reading and writing picture books and multimodal texts:
    Exploring intermodal and intramodal meaning in the
    emotional portraits and parallel stories of Margaret Wild* 41
Conclusion 51

2   Exploring multiple perspectives on reading and
    writing in culture: Arts as storied inquiry into
    aesthetic literacy and personal identity practice   56

   About this chapter 56
   About the authors 57
   Introduction 58
   *Aesthetic moments and strategic reading and writing in
       cultural stories: Observing and transforming literacy practice* 60
   *Exploring the work of Patricia Forde through inquiry-
       based approaches to reading and writing in culture:
       Literacy as a cognitive, psychological, linguistic,
       sociocultural and socio-political act* 64
   *Writing our lives as storied works of art: Arts-based
       inquiries as a theoretical lens for exploring identity
       and affect in the work of Máire Zepf* 76
   Conclusion 90

PART II
Reading and writing widely for personal purposes

3   Reading, writing and genre as personally resonant and
    sociocultural practices: Telling the human
    story of literacy as personal and social practice   97

   About this chapter 97
   About the authors 98
   Introduction 100
   *Understanding narrative and genre as frameworks for
       personal interpretation and social action within
       personally resonant and sociocultural reading and
       writing practices* 102
   *Narrating inner stories and relational identities: Text as
       a complex and flexible personal meaning making
       machine and the work of Todd Hasak-Lowy* 107

*Genre and (auto)biography as personal learning artefacts
for making the familiar strange in the scripts and
stories of Paul Fleischman 118*
Conclusion 129

4 Reading and writing for pleasure in reciprocal and
affinity-based story communities: Exploring digital
literacies, humour and authentic spaces for the sharing
of stories   133

About this chapter 133
About the authors 134
Introduction 135
*Affinity spaces for reading and writing for pleasure:
    Digital literacy in reciprocal reading and
    writing communities 136*
*From readers to writers: Exploring the stories of Joan
    Holub through fan fiction and remix in virtual and
    physical affinity spaces 141*
*The poems are told for you: (i)Poetry, parody and comedy
    in reading and writing for personal purpose and the
    poetry of KJ Shapiro 155*
Conclusion 165

PART III
Reading and writing deeply to transform understanding

5 Reading and writing through the lenses of critical
literacy, social justice and historical perspective:
Cultural, social and historical contexts for literacy and
identity   173

About this chapter 173
About the authors 174
Introduction 176
*Real world interventions as literacy practice: Connecting
    critical literacy, social justice and identity 178*
*Going deeper into history through narrative nonfiction:
    Learning as identity, critical literacy and social justice
    in the stories of Deborah Heiligman and Michelle Markel 182*

> From knowing to interpreting the past as an extended
>   present through historical fiction: Historical literacy
>   and social justice in the work of Marita
>   Conlon McKenna 194
> Conclusion 204

6 Culturally sustaining reading and writing practice:
    Engaging with funds of knowledge and popular
    culture literacies to negotiate curriculum design with
    learners   209

> *About this chapter 209*
> *About the authors 210*
> *Introduction 211*
> *The value of literacy in funds of knowledge-based*
>   *culturally sustaining pedagogies 213*
> *Exploring funds of knowledge and literacy values:*
>   *Collaborative explorations of authentic language,*
>   *culture and personal experience in the work*
>   *of Roddy Doyle 217*
> *Sharing words and worlds of experience in the work*
>   *of Judi Curtin: Popular culture and Negotiated*
>   *Integrated Curriculum (NIC) 224*
> *Conclusion 233*

7 Reading and writing about dark knowledge:
    Exploring alternative ways of knowing through
    philosophy, psychology and mental
    health literacy   237

> *About this chapter 237*
> *About the authors 238*
> *Introduction 240*
> *Exposing dark funds of knowledge as threshold concepts*
>   *for literacy and learning: Exploring school and*
>   *lifeworld knowledge and ways of knowing 241*
> *Communities of inquiry for reading deeply to transform*
>   *understanding: Philosophically oriented real*
>   *encounters with our world in the work of Kevin Brooks 243*
> *Authentic ways of knowing and deep funds of pedagogy:*
>   *Connecting education, emotion and lived experience*
>   *in the work of Neal Shusterman 253*

Living with dark knowledge within: Positive pedagogies for Mental Health Literacy and well-being and the work of Cethan Leahy 264
Conclusion 276

Index *281*

List of interviews

Five minutes with Shaun Tan	24
Five minutes with Margaret Wild	43
Five minutes with Patricia Forde	65
Five minutes with Máire Zepf	77
Five minutes with Todd Hasak-Lowy	108
Five minutes with Paul Fleischman	118
Five minutes with Joan Holub	144
Five minutes with KJ Shapiro	157
Five minutes with Deborah Heiligman	183
Five minutes with Michelle Markel	187
Five minutes with Marita Conlon-McKenna	197
Five minutes with Roddy Doyle	217
Five minutes with Judi Curtin	224
Five minutes with Kevin Brooks	245
Five minutes with Neal Shusterman	255
Five minutes with Cethan Leahy	268

List of boxes

From story fragments to multimodal maps: Exploring reading, writing and mode as tools for strategic and personal multimodal literacy development	38
Reading and writing multimodal text: Strategies for personal and collaborative intramodal and intermodal meaning making	49
Reimagining learners as art, story and word collectors: Reading and writing in culture through literary landscapes and literacy self-portraits	74
'Writing' beyond the blank page, upside down stories and imagination workouts (Written by Máire Zepf)	85
Strategic writing as inquiry into ourselves: The arts of learner lives	89
Voice and Narration in Children's and Young Adult Literature: Engaging with literacy as personal and social practice	116
Reader's theatre and writer notebooks: Listeners as co-narrators of the story	122
Experiments in genre and authentic language: Sociocultural frameworks for personal and social literacy practice	126
Narrating (auto)biography and life stories to interpret experience through a focus on the human aspects of literacy	128
From readers to writers: Exploring fan fiction and remix in affinity spaces and reading for pleasure communities	153
Writing widely for personal purpose: Humour, parody and (i)Poetry	164

Interrogating past and present experience through
narrative nonfiction, critical literacy and social justice:
Connecting real people, places and worlds   191
Participating in history through reading
and writing – Demystifying and dramatising
historical fiction and literacy   202
Funds of knowledge and culturally sustaining pedagogies:
Exploring our words and worlds through authentic
language and literacy practice   222
Popular culture and Negotiated Integrated Curriculum:
Researching ourselves, our worlds and the meanings of
childhood   231
Encountering difficult knowledge and experience
through philosophy and inquiry: What is time – The most
unreliable narrator of all to experience? (Philosophy with
a Big and little P)   251
Authentic learning contexts for deep funds of pedagogy:
Reimagining education through the lenses of emotion
and lived experience   262
Positive pedagogies for Mental Health Literacy:
Repurposing classroom literacy to normalise personal
struggles and foster positive identity development   274

Introduction

Going with the tiger: Reading and writing strategically, widely and deeply

Literacy is a complex and multifaceted concept, a movable target in our attempts at definition. Snow (2004) broadly identifies in education literature and research two divergent understandings of literacy. The first understands literacy as an instructed skill technically achievable by individuals in schools and classrooms in ways that are fixed and can be measured according to separate and specific component skills. The second imagines literacy as a social and cultural practice emerging and felt in and through particular literacy contexts and human relationships. Every day in classrooms teachers make choices about, plan for and define literacy in particular ways based on personal understandings of literacy and its position within these two divergent views. Engaging in these kinds of pedagogical decisions it is important to remember that how we choose to understand and define literacy matters, as language (just like literacy itself) is not only representative, but "frames the world, so that in particular ways the world becomes available to us" (Webb, 2011, p. 120).

In his short story *Cinnamon* Gaiman (2017) captures some of the mystery, magic and emotion at the heart of meaningful literacy practice in his retelling of an unsettling encounter between a young princess who does not speak and a man-eating tiger. This encounter takes Cinnamon beyond the boundaries of her world to new and imagined ones as language, feeling, emotion and experience connect in powerful ways in their unusual communication. For Gaiman (2017) literacy and stories are felt experiences, lived in the moment in ways that change our understandings of ourselves and our worlds.

'Pain' said the tiger, and it extended one needle sharp claw into Cinnamon's palm. It pierced her soft brown skin, and a bead of bright blood welled up. Cinnamon whimpered. 'Fear' said the tiger, and it began to roar, starting so quietly you could scarcely hear it, working its way up to a purr, then a quiet roar, like a distant volcano, then to a roar so loud that the palace walls shook. Cinnamon trembled.

'Love' said the tiger, and with its rough red tongue it licked the blood from Cinnamon's palm, and licked her soft brown face. 'Love?' whispered Cinnamon, in a voice wild and dark from disuse. And the tiger opened its mouth and grinned like a hungry god; which is how tigers grin.

(Gaiman, 2017, eBook)

This text understands literacy as an "open textured concept, meaning that the definition of literacy is constantly shifting dependent on its purpose, the people who use it and in what context it is consumed" (Freebody, 2007, p. 12). The term literacy itself represents, rather than any fixed understanding of reading, writing, speaking and listening, a socially contested site for learning where identified culturally valued skills sit embedded in the wide range of diverse practices that give them meaning. As Gee (1996) explains, definitions of literacy "ultimately comes down to moral choices about what theories one wants to hold based on the sorts of social worlds these theories underwrite in the present or make possible in the future" (Gee, 1996, p. 123).

This text defines literacy as a lived, sociocultural, value laden and contextually dependent practice where meaning is derived through relationships between people, settings and culture. Different social practices and human discourses facilitate and make meaningful specific literacy engagements as literacy is always about engaging in a particular way with a particular type of text or experience for a particular purpose. Reading takes on different meanings, for example, in the classroom, exam hall, bedroom or work place. As a result, literacy can only be fully understood in the unique context in which it is experienced and within the social, cultural, economic and historical practices of which it is a part.

Short (2011), applying this understanding of experience as situated to children's literature, asserts that "the opportunities that children have to read literature, the literature that is available, and the types of experiences children have with that literature shift along with the sociopolitical context" (Short, 2011, p. 55). Her discussion of how reading wars (Ylimaki and McClain, 2007) contest and politicise reading (and writing) spaces to such an extent that contemporary literacy research, literature and debate, particularly in the early years of education, are consumed not with how to teach reading but how best to teach phonics (Hall, 2007) forms the starting point for her exploration of the purposes of children's literature for literacy development. She argues that literature should not be seen as an accessory or add on but central to reading, writing and literacy practice in the classroom. She suggests that teachers play a key role in encouraging children and young adults to come to see literature as inquiry into life and integral to understanding themselves and their world. She believes that any literary text can "become a touchstone for literary understandings, political contestation, content knowledge and literacy strategies" (Short, 2011, p. 60).

Her identification of three distinct and different purposes of children's literature in the context of literacy education, namely reading strategically to learn about literacy and literature; reading widely for personal purposes; and reading deeply to transform understanding (Short, 2011), frame the discussion of literacy developed in this text. This text understands these purposes identified by Short (2011) within her own context of working with younger children as applicable to both children's and young adult literature. Each chapter of this text can be read independently and out of sequence (as can each author interview within) but together they develop a particular sociocultural perspective on the entangled and mutually constituting relationships between children's and young adult literature, literacy and learning.

The first part of this text, chapters one and two, explores reading and writing strategically to learn about literacy and literature. For Short reading strategically involves a pedagogical focus on two distinct yet mutually interdependent types of knowledge, namely literary knowledge and literacy knowledge. Literary knowledge refers to knowledge about literature as a narrative form, encompassing elements such as story, theme and language. Important here is not the identification of these and other story elements, but the understanding of how these elements influence the construction of meaning and story pathways within text. Within this perspective genre is understood as a flexible tool, rather than a prescriptive set of rules for meaning making. Literacy knowledge develops alongside literary exploration but focuses on reading and writing as processes and related literacy elements such as comprehension, sequence and vocabulary.

Strategic readers and writers develop simultaneously their literary and literacy knowledge through explorations of text focusing on the meaning making strategies of readers and writers and the many different reading and writing pathways offered within. Here and throughout this book, the word text is used in its broadest sense, to refer to anything that can be "read" or "written" to communicate meaning and includes written text, visual and moving imagery, oral and aural communication, digital representation, multimodal and aesthetic experiences and so on. These strategies for meaning making, identified collaboratively by learners and teachers in strategic reading and writing practice, encourage the development of personal repertoires for reading and writing, along with a desire to make reading and writing experiences a part of our own lives.

Chapter one explores diverse and authentic literary and literacy pathways within strategic reading and writing practice through a focus on multimodal literacies in the work of Shaun Tan and Margaret Wild. Reading, writing and mode are reconceptualised as strategic and personal tools for literacy development. New and emotional literacies are also considered in an interrogation of the complex relationships between reader, writer and text in children's and young adult literature. Keeping communication and meaning central this chapter understands reading and writing practice as supporting learners in the making of their own literary and literacy multimodal maps needed to help navigate later experiences and worlds outside of the classroom. Literary pathways are foregrounded in this first chapter as providing rich context for simultaneous literacy exploration.

Chapter two moves to look more closely at literacy pathways within the meaningful and authentic context of engagement with literary practice outlined in chapter one. Reading and writing as strategic processes are interrogated from multiple perspectives within their cultural contexts so as to better understand literacy as a shared and sociocultural practice. Inquiry based learning through the arts (incorporating modes such as dance, music, drama, poetry, mixed media and so on) across home, community and school settings is foregrounded along with the understanding that each of these cultural activities afford unique literacy pathways for reading and writing experience. Interviews with Patricia Forde and Máire Zepf reflect on the role of aesthetic and arts based literacies in the development of a multiple perspective inquiry approach to reading and writing strategically in the classroom.

The second part of this text, chapters three and four, explores how teachers can engage learners in reading and writing widely for personal purposes in and beyond classroom settings. Short defines reading and writing widely for personal purpose as involving not only personal enjoyment of reading, but social opportunities to share and become interested in a wide range of genres, authors and text. Choice and personal resonance (ranging from entertainment to deeper personal inquiry) are central to the reading and writing of texts that matter to learners from this perspective.

Reading widely has a range of benefits, including the promotion of positive attitudes about reading, the expansion of learner literary and literacy knowledge, the development of learner confidence in comprehension and interpretation, and the encouragement of lifelong reading and writing habits (Short, 2011). Reading widely involves immersion in stories and independent reading and writing pedagogies that extend reading, writing and literacy practice beyond school, and curricular settings and purposes. Read alouds are a central feature alongside many opportunities for dialogue based on different kinds of texts that ask learners to reflect on the meanings of reading and writing in their own lives.

Chapter three explores the human practice of literacy as learning through thinking and talking about ourselves, or telling our stories, in diverse personal and social contexts. Reading, writing and genre are reconceptualised as personally resonant and deeply sociocultural practices. The work of Todd Hasak-Lowy and Paul Fleischman exemplifies the many ways in which literacy is embedded in and inseparable from personal and social real world contexts and experiences.

Chapter four moves beyond traditional classroom contexts to explore opportunities for reading and writing widely for personal purposes within social reading and writing communities, such as affinity based and/or online spaces. Pedagogies for reading for pleasure, engaging with fan fiction, remix, parody and read aloud are developed through engaging with the stories and poetry of Joan Holub and KJ Shapiro.

The final part of this text, chapters five, six and seven, investigates collaborative opportunities for teachers and learners to read and write deeply to transform understanding of themselves and their worlds. Short defines this aspect of reading and writing practice as involving intensive critical inquiry into personal, societal, scientific and philosophical issues through texts that "have multiple layers of meaning, and challenge readers to linger longer over ideas, words, characterisations, setting descriptions and relationships among literary forms and themes" (Short, 2011, p. 61). Dialogue is encouraged during, rather than after, reading and writing practices. Curriculum content, learning intentions and purpose should be constructed with rather than delivered to learners in the classroom.

Chapter five explores reading and writing deeply to transform understanding through a focus on critical literacy, social justice and historical perspective in learning. Identity is foregrounded as a central theme in reading and writing deeply alongside stories of real people and/or true historical events in the narrative non-fiction and historical fiction texts of contributing authors Deborah Heiligman, Michelle Markel and Marita Conlon McKenna. Understanding our lives in the context of the lives and experiences of others this chapter affirms the effects of critical, social and historical literacies on personal identity and literacy development.

Chapter six continues an exploration of reading and writing deeply to transform understanding by examining opportunities for culturally sustaining reading and writing practice in the classroom with particular reference to funds of knowledge and popular culture literacies and contexts. Foregrounding the theme of co-constructing rather than delivering content and learning, this chapter investigates ways in which teachers can negotiate curriculum design with learners through Negotiated Integrated Curriculum (NIC), basing this negotiation on the many diverse ways in which learners themselves already engage with culture, language and literacy in every day contexts. Authors Roddy Doyle and Judi Curtin share their understandings and experiences of meaningful personal, community and cultural learning alongside their exploration of these key themes in their own work.

Chapter seven focuses explicitly on darker and more problematic knowledge and ways of knowing in its engagement with pedagogies for reading and writing deeply to transform understanding. Opportunities for engaging with philosophy, psychology and mental health literacy through children's and young adult literature are exemplified in the works of Kevin Brooks, Neal Shusterman and Cethan Leahy. In these works and the chapter itself lived experience is brought to bear on literacy, learning and identity in powerful and meaningful ways.

The depth and scope of understanding developing within these chapters would have been impossible were it not for the generous and insightful contributions from the children's and young adult literature authors acknowledged at the outset. Sincere thanks to each of you for your interest, time and engagement with this text and the ideas within. Without these contributions it would also have been impossible to achieve a key aim of this text, the closer connection of learner, teacher and author identities and worlds.

Exploring authentic reading, writing and literacy practices through the experiences of authors affords an evidence-based approach to engaging with children's and young adult literature for reading, writing, literacy and identity in the classroom. This addresses contemporary literacy trends that emphasise the importance of evidence based practice for literacy instruction in the classroom (Shanahan, 2003) and offers meaningful and identity affirming pedagogical alternatives for literacy to what Short (2011) terms the teaching of "isolated skills through hierarchical, sequential reading programs as stories are limited to excerpts in anthologies and controlled vocabulary stories for reading schemes" (Short, 2011, p. 49).

Each author interview includes lots of ideas for activities and related pedagogies for engaging with children's and young adult literature texts and key chapter themes from the authors themselves. These, and the other ideas for pedagogy and practice developed within this text, are not exhaustive and are meant only as starting points for thinking about opportunities afforded by children's and young adult literature to explore reading, writing, literacy and identity in the classroom. It is also important to note that in this text pedagogy itself is understood and developed as any practice that is or may be:

> salient to people as they engage in activity and develop competence in the practice in question… This deeper and broader notion of pedagogy, which is not confined to a particular place, setting, age or stage, draws attention to the identities which are variously valued, reproduced and transformed as people participate in activity. Whether the practice is in relation to becoming a reader, a learner of mathematics in school, a teacher, an architect, a hairdresser and so on, how the cultural practice is mediated by one's lived experiences becomes significant for one's ability to demonstrate oneself as competent and be recognized by others as competent in a given practice. Pedagogy involves an appreciation of the significance of experiences and meditational aspects as key to supporting learning.
>
> (Hall, Murphy and Soler, 2008, p. ix)

The bibliography of this text is separated by chapter so that readers may explore strategically, widely and deeply any chapter and particular named themes within that resonate with their own experiences. Readers will also find in this section a bibliography of the children's and young adult literature texts explored in this book along with additional lists of other suggested children's and young adult literature texts particularly apt for experimenting with key themes and ideas from each chapter.

As we journey through the storied landscape of children's and young adult literature and its three identified purposes for literacy education, it is important to remember that engaging with literacy in the classroom is more than just reading or writing the words. As Rhees (2006) explains, literacy is an act imbued with meaning as when someone learns to speak he or she does not:

> just learn to make sentences and utter them, he learns to say something. He learns what can be said; he learns what it makes sense to say… And because he learns to speak, and he learns what can be said, he can go on speaking and go on learning
>
> (Rhees, 2006, p. 29)

Returning to Cinnamon's intensely experienced and intimately felt sensuous encounter with a man-eating tiger at the beginning of this introduction, a metaphor for the peril and promise of the strategic, wide and deep literacy practices developed in this text, affirms this sociocultural understanding of meaningful literacy practice as moving beyond reading and writing words, to emphasise the power of story, identity and lived experience in literacy and learning.

'I can talk,' said Cinnamon. 'I think I always could.' 'Then why didn't you?' asked her mother. And Cinnamon said, 'Why not? Because I had nothing to say.' 'And now?' asked her father. 'And now the tiger has told me of the jungle, of the chattering of the monkeys and the smell of the dawn and the taste of the moonlight and the noise a lakeful of flamingos makes when it takes to the air,' she said. 'And what I have to say is this: I am going with the tiger.'

(Gaiman, 2017, eBook)

Introduction bibliography

Freebody P. (2007) *Literacy Education in School: Research perspectives from the past, for the future.* Canberra, Australia: Australian Council for Educational Research.

Gaiman, N. (2017). *Cinnamon.* UK: Bloomsbury Children's Books.

Hall, K. (2007). Literacy policy and policy literacy. In Openshaw, R. Soler, J. (Eds), *Reading across International Boundaries: History, policy and politics* (pp. 55–70). Charlotte, NC: Information Age,.

Hall, K. Murphy, P. Soler, J. (2008). *Pedagogy and Practice: Culture and identities.* UK: Sage.

Rhees, R. (2006). *Wittgenstein and the Possibility of Discourse.* Zephaniah, D. (Ed.). Philips. Malden, MA: Blackwell Publishing.

Short, K. (2011). Reading literature in elementary classrooms. In Wolf, S. Coats, K. Enciso, P. A. Jenkins, C. (Eds.), *Handbook of Research on Children's and Young Adult Literature.* Routledge.

Snow, C. (2004). What counts as literacy in early childhood? In McCartney, K. Phillips, D. (Eds.), *Handbook of Early Child Development.* Oxford, UK: Blackwell Publishers.

Webb, S. (2011). Selecting television programs for language learning: Investigating television programs from the same genre. *International Journal of English Studies, 11*(1), 117–136.

Ylimaki, R., McClain, L. (2007). Curriculum leadership and the current politics of US literacy education. In Openshaw, R. Soler, J. (Eds), *Reading across International Boundaries: History, policy and politics* (pp. 71–86). Charlotte, NC: Information Age.

PART

Reading and writing strategically to learn about literacy and literature

CHAPTER 1

Understanding reading and writing as multimodal literacies: Mapping literary and literacy pathways through text

About this chapter

This chapter explores literary and literacy aspects of strategic reading and writing practices for learning about literacy and literature through a focus on multimodal literacies and the reconceptualisation of reading, writing and mode as strategic and personal tools for literacy practice. Understanding reading as the active mapping of unique literary and literacy pathways through text readers and writers work together to cocreate meaning based on alternative perspectives and varied experiences. Multimodality is defined and explained, and pedagogies and activities that focus on multimodal literacy are exemplified through selected children's and young adult literature texts and author interviews. These multimodal (textual, aural, linguistic, spatial and visual) texts are discussed through the lens of multimodal, new and emotional literacies. Opportunities for multimodal reading and writing projects with learners that focus on understanding the complex relationships between reader, writer and text; and interpretation, knowledge and imagination are outlined. Picture books, as an example of multimodal text, are discussed, with a dual focus on potential author and illustrator literary and literacy pathways available within for strategic narrative development. Reading and writing pedagogies for engaging with picture books with younger and older learners in the classroom are also explored.

About the authors

Shaun Tan

Shaun Tan is a part-Chinese, Irish and English artist, writer, illustrator, director, theatre designer, concept artist and filmmaker. His work incorporates a variety of media and modes including writing, drawing, painting, sculpture, found objects and photography. Shaun has won innumerable national and international awards for his unique storytelling art including an Academy Award (Oscar) in America, the Astrid Lindgren Memorial Award in Sweden and the Kate Greenaway Medal in the UK.

Shaun's picture books are not written specifically for children and explore relationships between different modes of expression in meaning making and storytelling, where transformation through questioning is central. His website (www.shauntan.net) provides detailed information about and sample extracts from his work, comprising of text, image, video and sculpture. This chapter explores but a small selection of some of these texts and their possible purposes for exploring literacy in the classroom.

The Lost Thing, an Academy award-winning short film and picture book, tells the story of a boy's quest to find a place for a lost creature, the appearance of which no one else in the city seems to notice. *The Arrival*, a wordless graphic novel, explores what it feels like to be new and alone journeying through an unfamiliar world. *The Red Tree* presents a fragmented journey through the lighter and darker spaces of our mind, combining images and words in powerful and unsettling ways. *The Singing Bones* takes the fairy tales of the Brothers Grimm as inspiration for multimodal representations of the very essence of each tale, familiar and strange. *Tales from the Inner City* is an anthology of tales set in the imaginative and surreal world of nature, each story focusing on a different animal and its relationship with humanity past and present. In *Rules of Summer* each two-page image spread can be read as a chapter of a story, telling of an event and lessons learned.

Margaret Wild

Margaret Wild, born in South Africa and later immigrating to Australia, has worked as a journalist and book editor and is now a full-time writer. Her writing includes picture books, verse novels and novels, in which she experiments with meaning created through intersections of image, word, shape, thought and text. Margaret has won a plethora of awards for her writing including the Nan Chauncy Award and the Lady Cutler Award for her contributions to Australian children's and young adult literature. Most recently she has been awarded the 2020 Australia Council Award for Lifetime Achievement in Literature.

Margaret's writing explores themes of friendship, bullying, death and loss through unusual imagery, characters, language and form. Working in partnership with illustrator Ron Brooks, her picture book *Fox* appeals to a universal audience in its minimalist portrayal of the darker side of friendship, love and the human experience. *The Dream of the Thylacine,* a second Wild and Brooks collaboration, is a dream like lament to freedoms lost and a desire to return to a place long past but never forgotten. *Jinx* explores in verse the people, places and experiences in Jen's life, a young girl trying to make sense of her world and herself.

Introduction

The last century has seen significant shifts in the understanding and practice of literacy in our daily lives. More and more frequently images rather than words are used as a mode to communicate meaning with the screen replacing the page as the dominant medium for this communication to a wide variety of private and more public audiences (Kress, 2003). As a result in our everyday experiences multimodal and collaborative literacy practices enable individuals to develop and represent their knowledge in a wide variety of different ways. These developments in our everyday literacy practices posit learners as active and agentive literacy users, developers and creators with the purpose of meaningful communication at the core of literacy practice. Thinking about how younger learners may be supported in the development of these new literacies through literature Myers (2014) explains that:

> [Children] see books less as mirrors and more as maps. They are indeed searching for their place in the world, but they are also deciding where they want to go. They create, through the stories they're given, an atlas of their world, of their relationships to others, of their possible destinations… When kids today face the realities of our world, our global economies, our integrations and overlappings, they all do so without a proper map. They are navigating the streets and avenues of their lives with an inadequate, outdated chart, and we wonder why they feel lost.
>
> (Myers, 2014, p. 2)

These new literacies challenge classroom contexts to reinvent traditional school-based modal conventions to include new, multimodal and collaborative literacy practices, and suggest that classroom literacy emphases on language and words alone are incomplete. Wohlwend (2017), for example, evidences how formal school literacy practices result in some materials, modes and meanings becoming unavailable to learners in classrooms. She suggests instead that a pedagogical focus on collaborative play and exploration involving multiple modes, materials, spaces and textual forms affords learners opportunities to actively engage in authentic study of communication and, more specifically, the intertextual and intermodal relationships between texts, thoughts and experiences in the world.

Understanding literacy as strategic and successful engagement in meaningful, varied and diverse multimodal communication in our everyday lives is a central aspect of the conceptualisation of literacy developed in this text. Through the metaphor of maps this chapter explores experiential (literary and literacy) pathways through text, suggesting that a multimodal literacy focus in the classroom encourages learners to read, write and communicate authentically and differently, using a variety of unique modes, media and meanings. Building on Short's (2011) first purpose for children's and young adult literature in the context of literacy, the first two chapters of this text explore reading and writing strategically to learn about literacy and literature, focusing closely on the intertwined literary knowledge of narrative forms (such as understanding of story, themes and language) and literacy knowledge of textual structures and reading and writing processes (such as understanding comprehension, decoding skills and vocabulary). Understanding literary and literacy knowledge as interdependent and mutually constituting this chapter focuses more closely on literary knowledge and related pedagogical approaches and activities involving mapping literary (but necessarily also literacy) story pathways through text while the next chapter foregrounds literacy knowledge in our exploration of strategic reading and writing practices across a wide range of arts-based literacies in the classroom.

Strategic readers and writers reflect closely and collaboratively on their textual knowledge, using both cognitive and social processes for constructing meaning. As learners share stories and experiences in this way in classroom contexts, they choose their own pathways, drawing their own semantic maps and multimodal understandings of literature, literacy and learning through literature relevant to and made from their own life experiences, previous histories and imagination. This active and authentic engagement with multimodal literacies is essential for learners if they are to be able to create the kinds of multi-layered maps (and develop the kinds of multimodal literacies) they will need to navigate their worlds beyond the classroom in the future.

Worlds within texts are neither real or imaginary, they are representations offering ways of seeing and thinking about experience that can be remade from alternative perspectives. Engaging with multimodal literacies learners and teachers work together to identify new literary and literacy paths and opportunities for learning rather than meandering down old ones, using familiar texts and experiences to imagine new trajectories for learning and experience. Designing related pedagogies for learning teachers first need to understand that sharing a text in the classroom really means sharing a wide variety of different and unique literary and literacy story paths, as not all learners will experience the text in the same way. This chapter uses multimodality to explore some of these many different possible experiential pathways offered by texts and considers related pedagogies and activities for classroom practice.

Interrogating the complex and entangled relationships between texts, readers and authors, a recurring theme in this text, a multimodal literacy focus supports learners in understanding the many voices (including their own) present in text as well as imagining how they might voice their own stories in the future. As Shaun Tan, one of the children's and young adult literature authors contributing to this chapter tells us, "artists, writers, and readers are all thing-finders. We have some sense of direction but don't really know what's at the end of the journey; we walk beside our readers, not in front of them" (Tan, 2015, p. 112).

Multimodal pathways through the intuitions of childhood and young adulthood: Understanding text as a visual object, multimodal event and sociocultural artefact

Jewitt's (2008) multimodal understanding of reading across a variety of different cultural forms including textbooks, computer games and online websites, highlights the many different ways in which readers remake a text as they journey through it. As Jewitt (2008) explains:

> students need to learn how to recognise what is salient in a complex multimodal text, how to read across the modal elements in a textbook, how to move from the representation of a phenomenon in an animation to a static image or written paragraph, and how to navigate through the multiple paths of a text… Along with the choice of what mode to read, the structure of many [digital] texts opens up options about where to start reading a text – what reading path to take.
>
> (Jewitt, 2008, p. 259)

The understanding of multimodality as a theoretical and analytic lens for making sense of communication in terms of the many different and complex ways (or modes) individuals convey a particular message to others offers an active and reader centred starting point for developing multimodal literacy focused pedagogies in the classroom.

Multimodal texts experienced in our daily lives employ more than one mode (socioculturally shaped resources for meaning making, e.g. poetry, sculpture, photography, painting, dance) to make meaning (Kress, 2010) and require an understanding of multimodal or multiple literacies to interpret their intricate and interconnected messages. The concept of mutiliteracies was first developed by the New London Group (1996) as a response to multimodal understandings of communication and meaning making in changing cultural, physical, spatial and technological contexts for literacy.

A multiliteracy approach understands literacy as continual, supplemental, and focusing on enhancing or modifying established literacy teaching and learning (Rowsell, Kosnik & Beck, 2008). To this end multimodal literacies are fluid and plural repertoires of and for experience and encourage teachers to continually respond to and include in classroom pedagogies modes, media and multimodal literacies that learners are familiar with from out of school contexts.

Multimodal literacy practices also understand that language (as well as all other modes of meaning making) is itself partial as many modes of meaning making interact with readers and viewers in the kinds of multimodal texts and communications we encounter daily in our lives. Images in modern day texts, for example, do not simply illustrate the words. Elements within these images work spatially and simultaneously to make their own meanings later interpreted by the reader alongside textual, linguistic and sequential representation. The mode of film offers further differentiated opportunities for meaning making and interpretation, including movement, sound, speech, time and special effects.

Engaging in multimodal literacy practices in the classroom involves an exploration of how meaning is strategically produced through these texts intramodally (within modes) and intermodally (across modes) (Unsworth, 2006) and then in turn interpreted uniquely by individual readers and viewers. Modes interact with each other in ways that can change or modify the meanings inherent in each mode (Lemke, 1998) and meaning is not itself located solely in any one mode. Pedagogical approaches focusing on multimodal literacies involve strategies for exploring the integration of modes, media and knowledge alongside an understanding of the importance of the personal and emotional strategic interpretation of texts by individuals in the reading process.

Focusing closely on story interpretation strategies Serafini (2015) suggests that a central aspect to the development of multimodal literacy is our reconceptualisation of text as a visual object, a multimodal event and/or a sociocultural artefact. Viewed through these alternate lenses multimodal texts offer teachers and learners opportunities to discuss representations and interpretations of texts and the ways in which texts are produced strategically in sociocultural, political and historical contexts. Kress et al.'s (2001) ethnographic study for example reveals how different modes of representation in the science classroom (image, writing, three-dimensional model, computer CD ROM and the internet) affords very different learner constructions and interpretations of a cell, science and learning itself. As Jewitt (2008) explains:

> Each of these representational forms makes different demands on the learner. There was also evidence that different modes have different potential effects for learning, the shaping of learner identities, and how learners create pathways through texts. The choice of mode, then, is central to the epistemological shaping of knowledge and ideological design. What can be done and thought with image or writing or through action differs in ways that are significant for learning. In this regard, the long standing focus on language as the principal, if not sole, medium of instruction can at best offer a very partial view of the work of communicating in the classroom.
> (Jewitt, 2008, p. 256)

Jewitt (2008) here asserts that the modes and media through which knowledge is represented shape both what is to be learned (the curriculum content) and how it is to be learned (pedagogy and practice), explaining how classroom knowledge is shaped through teacher choice of some modes over others and the consequent affordances and constraints (Gibson, 1977) to learning and practice. Understanding the classroom itself as a multimodal environment she suggests that teachers and learners should take great opportunity to interrogate the ways in which all modes and media (multiliteracies) feature in the classroom. Her understanding that each mode offers particular and varying affordances and constraints in terms of both expression and interpretation allows teachers to think about literacy planning in new ways and underscores the significance of strategic modal (and textual) choice for learning about literacy and literature.

Kress and Jewitt (2003) present a possible framework for classroom interrogation of multimodal texts and multiple story paths in their definition of multimodal literacy as an understanding of the multimodal concepts of materiality, framing, design and production. Designing opportunities for engaging with multimodal literacy in the classroom begins with teacher and learner collaborative exploration of each of these four aspects of multimodal literacy and opportunities within each for reading and writing strategically to learn about literacy and literature, outlined in brief here.

Materiality refers to the intentional representations of meaning inherent in the materials from which the text itself is produced.

Important here is the understanding that the combination of modes to make meaning is a conscious and careful act on the part of the author and is motivated by a relationship with the reader. Materiality acts to stabilise individual representation and interpretation in ways that ensure textual messages are culturally defined and understood as possible literary and literacy pathways become recognisable within text. Kress explains further that different cultures express themselves in many different ways. While these meanings share similarities, their mode of expression across cultures varies. Thus modes are always situated within specific cultural, social and historical contexts in ways discussed in detail in part three of this text. Exploring the materiality of texts with learners connects closely with literacy aspects of strategic reading and writing practice, as it asks learners to consider how precisely and from what materials, ideas and understandings of experience the text itself is made. Interrogating a text in this way reveals new and multi-layered literary and literacy pathways through the story.

Framing, the second aspect of multimodality, considers more carefully how precisely the selected materials are used intramodally (within modes) and intermodally (across modes). The reader is encouraged to think about how elements of a composition may connect or disconnect to and from each other in a variety of structural, visual or semantic ways. Looking at the relationships between and across modes within text, learners are asked to consider how the story and its material elements are framed by its author in personal and cultural ways that combine individual literary and literacy aspects (or pathways) into the unique telling of a cohesive story, a narrative that offers a meaningful and communicative exchange between reader and writer.

Design, the third aspect of multimodality, encourages readers to think about conceptual aspects of expression to imagine how they and the author understand key textual messages, processes, themselves and the world. Readers may consider for example what affordances and constraints any type of expression facilitates (personally, historically and culturally) and how authors design text within (and outside of) these boundaries.

Finally, the understanding of the fourth aspect of multimodality, production, encompasses exploration of the creation and making of the text itself and the skills and techniques available to the author within his or her chosen modes for expression. In his interview Shaun exemplifies this well in his explanation of how different modes offer unique opportunities for imagination, creativity and storytelling.

Applying these multimodal concepts to our exploration of strategic reading and writing practice to learn about literacy and literature, teachers are encouraged to engage in collaborative reading and writing practices and discussions around individual interpretation and experience. Janks and Comber's (2006) Arndale Alphabet project exemplifies many of the key ideas of multimodal literacy-based classroom approaches and focuses closely on both literary and literacy pathways through text. In this multimodal project two culturally and geographically different class groups created alphabet books based on their own personal and neighbourhood experiences, available materials, designs and lessons in framing, each imagining the other class group as audience for their book. As a result literary and literacy practices and pathways across both communities were not just shared but explained, developing in many ways each of the participants' own individual and collective literacy resources and understandings.

Janks and Comber also highlight how this multimodal literacy project employs particular multiliteracy pedagogical approaches through a focus on four key multiliteracy components – situated practice (engaging learners in activities focusing on their own personal and community histories); overt instruction (teaching of key multimodal concepts in the moment to highlight opportunities for literacy and learning development); critical framing (the exploration of messages in texts from multiple perspectives); and transformed practice (taking our personal or shared understandings and placing these in juxtaposition with alternative understandings from different cultures and contexts) (New London Group, 1996).

A further multiliteracy focus on learner engagement through the exploration of personal multimodal histories and interests in the context of other people's stories, histories and cultures as evidenced in this project supports learners in ways that better prepare them to negotiate meaning making systems in the world beyond their own immediate personal, local and cultural contexts. Teachers could use this multimodal literacy research project as a model for designing their own similar projects across different class groups or schools.

Combining a variety of modes, multiliteracies and multiple meanings in this way, Jewitt (2008) suggests that using multimodal texts in the classroom can encourage learners to engage in nuanced, multiple and strategic readings and interpretation of text. Similarly, a focus on multimodality can encourage learners to explore new arenas for writing and expression, such as for example online spaces and fan fiction websites (explored in more detail in the second part of this text) where learners can experiment with a range of different identities – learner, writer, reader, editor. For Jewitt engaging with multimodal texts in the classroom affords teachers opportunities to connect more closely with the resources that learners themselves bring into the classroom through learner literacy worlds and their interests, experiences, resources and designs for learning.

Marshall's (2016) study of counter storytelling through graphic life writing with young adults evidences how "as writers and illustrators tell their coming of age stories in text and image, they call attention to alternative landmarks, lead readers to previously undiscovered locations and provide a new mapping of familiar experiences" (Marshall, 2016, p. 79), opening up new literary and literacy pathways for readers and writers. Additionally, this study suggests that engaging in explicit teaching about a range of different modes (or strategies) for storytelling may facilitate the development of multimodal norms and grammar similar to those existing currently for language. From this perspective a multimodal literacy pedagogical focus helps teachers reflect on and better understand reading and writing differences in the classroom as:

> how teachers and students use gaze, body posture, and the distribution of space and resources produces silent discourses in the classroom that affect literacy. Multimodality offers teachers the potential to reflect on their pedagogic use of the resources of their body, to critique and redesign these aspects of their practice.
> (Jewitt, 2008, p. 263)

The following principles from Larson and Marsh (2014) highlight the key literary and literacy aspects explored thus far in this chapter underlying a multimodal literacy pedagogical approach and are summarised here to focus the exploration of children's and young adult literature texts in the remainder of this chapter.

- Meaning making involves the use of a range of modes, not just language (Kress, 2010).
- Modes are socially, culturally and historically situated (Kress, 2010).
- Multimodal design involves intentional use of the modes that are to hand in any given context (Kress, 2010).
- There is a motivated relation between signifier and signified (Kress, 1993).

- The affordances of modes are not fixed but are situated in specific contexts of use (Kress, 2010).
- Children from a very young age produce multimodal texts that draw on modes in intentional ways (Kress, 2010).
- Analysing children's multimodal communication can provide additional insights into their learning that a sole focus on language would mask (Flewitt, 2013).

From breadcrumbs to story fragments: Mapping the worlds of Shaun Tan through an understanding of reading, writing and mode as strategic personal tools for thinking and meaning making

FIVE MINUTES WITH SHAUN TAN

You suggest that some of the traditional constructs we employ to organise and make sense of our experiences in and with the world, such as, for example, culture, family, nature, language and belief, could be better understood as ways of thinking, being and talking based in part on historic and geographic happenstance. Could you tell us a little more about your ideas here and what this might mean for our understanding of learning?

I'm no expert in anthropology but I am interested in cultural differences according to time and place, and what this tells us about our humanity. Perhaps we can't even know that humanity much without those relative differences, those alternative ways of being, different kinds of family, language, relationship to nature, social value and so on. Underneath all of our cultural constructs I do think there are some universal principles, and maybe those are genetic or otherwise fundamental, such as to do with being a thinking, sustaining, social creature. Things like love, compassion, a desire for fairness and law, but also fear, greed and other feelings that can be alternatively destructive or protective. It's all a big riddle – a fascinating one, in which things are both constructed and 'natural' for want of a better word.

I think there's also a lot of contradictory things that make us who we are, and that this troubles us but also drives us forward, is the basis for a lot of art and culture. How does this relate to teaching and learning? Maybe by looking more at differences and contradictions than similarities and consistent principles? I can only really speak with any confidence about art and literature, and I think the main thing there is to look at mixed feelings, at the inner conflicts that always seem present in any really good story or image. In my own work, I'm interested in stories that can be simultaneously positive and negative, that are somewhat ambiguous. Mainly because I think that's an accurate reflection of real life. I think for teachers and students being aware that any human values might be relative rather than absolute is important. That things could always be different, and that there may well be no such thing as 'normal'.

Could you tell us about how the ideas of literacy, meaning, imagination and experience blend for you in an understanding of reading?
I think the most simple way I like to discuss this is to consider the approach I take to fine art, that is, looking at paintings and visual images, which we also 'read' but maybe in a less prescribed way. My experience as an art student was that many works were quite obscure (especially contemporary art, but also art from any other period or culture) and were not always accessible by trying to 'read' them. I often lacked knowledge, theory, cultural experience. Alternatively, I found the act of very knowledgeable deconstruction left me a bit cold (as an Arts student), so that sometimes being able to 'read' a visual work really well in terms of ideology, technique, cultural context and so on was interesting but not moving.

I came to the conclusion that reading was more effective for me if it began first and foremost as self-reflection. That is, how does the work make me feel, and what does it make me think about. But the feeling is primary, and the same goes for written text. How it makes you feel is the necessary passage to meaning, either through thought or further research, and imaginative speculation. I felt that simple realisation was left out of a lot of my art and literary education. I like to think that the best critical literary involves not just asking questions of the text, but asking questions about yourself – to recognise yourself as the repository of all meaning, the source of all initial interpretation.

You state that your aim as a maker of text is to provide strange but compelling elements that draw narratives out of the reader. Could you tell us a little more about what you mean here? Based on this understanding, what for you are the key ingredients of a good story?
A good story just presents a series of interesting questions. It might be as simple as what happens next. I've noticed this again acutely when

reading or telling stories to my young daughter. She wants to hear about a weird problem first and foremost, and how that is then resolved, or better yet, gets even more problematic. Adult tales are the same. We love conflict and surprise, thwarted expectations, humour, luck, misfortune – basically the unexpected. There are a lot of other ingredients needed for a good story, including things like deeper metaphorical meaning or emotional resonance, but the key thing is that it sounds interesting, is unusual and yet still relates with real-life experience very well.

That's also true of a good illustrative image (by which I mean something that is more or less representational and narrative, a picture that tells a story, or a bit of a story). It should be interesting, unusual (often the same thing) and remind you strongly of something real. Real people, places, situations and feelings. But it must be strange in some way. Not too clear, but not too obscure. And I think not obviously resolved. An image that creates a feeling of curiosity, asks a kind of interesting question, and then leaves it for the reader to answer those feelings and questions, to imagine what the situation might be, who the characters are, what they might be feeling, what comes next or came before. And then, only later, perhaps what it all means (to the reader). I suppose it is a process of inviting the reader to ask as many interesting questions as possible, and then to seek their own answers, based on individual reaction and experience. Setting the stage to make the reader's experience a sufficiently complex and rewarding one – testing myself as a reader first to see if it works.

In terms of process with writing and illustration, for me it's a lot of trial and error. My drafts waiver between being too obscure or too obviously 'meaningful', and I'm trying to achieve something balanced in between. A story and/or image with enough for the reader's imagination to work with, but not too much that it becomes overwhelmed by strangeness or detail. I'm not sure there's an easy recipe or technique for this, but I know when something's working, and try lots of different sketches and drafts to get there.

Your stories are unusual in that they exist in multiple places, times and forms (books, films, paintings, exhibitions, apps, sculptures and theatres) and all narrate aspects of your tales in a variety of genres, modes and media to a variety of audiences. What opportunities does this multimodal approach to storytelling afford you as an author?

I never set out to work in different modes or media, but rather opportunities presented themselves and I was invited, often by others, to explore them. Film in particular is not something I've actively pursued, but have been a willing participant when asked to be involved by a producer or an art director. The same goes for the app, theatre adaptations and some exhibition and painting projects. My 'default' mode is probably landscape painting, and this may be the basis of all the other work, the thing I was most interested in during my adolescence.

So does a story change through transition between media and modes? Yes, a little, although I would suggest that I don't work in such a broad circle. For instance, the book *The Lost Thing* was inspired by film as much as illustration and adapting the story back into film was relatively straight-forward, conceptually if not technically. The biggest difference is the collaborative nature of film. It's several artists cooperating together. I learnt early on that being a good director is about letting other artists express themselves within the context of a given story. So the creative process is very different. I suppose the visualisation and meanings adjust a little too.

At the moment I've been working on a prospective adaptation of *The Arrival* as a possible TV series, and there are quite a lot of differences there, making concessions to a very different form, length, level of content. There are a lot of commercial and logistical considerations that are outside of creative problems, but certainly determine the ways in which creative problems might be set out and solved. And the story necessarily changes. But my main interest has always been the creation of a world conceptually and stylistically, and that is often highly adaptable. That is, once you know the kind of metaphor that a story is, the general stylistic approach, level of reality or displacement from reality, use of language and so on, you can change the story and still preserve the spirit of the original metaphor. It's a way of telling more than what's actually told that is most important.

Different media, especially film, offer a unique opportunity for sound, music and movement that's not available to me as a writer or illustrator. At the same time, the picture book offers a wonderful silence and slowness not available to the world of film and theatre. You can work with or against the strengths of either. I generally find myself returning to books and painting, my favourite media, I think because that silence and slowness is the most appealing to my particular imagination. It feels closer to something eternal, or endlessly open to interpretation. I notice that my books are often used by all kinds of students as the stimulus for creative writing exercises (for the same reasons that they are adapted by theatre companies quite often – they welcome adaptation and interpretation). Many of my stories are essentially incomplete, or only partially narrated, such as *The Red Tree*, *The Arrival* or even *The Singing Bones*. I'm very interested in story fragments as you can tell, and encouraging the reader to build on those.

You state that you feel like a translator of ideas as you work and that you are fascinated by imaginary and unreadable languages. What kind of an understanding of language do you see developing in your work? Does your work speak in one multimodal language/voice or many (text, image, object, intertextuality)? You talk about the idea of borrowing the language of objects such as old pictorial archives and family photo albums to tell your stories. What kinds of language do things have for you? How do you make these objects speak to you and to readers in your work?

That's a hard one to answer, because I work pretty intuitively. I guess comics, for instance, have a certain visual language, but I'm not sure how much of that is cultural convention and learnt, and how much is universal. Visual composition is a kind of language, lines and shapes, at least as I'm aware of it when drawing, akin to music. The arrangement of pictures is a language I suppose.

I tried to make *The Arrival* as universal as possible, for instance, to appeal to all readers, but it's hard to know if it entirely succeeds. I 'wrote' the book fairly intuitively and without an overall conceptual plan, I just put pages together in ways that worked most effectively, based on my own limited experience of film, television, comics, photo albums, museum displays, all the ways in which sequential pictures are organised into stories. I'll leave it to others to decide whether this is multi-modal or any other thing. All I can say is that I draw on a lot of visual sources, and then respond intuitively, with trial and error sketches and arrangements, often using cut-out elements. I often realise how it works later, but at the time of creation I'm not thinking much in terms of theory, just whether something feels right or seems like a good idea. The feeling of rightness is a kind of truth, that the work feels believable, as if it could be a real memory on the page, even though it clearly is not.

Your website is extremely comprehensive and you are very generous in your sharing of all aspects of your works with your readers, including in depth notes on individual texts. This unparalleled access to your strategic thinking and work behind the scenes, alongside supports for understanding reading, writing and illustrating, would allow teachers an excellent opportunity to complete an author study of you and your work in the classroom. Would you have any ideas for questions or activities that learners could use to guide their exploration of your work as an author study?

I can only think of maybe encouraging students to write and/or illustrate short stories following the approaches set out in both my books and notes. I think this is very much how I learned to paint and write, by examining the work of other authors and painters, and trying to imitate their approach. Not their style, just the approach. For instance, the use of unnarrated images or prolonged silence, the use of poetic metaphor, certain view points and so on. Perhaps my notes on my website (which are there primarily for students) help this. In most cases, I've tried to show an accessible process, where ideas can come from, referencing ordinary experience, the importance of research into the lives of others, and just trying to communicate clearly and unpretentiously. I enjoy demystifying the creative process and reducing any fear a student might feel toward writing and illustration.

It's actually not too difficult to do, to generate interesting texts. Each image in *Rules of Summer,* for example, could be viewed as a unique story and chapter. One student suggested to me the line 'Never check your mail after midnight', and I thought that was a good one. A good trick is to take a known rule, and change some elements of it, to make it absurd, but essentially very similar. So, 'Don't forget to feed the cat' could be 'Don't forget to feed the crocodile.' The absurdism frees up your mind to imagine an unexpected consequence, more so with a crocodile than with a cat, only because cats are overly familiar. Avoid easy solutions. You're just trying to get your mind to work in an unfamiliar way, by using a fairly familiar template.

Some unused 'rules' that I had scribbled down for *Rules of Summer* that students could experiment with are 'Never run away from a car crash' and 'Always pack your lunch the night before' (familiar rules that can be illustrated in a surrealist way), and variations on the familiar, such as 'Never bargain with an animal'. Students could also make up and illustrate their own rules. Another good exercise is just to cut up words as surrealists and many writers have often done, and shuffle them out to create unexpected combinations. You'd be surprised how effective and amusing this is. Again, it's just trying to 'derail' your brain from its usual tracks, and go down a less familiar road.

Shaun's understanding of reading and writing aligns closely with the strategic reading and writing practices to learn about literacy and literature developing in this chapter. His interview blends closely emotional and critical aspects of literacy as he considers self-reflection as central to our walking of literary and literacy textual pathways within moments where readers are forced to ask questions of ourselves: What do we feel? What do we think? Where are we going and what pathway are we going to take?

Engaging with Shaun's partially narrated stories, readers need to create their own personal meaning and literary path, drawing on previous experiences, feelings and understandings through the evocation of new, emotional and multimodal literacy practices and perspectives. Moving through and between modes, narrators and authors, Shaun's work offers a rich and fertile literary and literacy landscape to be mapped as it is experienced. The terrain is passable but the reader has to make a journey down a "less familiar road" (Tan interview, 2020). Reminiscent of Hansel and Gretel's breadcrumbs, Shaun's story fragments suggest possible literary and literacy pathways for readers to explore, but though reader and author make the journey together, decision and responsibility for the road taken lies firmly with the reader.

In his paper for *The Iowa Review* Shaun interrogates openly his work and process as an author and artist focusing on the question of whether or not others see and feel the same things as he does. He describes how:

> My real world, like that of most artists and writers, is one of idiosyncratic play, purposeless daydreaming, and a love of simple and ordinary things operating at a very small scale, a furtive scale, uncertain of itself. It's also very private and solitary. When I'm working, I'm more or less temporarily marooned on a desert island, only fleetingly wondering whether my work will be strong enough to float, like a message in a bottle, and be able to travel any distance at all, to reach anyone… Can a story move beyond my own private imagination, pass across oceans of language and culture, be understood by adults and children alike, perhaps even those living in distant places I have never visited?
> (Tan, 2015, p. 101)

Shaun's questioning of his own "readability" provides rich context for exploring the importance of strategic reading and writing practices in the classroom, alongside developing our own definitions and understandings of story, reading, writing and literacy. Interesting for Shaun is the notion of whether or not a story can go where an author has not and still hold resonance and meaning for readers in new spaces. This questioning turns traditional reflection on reading and writing on its head, as rather than thinking about how a reader engages with a story Shaun is concerned with how a writer engages with a world, or many, known and unknown. Though for Shaun this concern comes later, the immediacy lies in the act of story itself. Here, in his image of himself marooned on a desert island in the moment of expression, Shaun understands and actively uses literacies available to him as personal tools for thinking, meaning making strategies and opportunities experimented with in private spaces, rather than public and more visible markers of success or failure in culturally valued literacy practices and skills.

For Shaun traditional cultural constructs such as nature, family, belief, language and other socially accepted norms around which we structure our lives in any given community could be better understood as flexible realities and strategic ways of thinking about and organising our world and experiences. The ensuing riddle when we try to understand ourselves from a perspective of difference through imagination and interpretation is at the heart of Shaun's multimodal storytelling as he explores this experience in worlds familiar yet strange, real and less real. Connecting clearly with strategic reading and writing practice and multimodal concepts of materiality and framing Shaun considers what this riddle making may require of an author and explains that in relation to his own craft:

> each work contains many thousands of ingredients, experiments, discoveries and transforming decisions executed over several months, compressed into a very small space, 32 pages of words and pictures. Everything can be explained in terms of process, influences, developmental elaboration and reduction. What is original is not the ideas themselves, but the way they are put together.
>
> (Tan, 2002, p. 1)

Exploring further this strategic understanding of reading and writing as tools for thinking and meaning making in classroom practice teachers could employ Shaun's artist notes (available on his website) as models to engage learners in the development of their own artist diaries as they reflect on their own stories, reading and written. Shaun's notes explore in depth the multimodal aspects of materiality, framing, design and production in relation to a large number of diverse modes of artistic and creative expression.

Shaun moves fluidly between modes as his understanding of reading and writing as tools for thinking and meaning making extends also to the modes themselves. For Shaun each mode (and available literacies within) can be used as a tool by strategic readers and writers to sift for meaning in everyday experiences, but just like the differences between a shovel, a rake and a hoe, each tool will allow us to complete different kinds of tasks in different ways. Understanding multimodal reading and writing practices strategically as tools to be used rather than skills to attain (or fail to attain) is an empowering and agentic understanding of reading and writing for learners. With tools at our disposal in strategic reading and writing practice, literacy takes on new meaning as something to be played and experimented with, dug up and sown anew as we learn more about the ground, or literacy itself, and ourselves in the process.

Drawing himself as the displaced main protagonist in *The Arrival*, though he has never left his home country, Shaun suggests that for many people a clear identity or connection to place is not innate and sometimes requires invention, like writing a story or drawing an image. Despite his sometimes bleak portrayals he explains that optimism and opportunity for new understanding are evident even in his darkest texts as "such stories open the possibility of grafting childhood curiosity back into an adult consciousness, as much as it encourages young readers to hold on to those things that fascinate them and never let them go" (Tan, 2015, p. 106). Shaun's conceptualisation of childhood itself as a multimodal experience where imagination continually tests itself against reality in a search for meaning and some kind of fit in small creative acts offers powerful insights for our development of multimodal pedagogical approaches in the classroom. As he explains:

> It's a mistake to believe that childhood is just a series of educational stepping stones, something to be experienced and left behind as we graduate into adulthood. It's more like a bag of things you take on a long journey, always being careful not to forget where you put them. Ideally, our experience of life is an accumulation of things, all of which remain readily accessible.
>
> (Tan, 2015, p. 107)

Here Shaun speaks to a funds of knowledge approach (Gonzalez et al., 2005) to pedagogy (explored in detail in part three of this text), where learners themselves are understood as resources in the classroom, bringing with them abundant knowledge in the form of funds of knowledge from previous experiences and participation in home and community settings. From this perspective our childhood and young adult experiences become our "bag of things", our own personally selected and uniquely shaped tools for literacy learning and meaning making.

Shaun's work also touches on the concept of dark funds of knowledge (Zipin, 2009) (also explored in part three), as his multimodal texts provoke complex reflections on a variety of potentially dark and difficult themes for the classroom. Shaun's description of literature as "a condensed organization of ideas, a calm bay of interpretation in an attention-deficit-disorder world of mass media…a self owned experience" (Tan, 2015, p. 110) defines a space for literature and stories in the classroom where imagination and flexible realities intersect as from the safety of these calm bays of interpretation stories can be explored, made, shared and discovered, asking questions strategically rather than offering answers to readers. As Shaun explains: "I often think of a good story, whether written, illustrated, filmed or spoken, as really being a beautiful question. The most beautiful questions are actually a little unsettling, because at their best they have no simple answer" (Tan, 2015, p.110).

For Shaun a successful strategic reader and co-creator knows that imagination is more important than knowledge and understanding. Similarly, a successful strategic author knows that "the question of meaning must remain open, carefully passed to the reader intact, like a delicate object preserved in a jar" (Tan, 2015, p. 114). The reader is central to the meaning making process here as Shaun does not want the reader to reflect on what he was thinking but, using their own personal tools, what they are. As he explains in his interview multimodal, imaginative and emotional literacies are more important than knowledge and understanding for identifying and mapping possible literary and literacy pathways through his work. This is because Shaun's texts draw narratives from the reader and stand as experiments, windows for learning to read and write strategically using a variety of different modes and media.

Shaun further explains how each of his characters themselves in fact may represent the reader, allowing us for a time to take a walk in a stranger, but not an unfamiliar, space, as like us "they live in a place where language and wisdom can only take you so far; the rest must be imagined and relearned, as if you are once again a child" (Tan, 2015, p. 115). Applying these understandings to classroom practice calls for pedagogies that facilitate opportunities for learners to strategically and authentically experience, feel and journey across literary and literacy pathways through text rather than "knowing" it.

Shaun's book and Academy Award-winning short film *The Lost Thing* asks many questions to readers about the relationship between strategic reading and writing practices, knowing and imagination. Exploring the theme of strategic reading itself, this text could be used in the classroom as inspiration and scaffolding for learners to develop their own definitions and tools for strategic reading and writing practice.

Shaun himself explains how the story represents two oppositional ways of, or strategies for, seeing, reading and understanding the world. In the first literacy and understanding is based on fixed definitions and familiar things, while the alternative takes the shape of the lost thing itself, a disruptive and confusing presence in a world where everything has its place. The lost thing is unable to be read by the inhabitants of the world who lack the critical imagination, creativity and experiences required to play its meaning making game. His journey through their city and world centres on the necessity from the point of view of one young inhabitant to find him his place, in a world where such strange and unusual things have been forgotten. His placement in the Department of Odds and Ends satisfies, to some extent, the expectations of the many, but behind the closed doors of this imaginative and inventive space nothing has its own specific place or reason to be, alluding perhaps to the freedom of the imagination where there are not always right and wrong answers.

The Lost Thing and its film adaptation have been a focus of many multimodal literacy classroom research studies and offer myriad opportunities for the exploration of multimodal literacies and related pedagogies in the classroom. Dallacqua, Kersten and Rhodes (2015), for example, develop a number of activities for exploring modes and meaning in story based on these texts. Focusing on a number of different multimodal elements within (including audio, spatial, gestural, visual and linguistic aspects), they suggest a series of questions that could be used to guide and draw attention to reading and writing as strategic tools for thinking and meaning making in the classroom.

The Lost Thing, along with other pieces of Shaun's work, afford readers guided opportunities to strategically reconceptualise texts and stories across a variety of modes as visual objects, multimodal events and sociocultural artefacts (Serafini, 2015). Classroom discussions and projects asking learners to move fluidly within and across modes using reading and writing as personal and meaning making tools support learners in their identification and understanding of strategic literary and literacy pathways through text.

It is very interesting that Shaun suggests that books (including pen and paper alternatives) are a favourite of his because of their silence and slowness in developing ideas. Elsewhere Shaun tells how he regularly paints small observational scenes reminiscent of late 19th-century Australian Heidelberg paintings on cigar box lids in an effort to strip reality bare to its raw elements. Understanding his role of artist as one of translator and transformer, Shaun explains" "I don't think I've ever painted an image as a reproduction of what I'm seeing, even when I'm working in front of it. I'm always trying to create some kind of parallel equivalent" (Tan, 2001, p. 1).

This is very evident, for example, in his multimodal text *The Singing Bones,* where he has condensed each Brothers Grimm fairy tale into "the DNA of the tale, the core that haunts people forever" (Tan, 2016, p. 7), unsettlingly represented by a single sculptural image and a few lines of text. Within these pages familiar stories become visual objects, multimodal events and sociocultural artefacts (Serafini, 2015) in ways that model for learners how they might recreate their own stories as texts in the same way. Understanding stories as made up of many different fragments, modes, voices and experiences offer Shaun and his readers opportunities for strategically constructing and deconstructing literary and literacy pathways in ways that focus in on small creative acts. Each story, question or idea begins at some point on the blank page or canvas and, as Shaun emphasises, each retelling does not reproduce but reimagines the tale in some personal and meaningful way.

Shaun's multimodal approach to the creation of textual literacy pathways through the strategic juxtaposition of story fragments and asking the reader to build on these exemplifies storytelling on a small scale, beginning with many small words, images and ideas based on past experiences and combining interpretations of these in a variety of modes in interesting ways. Shaun's discussion of his writing of *The Arrival,* a wordless graphic novel documenting the journey of an immigrant in a strange and incomprehensible land, exemplifies his fragmentary approach to story making as he draws on his experiences of film, television, comics, photo albums and museum displays (and related literacies within) to name but a few. Moving elements around the page authenticity is a feeling rather than an aim as Shaun engages his literary and literacy understandings to play with "things" to tell his story in a way that will be universally, yet differentially, understood.

Authenticity for the reader is also a feeling as he or she intuits through familiar and strange literary and literacy landscapes. Shaun explains that viewers look for an average of eight seconds but the goal of his multimodal expression is to make us look for longer than that. He explains further

> if I draw a dog playing with a ball I'd never write 'the dog was playing with the ball' I'd write 'the cat was hiding nearby'. There has to be a visual and contextual discrepancy between words and pictures…surrealism helps because people aren't sure what they're looking at and details get people to go on a journey.
> (Tan, 2020, online)

The Arrival and Shaun's supporting artist notes available on his website offer further rich opportunities for exploring in depth strategic literary and literacy aspects of text focusing on story making through nonlinear and multimodal fragments with a particular focus on themes such as meaning, identity, migration and place.

Objects take on special significance in Shaun's multimodal approach to storytelling and the question of what things really are. "Wanting to know more about the tree-ness of a tree, the bird-ness of a bird, or the house-ness of a house; to not be fooled by the deceptive simplicity of words or labels" (Tan, 2015, p. 108) is a mystery to be unravelled in Shaun's work. For Shaun his talent for visualising objects and things to capture their flavour is not an innate skill but an excitement and attraction. His understanding of a skill as something that works to keep up with this excitement, "the watering can you reach for when you think about a garden" (Tan, 2015, p. 108), affords further opportunity and agency to learners and teachers, to explore first the excitement of the literary aspects of strategic reading and writing within multimodal texts, later scaffolding these experiences with "the watering" of developing skills and talents in ways that connect to now contextualised literacy aspects. Beginning in the classroom with a set of objects, around and through which our stories can be told would afford learners opportunities to think strategically about story, content, narrative, language and structure from literary and literacy perspectives in new and unique ways.

Rules of Summer (written text and iPad app) explores the friendship between two boys as they journey through a series of challenging situations. This text is structurally very interesting from literary and literacy perspectives as though a story emerges there is no precise narrative, instead the images are presented alongside a series of mysterious rules (for example, never leave a red sock on the clothesline). Readers are challenged to identify and follow their own pathways through the text and recreate the story for themselves in ways that mirror closely understandings of strategic reading and writing practice explored throughout this chapter. Within this text, objects tell their stories and reveal deeper meanings behind Shaun's unusual regulations in a truly multimodal and layered reading experience. Shaun himself suggests that each image could be read as a "chapter of an unwritten tale that can only be elaborated in the reader's imagination" (Tan, 2020, online website).

Shaun suggests *The Red Tree* as a possible companion read to *Rules of Summer*, as it explores the strangeness and darker aspects of an individual's inner life through metaphor, feeling and emotion, rather than the strangeness of relationships and shared experiences. The literary narrative here develops in a strange and dreamlike sequence of thought provoking and fragmentary images and statements that offers alternative approaches to traditional literacy understandings of story structure and framing in the classroom. This text would also facilitate a multimodal exploration of emotional literacies in the classroom as its images and text illustrate the darkly complex inner feelings and experiences of a young girl who feels that "sometimes the day begins with nothing to look forward to" (Tan, 2010, *The Red Tree*, opening line).

Looking to our relationships with animals, *Tales from the Inner City* reinvents traditional fables in an exploration of tensions between natural and artificial worlds, real and imagined. Fragmenting realities of human and animal relationships and experiences this text connects to broader themes of survival, extinction and sustainability in unique ways through a multimodal lens. Standing itself as a study of ecology this text could be explored in the classroom to support learner understandings of our own place in the world and our relationships with each other and our various interconnected local, national and global environments.

The following activities could be used with Shaun's texts (including those not explored in this chapter) or others to promote multimodal literacy through a focus on strategic reading and writing to understand literacy and literature in the classroom. Engaging in these kinds of activities Shaun reminds us that:

> We must accept that children today find themselves confronted by a confusing mix of reality and processed reality; this is what we have to live with. It's not necessarily bad, and humans have always been living with chaos and noise, blended truth and falsehood. Personal creativity can allow us to make sense of it: drawing, writing, looking, and reading within a thoughtful, attentive space. This is how we can catch our breath, collect our thoughts, test our ideas, and inevitably figure out who we are in the process. This is how we create our own personal map of the world.
> (Tan, 2015, p. 109)

FROM STORY FRAGMENTS TO MULTIMODAL MAPS: EXPLORING READING, WRITING AND MODE AS TOOLS FOR STRATEGIC AND PERSONAL MULTIMODAL LITERACY DEVELOPMENT

- **Make your own film or create a book trailer multimodal project:** Learners are asked to choose a book or story to imagine they will turn into a short film. Teachers share some of the following questions and activities as possible entry or starting points for learners: Can you create a storyboard for your short film? What will you have to think about (for example music, sound, image, colour, symbols, framing, movement, characterisation, narration)? Can you sketch some of the characters to be animated? How will they move, sound, talk? Can you record some sound effects for your film? What about special effects? What would be the key visual features of your setting? Audience? What will be the main differences between the text and your short film? Choose one scene in particular and think about this in detail. What different real life professions do you engage in in this project (filmmaker, director, writer, concept artist, musical director, sound and special effects artist)? Which ones did you like? Why?

    This project can be individual or collaborative. Some of the questions included here are adapted from the Australian Centre for the Moving Image

(ACMI) *From Book to Film: Educational Resource,* which is freely available online and includes a huge variety of activities on *The Lost Thing*. Additionally their website https://www.acmi.net.au/education/film-it/ is aimed at young people wanting to make a short film and offers a fantastic step-by-step exploration of screen writing, shot types, camera angles, movement, storyboards, cinematography, visual effects, sound recording and editing.

- **Annotated spreads (Farrell, Arizpe and McAdam, 2010) as multimodal maps of strategic reading and writing practice:** Learners are asked to select a number of images from the work of Shaun Tan and annotate them with questions, comments, images and sounds in a focus on close reading and the making visible of the learner's own strategic thinking and meaning making processes. Learners could be encouraged to consider in particular multimodal literacy elements (such as materiality, framing, design and production), or key principles of multimodality (for example intramodal and intermodal analyses, social, cultural and historical readings, relationships between reader, writer and message) or explore texts more freely in terms of their own personal experiences and possible literary and literacy pathways through text. Learners may also complete annotated spreads of other texts they are reading or writing. The following blog (linked from Shaun's website) is a lovely resource to support this activity https://blog.picturebookmakers.com/. In this blog picture book artists take learners around the world and behind the scenes through literary and literacy pathways of the illustration and narration of some of the most popular and interesting children's and young adult literature texts, including *The Gruffalo*.

- **Experimenting with literary and literacy pathways – 99 Ways to Tell a Story:** Learners are given different pages from Madden's *99 Ways to Tell a Story* (a series of one-page comics that tell the same story 99 different ways) and/or Queneau's *Exercises in Style* (again a retelling of one story in 99 different ways including haiku, blurb, mathematical formula). Collaboratively they are asked to consider the affordances and constraints of each mode of storytelling. What changes and what stays the same when we share our stories in different ways? Using it as a mentor text learners could write their own stories individually or collaboratively in a selection of different modes as a class project or assignment and reflect on what they have learned from considering their story in a variety of different modes. Learners could also be challenged to condense their stories down into one image/sculpture/representation as Shaun does in *The Singing Bones*.

- **Reading, writing and mode as tools for thinking, meaning making and identity – Peritextual, intertextual and artefactual reading:** Teachers and learners together engage in a series of tasks that ask them to explore the peritextual features (cover, endpapers, title page and any other textual or visual information not included directly in the story text of the book) of a selected text (such as Shaun's *The Arrival*). As learners read the text, they should be encouraged to search for links and references to other texts or stories. How and why might these be included in the text? What affordances and constraints do they offer? This activity could be further extended to a reading of objects as artifacts – modern day or from history, local or from other cultures. What might this object be called? What was it used for? Why? How could we use it to make a story? What stories would it have to tell of previous experiences? What meaning does this object hold? Learners could be encouraged to use pastiche, collage or multimodal texts to represent their strategic reading and writing experiences and identified literary and literacy pathways on this project.
- **Story fragments as flash fiction:** Learners are asked to write flash fiction stories, that is stories that are brief and limited to a certain number of words. The focus here is on paring down experiences to their essential meaning with each sentence moving the story forward in a particular way (layering the narrative similar to peeling back the skin of an onion – each sentence and layer must reveal something that was not known before). Wordcount can vary from 6 words (remembering "For Sale: Baby shoes. Never worn", authorship unsubstantiated) to twitterature at 280 characters, sudden fiction at 750 words and flash fiction at 1,500 words.
- **Author study as developing our tools for literary and literacy journeys:** The work of Shaun Tan lends itself very well to an author study because of the wide availability of online resources and multimodal and arts-based adaptations of his work. Reading Australia, for example, has published online a wide variety of detailed and engaging activities and ideas for a number of Tan's texts (https://readingaustralia.com.au/). In addition Shaun's own website https://www.shauntan.net/ shares openly and extensively his work, selected interviews, essays and presentations; extremely detailed notes on individual texts; and his creative process, alongside a plethora of resources and ideas for aspiring artists, authors and illustrators and is, in itself, a complete resource for an author study on Shaun Tan. Website materials could further act as mentor texts for how learners could think about their own creative processes, including

> how they can use reading and writing as tools for the development of literacy and literary pathways through text. Learners could also be encouraged to create artist statements exploring and mapping their own multimodal meaning making tools and strategies for thinking in and beyond the classroom. Completing this task learners could be asked to visualise what the reading and writing tools they think they need for engaging with literature and literacy might look like and communicate these to each other as visual objects, multimodal events or sociocultural artefacts (Serafini, 2015).

The texts explored in this part of the chapter offer a small taste of the richness of Tan's imagination, storytelling and worlds for exploring literary and literacy pathways through text. Tan's understanding of the collective theme of his work further suggests some of the ways in which we can support learners in multimodal literacy development and the making of new maps in new ways to represent their experiences as we move now to explore the work and words of Margaret Wild.

> If my work has a collective theme, it's something like this: "Reality is just another strange story." It's something we constantly narrate to ourselves through this peculiar invention of language and pictures, a project that begins in childhood and never really ends. Great books become part of our own map of experience: through reading we grasp the power and unity of our own thought and feeling. We are invited to empathize with others, to see the world from alternative angles, to wonder what it would be like to live differently, and to not feel alone when we constantly ask "What if?" …to a simple but profound realization: the world is what you make of it, a big, unfinished picture book inside your head.
>
> (Tan, 2015, p. 115)

Reading and writing picture books and multimodal texts: Exploring intermodal and intramodal meaning in the emotional portraits and parallel stories of Margaret Wild

A picture book is a multimodal text that makes meaning explicitly through the interdependence of pictures, words and other multimodal elements. As such it is a text type particularly well-suited to exploring multimodal, intramodal (within modes) and intermodal (across modes) meaning making and literacies in visible and less visible literary and literacy pathways through text. Additionally the sometimes taken for granted format of the book itself (the peritext – cover, end pages, title page and so on) hold great narrative significance and embody elements of materiality, framing, design and production in ways that allow learners to visualise, problematise and discuss innovative literary and literacy pathways through text. It is also important to note that picture books can be understood in their own right as authentic social, cultural and historical documents and provide opportunities for engagement of older as well as younger learners in the exploration of text as a visual object, multimodal event and sociocultural artefact (Serafini, 2015).

Picture books are not just for children. Challenging and controversial or crossover picture books (Evans, 2015) offer alternative storytelling structures that serve to condense serious real world problems for young and older readers (including illness, death, depression, abuse) in text accessible through multimodal engagement using techniques and in ways that are not possible in traditional literature texts. Kafka (1904) similarly highlights the power of story to reflect on darker experiences in his assertation that "we ought to read only the kind of books that wound or stab us. If the book we're reading doesn't wake us up with a blow to the head, what are we reading for? A book must be the axe for the frozen sea within us" (Kafka, 1904).

Learners respond strategically to the literary and literacy pathways within these multimodal texts in many different ways including exploring the book as visual object, multimodal event and/or sociocultural artefact; analytic responses to narrative meaning, illustrations and words; linguistic codes; intertextual responses by making connections to other texts; personal responses; transparent responses involving learners reacting as though they were living the story for real (such as emotional or physical responses) and/or interacting with story characters or reliving parts of the story; and performative responses involving premeditated and thought through engagement in activities around the text (Mourao, 2016). In her interview Margaret Wild draws on many of these reading strategies for engaging with multimodal texts to learn about literacy and literature alongside an in depth discussion of her own work.

FIVE MINUTES WITH MARGARET WILD

How do you think we can use stories and children's and young adult literature to encourage and support learning?

Learning is a life-long activity. At school and university, students hopefully learn how to think critically and how to analyse what's happening in the world. They can then apply these tools to their own lives and be less susceptible to propaganda, conspiracy theories and the ravings of tyrants. I think fiction has an important role to play in learning. Books help readers to immerse themselves in other people's lives and cultures. They give us the opportunity to walk in other people's shoes, helping us to realise that we are all essentially the same. No matter what race we belong to, we have the same hopes, fears and desires. In fiction we can see ourselves reflected and that makes us feel less alone. Stories engage our emotions, encouraging empathy, kindness and understanding. They stimulate our imaginations, opening us up to new possibilities and new ideas.

I love writing for children and adolescents because they are so receptive. As long as I can make a story credible and convincing, they are willing to enter into the worlds I create and engage with them. Of all my books, *Fox* is the one that has had the biggest response from very young readers to adults. I think this book can be read at different levels, but even the youngest reader seems to understand the themes of temptation, grief, love, loyalty and redemption. I think we need to trust children's ability to engage with complex ideas and themes. Readers are fascinated by the illustrations in *Fox*, as well as by the design and the placement of the spiky, hand-written text. The illustrator, Ron Brooks, wanted to slow down the reading of the story so that it echoes Magpie's physical and emotional journey, and I think his approach works brilliantly.

Do you have any memories of reading children's literature as a child? How do you understand reading?

I don't remember ever being read to as a child. My father was a typical 1950s man who went to work, came home, had a sherry and read the newspaper. My mother, who had been unwell with a heart complaint since she was young, had five small children so she simply didn't have the time or energy. When I was a teenager, she trained as a kindergarten teacher, and this was my first real exposure to a range of picture books. It was one of my grandmothers who sparked my interest in stories. We only saw her once a year because she lived very far away.

At bedtime she would regale us with exciting, funny tales about African animals. We were entranced. I wish I could remember her stories, but it is her voice, her expressions, her animation that I mainly recall.

Growing up, I had many favourite books, including by Enid Blyton, of course. I was seven when I picked up one of my brother's *Secret Seven* books. I was hooked from the first sentence, and I still remember my feeling of power (and astonishment) that I could read fast and fluently. I read all of Blyton's books and then went on to books such as *Seven Little Australians*, the *Anne of Green Gables* series, *Little Women*, and so on. As I had no one directing my reading, I started borrowing adult books quite young. *Jane Eyre* was one book I went back to time and again.

But it was fairy tales that sparked my imagination and have stayed with me ever since. Books like *The Snow Queen, The Little Mermaid* and *Beauty and the Beast*. They were strong, unsettling, nightmarish stories. Who could ever forget images such as the splinters of glass that penetrate Kay's eyes and heart? Or the Little Mermaid losing her tongue and voice in exchange for legs, but when she dances, it is as if she is dancing on sharp knives? Fairy tales are powerful and spell-binding, full of love, death, sacrifice, terror, loss of innocence and redemption. Great stuff! Books lead to other books. Older readers may want to try Angela Carter's powerful updating of fairy tales. Or look at Carol Ann Duffy's work. She has written marvelous poems such as *Mrs. Midas* and *Little Red-Cap*.

What do you think about when you write texts for children and young adults?

With picture books, the aim is always to try to integrate text and illustrations. They complement and extend each other. Each is integral to the other. Because picture books often don't have many words, each word must count. When I'm writing a story I always have the illustrations in mind. In that way I can leave gaps, leave out descriptions, leave out everything that will be better told in pictures. This makes my texts quite spare, allowing the illustrator plenty of room to contribute their own vision of the book.

My first book, *There's a Sea in my Bedroom*, was published in 1984. At the time I was working as a book editor and I continued this career for many years. I felt very lucky to have a "proper" job because it meant I was free to write the stories I wanted to write. I wasn't dependent on the whims of the market or the demands of a publisher. If a story was rejected, so be it. I just wrote another one. I wrote about things I found compelling, such as death, divorce, homelessness, grief, and ageing. These are serious topics, but I was very conscious that the stories must, above all, be well told and entertaining. I did not want them to be didactic, or what some critics call "teachy preachy". If there was a message or theme, it needed to be understated. I've always strived for honesty, though when I can, I will try to end the story on an ultimately hopeful note.

I never set out to write a particular story. I wait for the germ of an idea. It might be something I see or hear or experience. *Fox* came from a few sources. I'd listened to a radio program about vets and the animals they treated. A maimed dog and bird were mentioned, which caught my imagination. The other element was the bush fires that were dangerously encroaching on Sydney at the time. And I'd known someone was very unhappy, and this unhappiness made him sometimes act cruelly. He became the character of Fox. The idea for *The Dream of the Thylacine* came from a short, black and white film I saw at an art gallery. It was about the last confirmed surviving thylacine which died in the Hobart Zoo in the late 1930s. I was mesmerized by the pacing of the animal in the cage, and as I watched the film, a story was beginning to take shape in my mind.

I tend to write my stories in my head. Only once I know how it begins, more or less what happens in the middle, and how it ends, do I sit down at the computer. I do many drafts, rewriting endlessly, until I feel I can't make it any better. Once the stories are published, I never re-read them. With hindsight, I can see how they could be improved, but of course it's too late, so I just have to let them go.

Could you tell us a little about your experience writing in verse?

I have written two verse novels, *Jinx* and *One Night*. This was a new departure for me. I had tried writing novels in prose, but I felt exhausted by the pressure to produce so many words! I loved a verse novel, *Onion Tears*, written by a close friend, Diana Kidd. She told me about how she approached writing her novel – in fragments, piece by piece. I realised that this approach was perfect for a picture book writer like me.

In *Jinx*, once I'd written the first verse, I was on my way. I wrote the following pieces in no particular order, just what I found interesting on the day, knowing that later I could shuffle them around and see how they would best fit together. Each piece was like a little snapshot. It is an economic way of storytelling which suited me perfectly. With an overarching narrative structure to link everything together, I was able to create individual voices, a sense of place and community, as well as developing the characters, with the main focus on Jen. I found *Jinx* and *One Night* very enjoyable, but difficult to write. Because each piece was so short, the wrong word or a jarring phrase would stand out. So I rewrote constantly, looking at each word, each line length, trying to get it as right as possible. Both these books are fairly quick reads which made them attractive and accessible to a range of readers, especially, I think, to reluctant readers.

Do you have any advice or activities for aspiring writers?
I really don't know what advice to give aspiring young writers, except read, read, read! If you read good literature, you will be inspired to try to write better yourself. Don't just read prose. Immerse yourself in poetry as well. Great works feed your imagination, stimulate your thinking and make you strive to write the best story you can. Write from the heart. Write about something important to you. Strive to be truthful and emotionally honest. For me, some of the ingredients of a good story are engaging characters, an intriguing/involving plot and a satisfying ending. Above all, I want to be moved – to laugh or cry. I want to read books that haunt me for a long time. Those are the books I will re-read every few years. All my stories start with a germ of an idea. Gradually, over days, weeks, even years, I think about the idea until it evolves into a story I want to tell. In each story – even books for babies – I am only interested in writing it if there is an emotion attached – joy, love, grief, fear and so on. It is the emotion I want to explore.

Margaret's affirmation of the role of fiction in learning about ourselves, our world and the worlds of others aligns with Shaun's understanding of culture as a flexible reality and a way of thinking about our experiences. Her belief that we need to trust readers and their ability to engage with more deeply complex literary and literacy texts in the slow spaces of literature is also reminiscent of Shaun's ideas and connects closely with the theme of reading and writing strategically through a focus on multimodal literacies and story paths. Emotion is central to Margaret's storytelling and her remembrance of her grandmother's voice, expressions and animations rather than the childhood stories she shared highlights further the performative and emotional nature of storytelling and the importance of the modes chosen for the telling of our stories, as here these modes are what remain rather than the text itself. Margaret's picture books are not easy reads, but deeply complex tales and texts about the feelings and emotion of human experience.

Margaret's *Fox*, for example, can be read on many levels as a crossover picture book. The story of an envious Fox, an injured Magpie and a one eyed Dog is told in sparse yet concise narration and an unusual array of illustrative techniques of both text and image. Margaret's discussion of her development of the text for her picture books and how every word must count offers an important focus for engaging in multimodal strategic reading writing activities in the classroom. Slowness and smallness are again emphasised here as the writer engages closely with the central themes, ideas and words of their stories and what these could and should look like in the final text. Editing is central to the process as well as time to think about and develop ideas for creating our own literary and literacy pathways through text-based on authentic and meaningful real world stimuli.

Writing multimodal text in the classroom offers learners opportunity to focus more closely on the relationships between intramodal and intermodal literacies and how meanings are derived within and across modes, for example the weight of words to carry particular meaning where wordcount is limited, and simultaneously the interaction between these words and other multimodal elements to tell a story. Often in the classroom our focus lies on writing more and/or as much as we know on particular themes or ideas. Taking opportunities to focus in on the meanings carried by individual words and our deliberate and careful selection and combination of these focuses learners on writing less, conciseness and visualising the very essence of the stories they tell.

Developing alongside this written text a consideration of complementary images calls for careful, thoughtful and strategic reading and reflection of the text itself, as evidenced in Margaret's discussion of how her illustrator Ron Brooks responded to her text in particular ways in the process of illustration. Her explanation of how the placement and shape of text merged with the layered and multimodal illustrations to slow down the reading and experience of the story in an effort to mirror the slowness and depth of Magpie's physical and emotional journey exemplifies the development of intermodal and intramodal literary and literacy pathways through text.

In *Fox* the words of the story themselves become a part of the illustrative process and appear as skewed, scribbled and vertical scrawls varying in font and direction across the pages, inviting readers to find and navigate their own individual pathways through the work. Highlighting the multimodality inherent in all storytelling Margaret also stresses the key narrative role of illustrator Ron Brooks in the text and particular decisions made by him in his role as illustrator to move the story forward in unique and important ways.

Leigh (2010) explores ways in which access to a variety of writing and drawing media enables the development of new and innovative literary and literacy pathways for expanding meaning making in self-expression. Drawing on the work of Eisner and aligning with Shaun and Margaret's understanding of culture, she explains that what we come to know about the world is largely influenced by the tools we have available to us. She suggests that children, when given rulers, will be able and most likely to measure their world, but if rulers are our only tool for exploring our worlds then our knowledge of these worlds becomes limited to numbers and scale. So is it with our (over)use of language in the classroom. In her research she highlights a question from a young boy Marcus, who asks "Does anyone have violent red?", explaining how access to a range of red allows him to think more deeply and strategically about colour.

The Dream of the Thylacine, another multimodal picture book collaboration between Margaret and Ron Brooks and is a poetic lament to the last thylacine, the Tasmanian tiger, seen in captivity at the Hobart Zoo in the late 1930s. Keeping emotion central to the experience of writing, Margaret's stories are inspired by events that move her and the feelings inherent in these experiences. In her discussion of this text Margaret again highlights the time needed for the germ of an idea to develop from feelings and emotions into a story, noting that she begins to write only when she has imagined or written the story first in her head. Getting the story onto the page further requires endless rewriting and redrafting – a part of the experience and work of a writer not often focused on in detail in the classroom.

Themes of freedom and captivity, extinction and environmentalism are writ large in this extremely concise text. It is only through death that the thylacine's dream to be reunited with the wild can be achieved in the parallel stories of what was and what was wished to be. In a text so economic with words this story asks us to think carefully about the choice involved in every word or mark we read or make on the page. Emotion is central to both the story and how it is told as original photographs are layered with paint, mixed media and collage providing texture to the experience of reading a book. Engaging with this text in the classroom, learners should be encouraged to think about the architecture of this book and later their own stories – what is the shape of the text (from literal, literary and literacy perspectives)? How are perspective and spatial relationships used to make meaning? What changes and continuities are there between the different landscapes of the text?

Identifying as a picture book writer, Margaret, similarly to Shaun, conceptualises the writing process as fragmentary, involving the gathering, developing and putting together of many different ideas and pieces of texts to make a story whole. Understanding stories as simultaneously fragmented and themselves fragments of larger shared human narratives of experience across cultures, Margaret describes her approach to writing her verse novel *Jinx* in a nonlinear way, later putting the pieces together into a coherent and meaningful story shape. This bite size snapshot approach to writing in multimodal pieces could be adapted to classroom practice to encourage disinterested and less confident writers in writing mosaics and alternative modes for self-expression. Margaret's advice to read poetry as well as prose is very important and calls into question the extent to which we provide opportunities in classroom practice to also write in a variety of different styles including poetry.

READING AND WRITING MULTIMODAL TEXT: STRATEGIES FOR PERSONAL AND COLLABORATIVE INTRAMODAL AND INTERMODAL MEANING MAKING

- **Media, mode and me – Personal strategies for intramodal and intermodal meaning making:** Learners are encouraged to explore their own relationships with, and understandings of, the media and modes they use to communicate in and out of school through reflective journaling or other similar pedagogical approaches. Considering art and language as complementary ways of knowing and opportunities for constructing meaning, this project invites learners to experiment with a variety of traditional and nontraditional modes in their self-expression. Using *Fox* as an example learners could be first asked to consider what kind of reading and writing tools writers use and why. Do writers only use one kind of tool for reading, writing and expression? What tools can we use in the classroom to read and write strategically and how do we identify, select and develop these tools? What tools (and modes) best express emotions? Thoughts? Characters? Later learners will develop their own story collage using a variety of different modes together to tell their story. As a part of this multimodal journaling learners could use online multimedia tools such as Doodle Splash (an online tool combining drawing with analytical thinking around writing prompts to encourage the making of connections between image and text) to make their multimodal tools for thinking and meaning making visible to others.

- **Meaning and moving between modes – Responding creatively to multimodal texts:** Learners are asked to watch the YouTube video of the thylacine that inspired Margaret's text. In what ways does *The Dream of a Thylacine* capture aspects of this video – physicalities, feelings, emotions, movement, space, colours and shades? Can you develop your own creative response to the video? What story and parts of the experience do you want to share? How? Why?

- **Literary and literacy pathways of authors and illustrators – Collaborative make a book project:** Modelling the close working relationship between Margaret Wild and illustrator Ron Brooks learners each plan, write and illustrate their own picture book. As a first step each learner plans and writes the text (words) of their multimodal story. Learners are then paired and swap their pieces of text. At this second stage learners move from being authors to illustrators and work to collaboratively illustrate each other's textual stories. Johnson's (2000) *Making Books* further explores a range of practical book making ideas for young people focusing in particular on how books work and relationships between author, illustrator and audience.

- **Critical thinking and book talk:** Roche's 2015 text *Developing Children's Critical Thinking through Picturebooks* provides a wonderful resource for engaging learners in critical thinking and book talk activities using picture books. Central to this approach is the understanding that reading a story is only the beginning of learner engagement with text and reading. Discussion and dialogue are also modes essential to our meaning making in and from text. Learners explore books together as a group in detail, discussing and questioning any and all aspects of the work that interests them. Listening and connecting to the ideas of others in the group is also very important. This text is very highly recommended for teachers interested in engaging learners in a wide range of critical thinking and talking related activities that explore literary and literacy pathways in literature in the classroom.

Conclusion

This chapter explores literary and literacy aspects of strategic reading and writing practices through a focus on multimodal literacies. Understanding reading as the active mapping of unique pathways through text readers and writers work together to cocreate meaning based on alternative perspectives and varied experiences. The concept of multimodality is discussed in detail with a particular focus on how multimodal literacies experienced in daily life can be employed in classroom pedagogies and practice. Language is understood as one mode that may be employed to make meaning but is itself partial unless considered in relation to its interaction with other modes in communication and meaning making. As Shaun clearly highlights in his 2020 acceptance speech for the Kate Greenaway Medal, what is of prime importance is that:

> how those young individuals define and navigate a path through these competing forces of enlightenment and darkness is not for any artist or writer to say. No instructions are necessarily going to help, no moral fable, no emergency plan, no bullet points, no algorithm. When the next unpredictable 'black swan' event reshapes our collective future, who is to say that even our current ideas of progressive thinking, so self-evident now, may become rapidly antiquated. Future generations will always have to figure it out for themselves, with what they already carry in the tangled DNA of their minds and hearts. How they think and feel, how the truth of reason relates to the truth of emotion, how far their imagination can reach or not reach, how they can perceive a problem in order to solve it, how they can see the things from a different point of view, enough to know there is a problem in the first place. They have to find their own way, a good way, whatever that is.
>
> (Tan, 2020, Kate Greenaway Medal acceptance speech)

The interviews and work of the children's and young adult literature authors featured in this chapter offer many opportunities for the development of multimodal literacies and related pedagogies that focus learners on reading and writing strategically in the classroom. This focus asks learners to reflect on literary and literacy aspects of text and is supported by learner engagement with new and emotional literacies. Reading and writing strategically learners reconceptualise text and story as visual objects, multimodal events and sociocultural artefacts (Serafini, 2015) in an attempt to better understand how and why stories are told. From this perspective, learners and teachers come to understand literacy, reading, writing and mode as strategic tools for thinking and personal meaning making rather than public markers of achievement or failure.

Understanding, as interrogated in this chapter, lies somewhere in the spaces between knowing and imagining as these multimodal texts preserve their meanings intact and ask the reader to question, interpret and to dream to become themselves a part of the narrative and choose their own literary and literacy story paths. In any given text, but multimodal texts in particular, many different pathways exist for the reader and their engagement with the story, paths that branch outwards, upwards and inward and, as Shaun suggests, ask the reader (just as has been asked of the author before) to walk the path less travelled and find their own way, whatever that may be and where ever it may lead, making their own maps along the way.

> Shapes and words dangle on the pages of my current sketchbooks like fishing line, the tip of a pencil able to hook submerged memories and impressions from very long ago, things that are otherwise inaccessible to the more conscious, purposeful parts of my mind. I try not to worry about what my drawings actually mean; I just follow them where they go.
>
> (Tan, 2015, p. 106)

Bibliography

Children's and young adult literature explored in this chapter

Donaldson, J. Scheffler, A. (2017). *The Gruffalo*. UK: MacMillan Children's Books.
Tan, S. (2018). *Tales from the Inner City*. UK: Walker Studio.
Tan, S. (2016). *The Singing Bones*. UK: Walker Studio.
Tan, S. (2014). *The Arrival*. UK: Hodder Children's Books.
Tan, S. (2013). *Rules of Summer*. UK: Hodder Children's Books.
Tan, S. (2010). *Lost Thing*. UK: Hodder Children's Books.
Tan, S. (2010). *The Lost Thing*. Animated short film.
Tan, S. (2010). *The Red Tree*. UK: Hodder Children's Books.
Wild, M. (2013). *The Dream of the Thylacine*. UK: Allen and Unwin.

Wild, M. (2008). *Fox*. UK: Allen and Unwin.

Wild, M. (2004). *Jinx*. UK: Simon Pulse.

Other possible texts for exploring literacy ideas and pedagogies highlighted in this chapter

Erlbruch, W. (2008). *Duck, Death and the Tulip*. Auckland: Gecko Press.

This beautiful and philosophical picture book explores themes of life, death, love and loss through a focus on the complex relationship between Death, Duck and the worlds around them.

K. O. Karrebaek, D.

This married couple from Denmark create dark and haunting picture books on a number of difficult and emotive themes. Below listed are just some examples of their work.

O. Karrebaek, D. (2008). *Bornenes Bedemand (The Children's Undertaker)*. Copenhagen: Rosinante & Co.

This text tells the story of a children's undertaker as he goes about his busy work.

K. O. Karrebaek, D. (2008). *De skaeve Smil (The Crooked Smiles)*. Copenhagen: Rosinante & Co.

This text is populated by aborted foetuses who try to understand why they were not born and given a chance to live.

K. O. Karrebaek, D. (2009). *Idiot*. Copenhagen: Rosinante & Co.

This text deals with the themes of bullying, murder-suicide and disability.

Macauley, D. (2005). *Black and White*. UK: HMH Books.

One of the first postmodern picture books, this multimodal text tells four (interconnected?) stories across a nonlinear storyline, multiple perspectives and peritextual elements.

Williams, M.

In her wide variety of innovative and interactive multimodal books Marcia Williams explores many different worlds and themes: ancient Egypt, Vikings, Tudor England, Rome, Greek myth, Shakespeare, Dickens, Austen, World War I and II, Les Miserables, monsters.

Chapter bibliography

Australian Centre for the Moving Image (ACMI). (2019). *From Book to Film: Educational resource*. Available at https://2015.acmi.net.au/media/428194/shaun-tan-ed-kit.pdf.

Australian Centre for the Moving Image (ACMI). (2020). Film it resource. Available at https://www.acmi.net.au/education/film-it/.

Dallacqua, A. Kersten, S. Rhoades, M. (2015). Using Shaun Tan's work to foster multiliteracies in 21st century classrooms. *The Reading Teacher, 69*(2), 207–217.

Evans, J. (2015). *Challenging and Controversial Picturebooks: Creative and critical responses to visual texts.* UK: Routledge.

Farrell, M. Arizpe, E. McAdam, J. (2010). Journeys across visual borders: Annotated spreads of 'The Arrival' by Shaun Tan as a method of understanding pupils' creation of meaning through visual images. *Australian Journal of Language and Literacy, 33*(3), 198–210.

Flewitt, R. (2013). *Multimodal Perspectives on Early Childhood Literacies. The Sage Handbook of Early Childhood.* UK: Sage.

Gibson, J. J. (1977). The theory of affordances. In Shaw R. E. Bransford J. (Eds.), *Perceiving, Acting, and Knowing.* Hillsdale, NJ: Lawrence Erlbaum Associates.

González, N. Moll, L. & Amanti, C. (Eds). (2005). *Funds of knowledge: Theorizing practices in households, communities and classrooms.* Mahwah, NJ: Erlbaum.

Janks, H. Comber, B. (2006). Critical literacy across continents. In Pahl, K. Rowsell, J. (Eds.) *Travel Notes from the New Literacy Studies: Instances of practice.* UK: Multilingual Matters.

Jewitt, C. (2008). Multimodality and Literacy in School Classrooms. *Review of Research in Education*, Vol. 32, p. 241–267.

Jewitt, C. Kress, G. (Eds.). (2003). *Multimodal Literacy.* New York: Peter Lang.

Johnson, P. (2000). *Making Books.* UK: Bloomsbury.

Kafka, F. (1904). Personal correspondence.

Kress, G. (2010). *Multimodality: A Social Semiotic Approach to Contemporary Communication.* London: Routledge.

Kress, G. (2003). *Literacy in the New Media Age.* London: Routledge.

Kress, G. (1993). *Language as Ideology.* London: Routledge.

Kress, G. Jewitt, C. Ogborn, J. Tsatsarelis, C. (2001). *Multimodal Teaching and Learning: The rhetorics of the science classroom.* London: Continuum.

Larson, J. Marsh, J. (2014). *Making Literacy Real: Theories and practices for learning and teaching.* UK: Sage.

Leigh, R. (2010). Violent red, ogre green, and delicious white: Expanding meaning potential through media. *Language Arts, 87*(4), 252–262.

Lemke, J. (1998). Multiplying meaning. In Martin, J. R. & Veel, R. (eds.), *Reading Science: Critical and functional perspectives on discourses of science* (pp. 87–113). New York, NY: Routledge.

Madden, M. (2006). *99 Ways to Tell a Story.* USA: Jonathan Cape.

Marshall, E. (2016). Counter storytelling through graphic life writing. *Language Arts, 94*(2), 79–93.

Mourao, S. (2016). Picturebooks in the Primary EFL Classroom: Authentic literature for an authentic response. *Children's Literature in English Language Education, 4*(1).

Mueller, L. (1996). *Alive Together.* USA: LSU Press.

Myers, C. (2014). The Apartheid of children's literature. *Sunday Review.* NY: The New York Times.

Queneau, R. (2016). *Exercises in Style*. UK: Alma Books Ltd.
Reading Australia. (2020). Various resources on a selection of Tan's texts available at https://readingaustralia.com.au/.
Roche, M. (2015). *Developing Children's Critical Thinking through Picturebooks: A guide for primary and early years students and teachers*. Abingdon Oxon: Routledge.
Rowsell, J. Kosnik, C. & Beck, C. (2008). Fostering multiliteracies pedagogy through preservice teacher education. *Teaching Education, 19*(2), 109–122.
Serafini, F. (2015). Multimodal literacy: From theories to practices. *Language Arts, 92*(6), 412–423.
Shanahan, T. (2003). Research Based Reading Instruction: Myths about the National Reading Panel Report. *The Reading Teacher, 56*(7), 646–655.
Short, K. (2011). Reading literature in elementary classrooms. In Wolf, S. Coats, K. Enciso, P. Jenkins, C. (Eds.), *Handbook of Research on Children's and Young Adult Literature* (pp. 48–63). London: Routledge
Tan, S. (2020). Artist website available at https://www.shauntan.net/.
Tan, S. (2020). Winner speech Kate Greenaway Medal. Available at https://carnegiegreenaway.org.uk/2020-cilip-kate-greenaway-medal-winner-speech/.
Tan, S. (2020). Lowensteins Artist Profile. Available at https://www.lowensteins.com.au/news-resources/blog/artist-profile-shaun-tan.
Tan, S. (2015). The Purposeful Daydream: Thoughts on children's literature. *The Iowa Review, 45*(2), 100–115.
Tan, S. (2002). *Originality and Creativity*. Available at https://www.shauntan.net/essay-originality-and-creativity.
Tan, S. (2001). *Locus Online*. Interview with Karen Haber available online at https://locusmag.com/2001/Issue12/Tan.html.
The New London Group. (1996). A Pedagogy Of Multiliteracies: Designing social futures. *Harvard Educational Review, 66*(1), 60–93.
Unsworth, L. (2006). Towards a metalanguage for multliteracies education: Describing the meaning making resources of language image interaction. *English Teaching: Practice and Critique, 5*(1), 55–76.
Wohlwend, K. (2017). The expression of multiliteracies and multimodalities in play. In F. Serafini & E. Gee (Eds.), *Remixing Multiliteracies: Theory and practice from New London to new times* (pp. 162–175). New York, NY: Teachers College Press.
Zipin, L. (2009) Dark funds of knowledge, deep funds of pedagogy: Exploring boundaries between lifeworlds and schools, *Discourse: Studies in the Cultural Politics of Education*, 30(3), 317–331.

CHAPTER 2

Exploring multiple perspectives on reading and writing in culture: Arts as storied inquiry into aesthetic literacy and personal identity practice

About this chapter

This chapter builds on the sociocultural understanding of reading, writing and mode as strategic and personal tools for thinking and meaning making outlined in chapter one. Reading, writing and literacy are set within wider cognitive, psychological, linguistic, sociocultural and socio-political contexts so as to better understand reading, writing and literacy as sociocultural practice. The integration of the arts into literacy planning is explored as a way for teachers to focus more closely on diverse literacy aspects of strategic cultural reading and writing practice using children's and young adult literature. The arts here is employed as an umbrella term to encompass dance, music, drama, poetry, media, film, literature and the visual arts.

Research, literature and children's and young adult literature authors included in this chapter define a distinctive mode of literacy learning for arts-based pedagogies that complements the sociocultural understanding of literacy as a lived practice emerging from the previous chapter and centres on multimodal, aesthetic and sensuous knowing derived through observation, interpretation and imagination of culture and self. Understanding that we all know more than we can tell in particular contexts is a fundamental premise of an arts-based approach to literacy learning.

Sample pedagogical approaches discussed here explore personal and collaborative inquiry, questioning and reflection and suggest that teachers and learners should seek to share experiences, literacies and learning in a variety of alternative and multimodal ways and forms beyond language in the classroom.

About the authors

Patricia Forde

Patricia Forde is an Irish author, playwright, scriptwriter, former teacher and director of the Galway Arts Festival, Ireland. Patricia writes in both the Irish and English language and across a variety of genres, her stories testifying to the power of the arts and language in understanding our experiences. Patricia has received several awards including the White Raven Award from the International Youth Library and the Dublin UNESCO Citywide Read 2019 award. *The Wordsmith* (published under the title *The List* in the United States) has also been shortlisted for the Irish Children's Book of the Year Award and is an American Library Association Notable Book for Children.

Patricia's stories reveal a profound respect for and understanding of language, heritage and the arts in personal and creative writing and expression. Written to commemorate Galway's achievement of European Capital of Culture 2020 *An t-Oileàn Thiar* (*To the Island*), for example, connects young readers and writers back to Patricia's own beginnings and childhood and her sense of longing to see and be a part of something more than was in front of her eyes. *The Wordsmith* and its sequel *Mother Tongue* (published as *The Last Lie* in the United States) explore dystopian worlds (though perhaps closer to our own than we might like to admit) where the arts are taboo and language use is limited to a list of only 500 words. For more information see www.patriciafordeauthor.com.

Máire Zepf

Máire Zepf is a Northern Irish author and was the first Children's Writing Fellow for Northern Ireland (2017–2019) at the Seamus Heaney Centre for Poetry at Queen's University Belfast. Supported by the Arts Council of Northern Ireland in this role Máire promoted children's and young adult literature, reading and writing with young people of all ages and continues to do so. She is currently the Artistic Director for Quotidian – Word on the Street (an arts production company dedicated to putting literature, especially poetry, into public spaces in innovative ways, www.quotidian.ie). Máire writes in a variety of genres including picture books and historical fiction, and has written the first Irish language verse novel. Máire has won numerous awards including the Réics Carló Book of the Year Award (awarded for the Irish language children's book of the year), the KPMG Children's Books Ireland's Book of the Year Award, a White Raven award, the Literacy Association of Ireland Children's Book Award and the Oireachtas Award for fiction and has been honour listed by the International Board on Books for Young People.

Máire's work has been translated into a number of languages and celebrates the arts and the Irish language in particular as beautiful and powerful media for self-expression, identity development and learning. Her Irish verse novel *Nóinín*, spoken in two voices, tells first the story of Nóinín as she meets and falls for a boy online, while her relationship with her best friend Eimear deteriorates. Later Nóinín will go to meet Oisín and never return. The second half of the novel explores the aftermath of this encounter, from the point of view of her best friend Eimear. Breathing new voice into Irish myth and storytelling *An Féileacán agus an Rí* (*The Butterfly and the King*) recasts an ancient Éadaoin as a powerful and agentic young woman vying for her own freedom and has been adapted to dance at the Belfast Children's Festival. For more information see www.mairezepf.com.

Introduction

As a society we tell our stories through the arts. Books, plays, poetry, films, musicals, ballets, concerts and exhibitions all serve to publicly narrate personal stories of shared cultural histories and experiences of groups of people in a variety of different ways. These stories, and the diverse literary and literacy pathways within, when read or experienced generate new ones, intertwining with and reshaping collective understandings of literacy, identity and culture as we teach and learn about ourselves and others in and through these storied spaces. Patricia Forde, one of the children's and young adult literature authors contributing to this chapter, summarises this experience very well in her interview when she talks about how, as she was growing up, stories were all around her.

Building on the sociocultural understanding of reading, writing and mode as strategic and personal tools for thinking and meaning making outlined in chapter one, this chapter places these tools within wider social, cultural and historical contexts. While the previous chapter foregrounds experiential pathways in engagement with literary and narrative aspects of multimodal texts, this chapter explores reading, writing and mode in the context of culture so as to better understand the many diverse literacy practices within as shared and sociocultural processes.

A study of (and through) the arts is uniquely placed in this regard, as the storehouse of the arts itself serves as a repository of collective and culturally accepted, desired yet dramatically diverse modes, literacies and knowledge. By focusing explicitly on the arts as collective aesthetic learning, this chapter situates its exploration of literacy in modes encompassing not only language, but also for example music, dance and performance. Classroom practices that cultivate literacy in all its forms to open up new identities, experiences, meanings and spaces for reading and writing our worlds, are a central focus of this chapter. As Eisner suggests:

> Education can learn from the arts that the limits of language are not the limits of cognition. We know more than we can tell… what schools need to attend to is the cultivation of literacy in its many forms. Each form of literacy provides another way to be in the world, another way to form experience, another way to recover and express meaning.
>
> (Eisner, 2002, p. 5)

Exploring reading, writing and literacy in culture teachers should encourage learners to understand that the classroom is not the only place where stories are shared. Engaging strategically with cultural stories and their diverse literary and literacy pathways in a variety of settings beyond the classroom (such as home, community spaces, libraries and dedicated arts buildings) opens up new possibilities for literacy learning, along with how and where as a culture our stories are told, remembering that those who will tell our stories tomorrow are sitting in classrooms today. Understanding reading, writing and mode within the context of culture, affords learners opportunities for authentic inquiry into real worlds, words and literacies that are unfamiliar and otherwise inaccessible. Connecting cognitive, psychological, linguistic, sociocultural and socio-political contexts for literacy development through arts and inquiry-based learning involves pedagogies that focus on stimulating curiosity, questioning, investigation, critical thinking, reflection, collaboration, discussion and the sharing of personal experiences in the classroom.

Aesthetic moments and strategic reading and writing in cultural stories: Observing and transforming literacy practice

Foreshadowing Patricia Forde's symbolic remembrance of the island of Hy Brasil in her interview, looking to what may lie beyond the moment's grasp is for Greene the essence of aesthetic learning as she highlights how:

> there is always more to be found, horizons to be breached, limits to be broken through always untapped possibilities. [In] a world so focused on objectives and results, efficiency, effectiveness and the rest, I would lay particular stress on what lies beyond the moment's grasp, on the uses of defamiliarising the over familiar (and thus invisible, inaudible) world.
>
> (Greene, 2001, p. 206)

Aesthetic education, or the study of the arts, "is an intentional undertaking designed to nurture appreciative, reflective, cultural, participatory engagements with the arts by enabling learners to notice what is there to be noticed" (Greene, 2001, p.6) requiring its own distinctive mode of literacy. Understanding cultural activities such as dance, music, drama, media, film, literature and the visual arts as modes of aesthetic (Eisner, 1985) and sensuous (Abbs, 1987) knowing necessitates pedagogical approaches that focus on a variety of arts-based literacies existing beyond the limits of language (Barton, 2013).

Each of these cultural activities offer unique literacy pathways for understanding experience. The theme of war, for example, can be explored through dance, music, drama or literature but each mode will afford and constrain authorial voice and agency in particular and uniquely different ways. Exploring the arts in the classroom allows teachers to make available to learners new and innovative ways of experiencing (reading) and creating (writing) stories and focus closely and explicitly on the literacy aspects involved in learning to read and write strategically across a range of modes, cultural activities and stories.

These multiple and multimodal ways of knowing, or stories, are themselves informed by dynamic understandings of culture, history and experience as learners both shape and are shaped by (classroom) practices and worlds. Understanding, as Eisner suggests, that alternative arts-based literacy forms offer other ways to be, make sense of and write about our experiences this chapter affirms the potential of the arts to support learners in the production of new kinds of literacies, texts and understandings that "give shape to formless ideas... [and are] a vehicle by which we can express our growing awareness of ourselves and the worlds in which we live" (Wright, 2012, p. 4).

For Greene coming into contact with any form of art is like meeting another human being and different art forms (sculpture, film or music for example) each elicit unique experiences and feelings. Understood in their particular sociocultural context she cautions that each form or mode also requires specialist and particular language (and literacy) "to notice, to see, to hear, to attend" (Greene, 2001, p.6) opportunities for learning within these "aesthetic moments" (Greene, 2001, p. 12). Moving away from habitual classroom curricula and routines literacy practices within these aesthetic moments challenge learners to notice the power of affective experience in literacy and literature and reflect on their own understandings and experiences in new ways.

Greene's foregrounding of the importance of affect, noticing and attending to story makes visible the reciprocal and transformative nature of an encounter with the arts. Noticing and reflecting on literary and literacy pathways within these culturally shaped "texts" expands the range of learner literacies and experiences, "opening perspectives... enlarg[ing] the spaces – the perceptual, imaginative, and conceptual spaces – in which the young come in touch with and try to interpret their worlds" (Greene, 2001, p. 139).

An aesthetic approach to reading and writing strategically to learn about literacy and literature focuses on inquiry, imagination, curiosity, collaboration and personal experiences as when "one attends, one lends the work one's life. Or one brings it into the world through a sometimes mysterious interpretive act in a space between oneself and the stage or the wall or the text" (Greene, 2001, p. 128). For Greene breaking with ordinary or traditional literacies and ways of seeing and hearing in this way and living for a time in an imaginary world engages learners in a distinctive mode of literacy as we "lend works of art [our] lives and respond with [our] own creative expressions" (Gulla, 2018, p.109).

Building on these understandings Gulla (2018) introduces some central concepts for developing pedagogies for arts-based literacy learning. These include a focus on collaborative inquiry; guided discussion; making connections; questioning for critical and complex thought and language development; the power of symbol and metaphor for personal reflection and expression; and hands-on exploration and making of text in an approach to literacy that she describes as a kind of apprenticeship in observation (Gulla, 2018). The purpose of these observation-based pedagogies is to help learners "to break with compartmentalized viewing, to take new standpoints on the world" (Greene, 2001, p. 318). Gulla also affirms that the telling of our own stories in response to particular works of arts requires courage and is far more than an academic exercise. In this way aesthetic literacy observation and practice is transformative as we imagine new possibilities for sharing our stories and experiences with others through reading and writing in culture. As Gulla explains:

> This is a mode of teaching that focuses on the live transaction between the work of art and a person… The goal is not to become an expert; it is to become awakened to possibilities. When we bring students into an encounter with a Jackson Pollock painting our purpose is not to talk about what we know about Abstract Expressionism. In an aesthetic education context, we take the time to guide them to notice patterns in the movement of the paint. We encourage them to sweep their arms to follow Pollock's movements to have the sensation of this unique and muscular approach to painting, and through this movement we observe the deliberate choices the artist made, the rhythm, the way he danced with paint. Through guided questioning and

art making experiences, we teach students to actively encounter the work, trying to empower students to see for themselves.

(Gulla, 2018, p. 112)

To engage learners in the kinds of arts-based literacy practices introduced thus far, teachers need to understand that when readers and writers engage in literacy practices in the classroom, they engage in a cultural practice using the particular values, tools, resources and histories available to them. While learners might not be able to voice a definition of abstract expressionism they can employ aesthetic and sensuous knowing to explore the media, colours, movements and forms personally and collaboratively to observe, interpret and imagine their previous experiences in dialogue with art in new ways. (Classroom) learning can therefore be understood as culturally shaped by the practices and histories of its participants. Culture is defined here as encompassing the activities, identities and contexts of particular groups of people as they engage in meaningful and situated learning practices and there may be many different cultures (in terms of groups of people and practices) present in any classroom setting.

When all learners do not have equal access to valued classroom literacies in their previous histories and out of school experiences, difficulties arise in classroom settings where, more than any other place, successful participation "insist[s], slowly but inexorably, that the world cannot be known other than through the abstractions of written language" (Kress, 1997, p. xvii). For example, Smith (2016) reveals that in the context of Ireland there is significant social and gendered differentiation in what kinds of tools are available to children from different social and economic backgrounds and in their overall cultural participation. Her study suggests that in home settings children in lower socioeconomic groups are far less likely to be exposed to reading and other cultural activities and that girls are far more likely than boys to engage generally in arts related activities. A broad focus on the arts in classroom practice addresses some of these social, economic and gender gaps in cultural participation and resulting inequalities in education, affording all learners opportunities to explore new literacies, cultures, tools, meanings and learning.

This sociocultural understanding of culture as an emergent, social and interactive process defines culture as "not so much a product of sharing as a product of people hammering each other into shape with the well-structured tools already available" (McDermott and

Varenne, 1995, p. 325). As people hammer each other into shape in culturally significantly and meaningful ways, the culture itself as well as the individual learner is transformed (learns).

Máire Zepf's engagement with Irish culture and tradition for example, has provided her myriad opportunities for creative storytelling but beyond this, her writing of the first Irish language verse novel, has also changed that Irish culture and tradition for current and future participants (including readers and writers) in terms of the kinds of stories now imagined and how they might be told. This dynamic understanding of culture suggests that the more opportunities learners have to engage with meaningful ideas and alternative literacies beyond curriculum content in the classroom, the richer the possibilities for and experiences of engagement, learning and transformation of the individual, local and wider geographical and historical cultures.

Exploring the work of Patricia Forde through inquiry-based approaches to reading and writing in culture: Literacy as a cognitive, psychological, linguistic, sociocultural and socio-political act

Arts-based pedagogies offer learners opportunities for reading and writing in culture in ways that foster authentic connections with shared histories, cultures and literacies. They also invite us to join existing conversations knowing more than we can tell but using new literacies, knowledge and ways of knowing to share something of our own experiences. Understanding children's and young adult literature itself as a cultural endeavour, activity and practice, this chapter begins its exploration of reading and writing in culture with a focus on these cultural stories, questioning how and why these stories (and not others) are defined, accepted and valued as children's and young adult literature.

Though sometimes relegated to the margins of classroom experience (Dowling Long, 2015) the children's and young adult literature authors contributing to this chapter champion the possibilities of these stories and the arts and aesthetic literacies within for engaging learners in meaningful reading, writing and literacy practice in culture. They understand that "engaging with the arts as students journey through learning opens windows to multiple worlds, and provides bridges to understandings whether they are in other content matter, or to other peoples and cultures" (Goldberg, 2017, p. 12).

FIVE MINUTES WITH PATRICIA FORDE

How do you think learning through the arts can be encouraged and supported in the classroom?

I read somewhere that learning is that which changes us. I think learning happens, when we are given information or experience, that combined with what we already know, changes the way we think about something. Personally, I think experiencing something is the most powerful way to learn, and reading and drama offer us all a way to experience things we might otherwise never experience. What is important is that the transformation of the learner is permanent which is why cramming for exams is not a valid learning experience. You have to get past peoples' defences and prejudices, to teach them something, and because you are asking them to change, they have to have trust in the teacher.

The arts are a powerful tool to help young people find a voice and an identity. The arts help young people express themselves and this in turn helps with their own sense of self. Writing helps children to express themselves, to hear their own voice and can help them to see things from a slight remove. Reading helps children to discover that they are not alone in the world, that there are other people just like them. It teaches them empathy and helps them learn what it is to be someone else with a very different set of challenges. Reading a story allows us to inhabit a new setting, to become another character, to grapple with problems, and experience the pleasure of resolution. A book is an escape hatch, a portal to somewhere else and as such is an essential life skill. For me reading is made up of two distinct parts. The first part is the ability to understand the code, to learn the relationship between letters and individual sounds, and the ability to blend those sounds into words. This is the part of reading that first most occupies teachers, parents and children. The second part is the ability to follow a story, to suspend disbelief, and to become immersed totally in narrative. This only comes with experience and guidance. I want readers to find characters with whom they can identify, because that is a crucial gift that reading can offer.

I want children to love the story I am telling. It is of no concern to me whether they read the story themselves, or someone else reads it to them. I want to share the story, to invite them into the world that I have created, and then through storytelling, keep them there, eagerly pursuing my heroine, caring about her, and determined to know her ultimate fate. I want them to feel at home in my book, to believe they are there, making friends with my heroine, having experiences both familiar and strange.

Through reading, children see that characters have many layers, people are not necessarily all good or all bad, and that we are all capable of making mistakes. Characters in books become as real to them as their siblings or friends. This is a powerful tool for parents and teachers. In a world, where children have never been further away from the influence of adults we can speak to them through the pages of a book. I think the most important thing is to harness natural curiosity. Reading an historical novel, for example, will often lead the class to research that historical period further. History, English, Irish, Geography and Science could all find jumping off points within the canon of literature written for children.

The tradition of storytelling in Ireland greatly influences your writing and themes. Could you talk to us a little more about this?
I was lucky to attend a small country school and be taught by a teacher who loved stories. Later we moved into Galway town and there were stories all around me. Our house had once been owned by one of the fourteen tribes of Galway. From our upstairs window, we looked down on a cobbled yard, where once the horses from Lynch's castle were exercised. From neighbouring Mayo, we had a famous pirate, called Gráinne Mhaol or Grace O'Malley, stalking the bay in the 14th century. Oliver Cromwell, sent his forces to lay siege to the town in the 17th century, and after many months of holding the line, the citizens were forced through starvation and an outbreak of the Bubonic Plague to surrender. Down in Kirwin's Lane, where my sisters and I played hopscotch on summer evenings, was the home of Dick Martin (or Humanity Dick) who fought for animal rights in the 19th century. On one famous occasion, we were told, he brought a donkey into court as a witness. Whether or which, he was responsible for the first prosecution for animal cruelty in the world. I didn't read any of those stories. I heard them. Listening to stories sentences and paragraphs have a shape and the telling and retelling of tales emphasises this. It's a bit like music. After a while you can hear where there's a wrong note. It's why I read my work aloud to make sure that the voice is always in tune with itself.

At around the age of ten, I read a lot of folklore and mythology. I loved old maps of Galway, and Enid Blyton style, I was always hoping to find a secret passage, in our three hundred year old house. I can't remember when I first heard about Hy Brasil but it feels like I've known that story all my life. Hy Brasil is an island that is said to appear off the west coast of Ireland every seven years. For the remainder of the time, it is shrouded in a mysterious mist, which conceals it from the eyes of mortals. I regularly went down to the Claddagh, to gaze out on the broad Atlantic in the hope that one day I would see this magical place. I can still remember that longing. When Galway became European Capital of Culture in 2020, I was commissioned to write a Picture Book that would be given free to every child who started school in Galway in 2020. It was a great honour to be asked, and I wanted to make a book, that would say to those five year olds, that this is important. Books are important, stories are important, believing in something that you can't always see is important, and most especially in this momentous year for Galway, children are important. It was published in Irish and in English by Little Island under the title *To The Island/An t-Oileán Thiar*.

You have stated that for you writing often begins with a single image. Could you tell us more about your writing process?

I have never understood where that initial image comes from even though I can see that in part it comes from my own experience. With *The Wordsmith*, for example, I saw Letta behind a counter in a shop. My father was a shopkeeper and we lived over the shop. I spent time behind the counter, so that was a world I was familiar with. Letta was selling words which meant that the words had a value. I had been thinking a lot about the Irish language at the time, and I was wondering about the value of the words we were losing from the language. If there is no word for something, does the thing itself become less valuable? After the initial image, it's all about discovery. I asked myself why the girl was selling words. I realised the book would be some kind of fantasy and took it from there. I don't plan much when I am writing my first draft. I follow the thread and see where it takes me. In the next draft I do some retrospective planning. I might draw a map or write back stories for the characters. It is only when the book is written that I can identify themes and messages that the reader will find but that crept in unconsciously as I was writing.

I also think you learn from each of the different forms and genres in which you write. Film and television teaches you to think visually, which helps when it comes to writing picture books. When you are *only* writing the text for the picture book, and someone else is doing the illustration, you have to learn to leave room for that other person. If I put all the description into the text, I leave nowhere for the illustrator to go. Equally, television is a team sport, and you learn very quickly that you, the writer, are not at the top of the pecking order. Writing soap opera teaches you to come up with ideas quickly. Soap opera is a beast that needs feeding all the time. A novel is a major undertaking and I view it as more of a marathon than the other forms. Irish is a very visual language, I think, and I love to write Irish language picture books. I love playing with words regardless of language and being able to work in two languages adds to that pleasure.

Good stories begin with the character and the inner life of the character. If that part of the story is strong and convincing the story will work for me. After that, I want sentences that sing and words that are well-chosen. I also love fantasy and especially invention. What does the hero want? This could be a want to go to America, to be rich, to be loved by her mother. But we also need to know what the hero *needs*. Does she need to learn courage? Does she need to learn that some people will never change? The story works in that space where the tension is – the tension between the want and the need. Letta in *The Wordsmith* wanted a quiet life but she needed to fight to change the injustices all around her. The hero always needs a challenge. I would advise young people to keep a diary and to record emotional adventures. Tell yourself, not what you did, but what you felt. As a writer, you will be concerned with the interior life of your characters and *you* are the character you know best. You can imagine how that diary would change between the age of seven and seventeen. If you decide to make a career of writing for young people information like that would be pure gold!

What advice do you have for using children's and young adult literature in the classroom?

Literature is a safe space. Learners and teachers can discuss the issue in relation to the character in the book in an age appropriate way. Unfortunately, a lot of young people experience dark times in their lives and literature can help them to realise that others have been in these situations before them, and more will be there after them. Books provide starting points for conversation. I hope that we are better at identifying children who are in trouble and be able to do practical things to help them, but unfortunately the dark side of life is often very well-hidden, and educators operate in a space where information is often very limited. And maybe that is where books are useful, reaching out to children in a quiet intimate space and speaking directly to them.

Present children with a vast variety of books. I would rather read one chapter of a different book each day than have the entire class work on the same class novel. I love to introduce a novel to children as you would pitch a book to a friend. Give a thrilling synopsis. Then read the book to a point that leaves the reader wondering what happens next. Reading a different book daily for a month casts the net wide. Somewhere during that month you may just find a book to suit each child. This should also include nonfiction books and poetry anthologies.

I would also look at what writers do and discuss that in the classroom, encouraging speculation. What do you think happened before this story started or after this story finished? I have had great discussion about *The Wordsmith* in this way. We try to imagine what the last days before The Melting were like. We acted out news programmes where John Noa was interviewed and where he warned people that the end was nigh. This kind of discussion will help children with their own writing too and draw their attention to things they may have missed on first reading. I always think that reading is like riding a bicycle. You need to develop confidence and you need to practice.

Writing is an extension of reading and there are many different types of writing all requiring different skill sets. I try to present creative writing as an extension of play. Here is a space to invent our own world. What kind of school should we have? Could we design a uniform or have no uniform? What kind of animals and birds are there here? What religion holds sway? What laws are there? What is the greatest threat? Giving young people the opportunity to brainstorm like that, ignites their own inherent creativity. In my experience, the ability to think and dream is more important, on the training slopes of writing, than actually making lovely sentences.

Images are central to your writing process. Can you share an image with us that you think could form the basis of a creative writing exercise for our readers?

Aoife smiled at the children and held out her arms to them. But the children were wary. They did not like Aoife's hard green eyes. They didn't like her high, spiky shoes, or the smell of cold, damp days that surrounded her. *OR*

The owl widened her eyes. The spider was draped in a sparkling web – a shimmering shawl, made for a bride. *OR*

The Museum of Love and Loss looks like any other house in the lane if any other house had a door that came and went as it pleased.

Patricia's discussion of reading as both an escape hatch and life skill connects literary and literacy aspects of reading and writing and posits reading children's and young adult literature as a real experience that is retained afterwards in a way that transforms the reader's understandings of themselves and the world. Her distinction between understanding form and meaning, the code and the story, affords an opportunity to explore in more detail some literacy aspects of the cultural stories that make up children's and young adult literature, a practice often engaged in by teachers in traditional classroom practice. Reading and writing strategically, however, as previously highlighted, asserts that this exploration of literacy must occur with the simultaneous and supporting contextual investigation of literary aspects of text.

In traditional classroom practice teachers often focus on reading and literacy through either bottom up or top down approaches. Bottom up approaches focus readers on building up the text by reading word by word, sentence by sentence and so on. Top down approaches focus on meaning and believe that it is the individual reader and not the words on the page that make sense of the text. Alderson (2000) combines these approaches in an interactive model for reading where every component in the reading process interacts with each other as active top down approaches predicts meaning while bottom up approaches work to check these predictions. The words (literacy aspects) and the worlds (literary aspects) of the text are both of high importance in the experience of reading within this view as reading itself is understood as an interactive personal, social and cultural space. From this perspective teachers should look for opportunities to provide a range of supports through a variety of multiple perspectives for literacy as learners engage with meaningful and authentic reading and writing cultural practice.

Hall's (2003) *Listening to Stephen Read: Multiple perspectives on literacy* exemplifies well a multiple perspective inquiry approach to reading in her exploration of reading practice from cognitive psychological, psycho-linguistic, sociocultural and socio-political perspectives. Each of these four perspectives are briefly summarised separately here to exemplify their possible application in classroom practice but together they work to reconceptualise reading, writing and literacy as powerful cognitive, psychological, linguistic, sociocultural and socio-political acts. These sociocultural acts of knowing (about particular things and in particular ways) necessitate an inquiry-based approach to reading that focuses learners on the strategic unearthing of layers of semantic, linguistic, social, cultural and historical meaning inherent in the literacy and literary pathways of cultural texts. Following the summary of these four perspectives on reading in culture is an exemplification of what each might look like in classroom practice using Patricia's text *The Wordsmith*.

Firstly, the cognitive psychological perspective understands reading as a staged and developmental process where the word and attention to sound (phonological awareness) helps readers decode words through a focus on the alphabet and individual letters. Pedagogies here are built around the development of mental imagery through graphic organisers, summarizing, asking why questions and explicit attention to words of the text. From a contrasting psycho linguistic perspective rather than something that can be taught we learn reading best by engaging in reading itself. Non-visual resources such as context and prior knowledge act as cues for readers who problem solve and construct meaning around whole and authentic texts. Pedagogies supporting this perspective are interactive and include a focus on shared reading experiences, literature circles and personal response-based activities to story.

The sociocultural perspective on reading focuses our attention on the social and cultural contexts in which reading occurs and asks individuals to define the meaning and purpose of reading in each context in which it is encountered. Reading in an English classroom, car garage and at home, for example, are understood as being very different in form, function, purpose and meaning. Pedagogical approaches sensitive to this perspective ask classroom reading communities of practice to carefully consider what reading is for and how it is done (including reflecting on agency, power and value) in a particular context.

Finally the socio political perspective understands that no knowledge is neutral and a very important part of learning to read is being able to determine underlying assumptions and biases in text. Readers are urged to take a critical stance towards textual images and worlds and think about how texts work to achieve certain effects. Pedagogies from this perspective work to make explicit relationships between language and the world, specifically how personal and cultural attitudes and beliefs are presented in language. Developing critical literacy through explorations of power, intertextuality and the referencing of other worlds, ideas, beliefs and understandings in texts are central to classroom activities within this approach.

Patricia's description of the many historic and contemporary cultural stories that existed all around her growing up and their impact on her childhood experiences exemplifies how personal and cultural stories interact in the development of self and identity and shifts focus from written to spoken language. Within the world of her novel *The Wordsmith,* language, identity, culture and the arts are closely bound together in one community's meaning making in the aftermath of environmental disaster. Identifying our own world and familiar types at a remove in the story, readers experience characters and the dystopian world of Ark as both familiarly strange and strangely familiar, where ways of living are interrogated through the lens of arts and culture. This aligns with Patricia's understanding of books and story as important points of meaningful connection between young learners and adults in a world where space for these kinds of cultural interactions are becoming ever more limited.

Within the world of Ark words are powerful and dangerous and all artistic expression is banned. Controlling the language spoken (by limiting those living there to speak List, a language of only 500 words) allows John Noa to control the people, their experiences and the world itself. Desecrators, living outside of the community of Ark, face severe punishment for celebrating the experiences offered by music, art and culture. The wordsmith of Ark searches for, collects, groups and sells words. Alongside clothes, food and water words and language are rationed among individuals for the greater good of all.

Reading the cognitive, psychological, linguistic, sociocultural and socio-political contexts of *The Wordsmith* opens up myriad questions for personal and collaborative inquiry-based activities around language, environmentalism, climate change, the power of words, censorship, the role of the arts in life and learning and much more. The close focus on words and vocabulary (each chapter for example beginning with a numbered list or non-list word and its definition similar to the cards the wordsmith makes) and the underlying question of how many words we need to survive aligns with a cognitive psychological perspective in its emphasis of the spoken word as a means of communication between people.

These themes connect closely to Patricia's own discussion of how the spoken word and the oral culture of storytelling in Ireland is central to her identity and practice as a writer. Aligning storytelling with culture, sound and music as she reads her own writing aloud to herself extends the different kinds of arts-based literacies we can bring to bear on a study of words and language to develop narrative voices that are always in tune with themselves. As teachers we might consider, for example, the opportunities learners have in our classrooms to engage with older cultural literacy, reading and writing traditions such as oral storytelling. Learners could themselves also be encouraged to read aloud and share their own writing as a part of the writing process itself rather than at the end and reflect on how they might understand this as time for interpreting and imagining their characters and stories anew.

The idea of word lists/collections for different professions and contexts could also be adapted to classroom vocabulary or key word learning where learners are encouraged to develop literacy practice by collecting their own personally relevant and meaningful word lists. Learners could also engage creatively with word listing tasks, considering and justifying for example what 100 words they would include if language in the classroom, home, sports field, youth club etc... was to be limited. Could we survive a week in the classroom using only these words? Could we create our own world in a creative writing task where language is similarly limited? What kind of world would we create? What language would be needed here and why? What texts could we base our own worlds on? What do we think about the concept of economy of expression? Can words say too much? Or too little?

These wider reaching activities move literacy and learning towards more psycho-linguistic understandings as learners are asked to use and research familiar texts to problem solve and learn through creating unique and personally resonant worlds with their own unique characters and language. Taking time to imagine and live with our ideas, and experience them through a variety of modes and media (for example words, images, maps, people), is an essential aspect of arts-based literacy practice. As Patricia explains, thinking and dreaming on the training slopes of writing is an essential part of the observation, interpretation and imagination required to notice what can be noticed beyond the moment's grasp (Greene, 2001). Her bite-size approach to text, including a wide variety of text types and worlds in classroom practice, along with her playful approach to language (as something that can be chosen and so redefined for example) similarly supports this personal, aesthetic and affective engagement and ways of knowing and opens up opportunities for the production of new kinds of texts using a variety of arts-based literacies beyond the written word.

Sociocultural approaches to reading *The Wordsmith* could ask learners to think about how language is used and for what purpose in the different communities and settings of Ark. This question could be broadened to our own world, asking learners to consider how and why their use of language differs in varied contexts, cultures and settings. Connecting with the arts (including dance, drama, music, film) as a setting and context for the telling of personal and cultural stories learners could also be encouraged to think about language and literacy paths in these contexts and more broadly (aligning with Greene's suggestion of unique arts-based literacies) learners could consider how dance, music, film and so on themselves offer their own unique languages and literacy paths for communication of experiences through these media.

Finally, the main themes of *The Wordsmith* explicitly focus readers on the socio political nature of texts, namely that knowledge and language are never neutral, and part of our work as readers is to more deeply understand the relationships in texts between language and the world. The world of Ark echoes at a safe remove experiences, concerns and real life problems of today's world. The Melting, the environmental disaster leading to the founding and philosophies of Noa's Ark, is remembered in ways that ask us to question our own beliefs about global warming, climate change, environmentalism and activism but also how language is used in our world to talk about and position ourselves and our practices in relation to these current issues. Hope is defined as a relic of another time where language could be understood as just as subversive, useless and dangerous as in the world of Ark. How can we understand the role of the arts in the development of cultures, identities and personal experiences of learning?

REIMAGINING LEARNERS AS ART, STORY AND WORD COLLECTORS: READING AND WRITING IN CULTURE THROUGH LITERARY LANDSCAPES AND LITERACY SELF-PORTRAITS

The Wordsmith (Patricia Forde)

One of the tasks of the wordsmith in Patricia's story is the collection of words and their meanings. In her interview Patricia tells of her own childhood experience as a collector of the stories all around her experienced through the voices of others. Charting the stories of a class group, local area, school or community asks learners to engage with stories and texts outside of the curriculum in an arts-based pedagogical approach that centres on an immersion in narrative, history and culture and offers authentic opportunities for learners to create individual and collective literacy self-portraits.

- **My reading history in people and places:** Ask learners to think about their reading practices and histories at home. What memories of childhood reading and storytelling do you have? What have you read? Where (bedroom, kitchen, outdoors) and with whom (alone, siblings, grandparents)? When did you read and/or listen to stories? How do these answers compare to your experiences of reading now? And in school?
- **Story 24:** Keep a log over the next 24 hours of anything you read and any stories you hear. In small groups share and discuss these logs and create a collaborative story collage representing the experiences of the group. What words are most common in your discussion? Include these as a central aspect of your collage. Using the internet research how many words make up an average young person's vocabulary. On average how many words do they use a day? What kinds of words? How does this compare to our own experiences? What words could we not live without? Why?
- **Collecting stories all around me:** Ask learners to research local stories. Just as Patricia found stories all around her, encourage learners towards natural inquiry of the objects, places and spaces close to them. Can you research your house, your neighbourhood, a family heirloom? What stories are all around you?
- **Book/story landscapes:** Create a landscape of books/stories laid out across the classroom space. Take a thematic approach and try and group similar books/stories and authors together in one area (two to three books per table for example), taking learners on a journey through connected landscapes of stories. Allow learners plenty of time to explore and discuss this landscape and think about specific spaces within it – where are their favourite, familiar and strange places? What might these stories look like as a real landscape? What kind of world would all these characters live in together and how might they interact with each other? How would learners group these books themselves? What would individual learner's personal reading landscapes look like? Which of your classmate's reading landscapes would you like to explore more? Why? How?
- **The 50-word story bet:** Share the following 50-word list with learners: List: a, am, and, anywhere, are, be, boat, box, car, could, dark, do, eat, eggs, fox, goat, good, green, ham, here, house, I, if, in, let, like,

may, me, mouse, not, on, or, rain, Sam, say, see, so, thank, that, the, them, there, they, train, tree, try, will, with, would, you. Encourage discussions about the words. What do you notice? Are any of the words familiar? Why are we looking at this list of words? Could you write a story using these words? Could you write a story with a very limited vocabulary? As a class can we come up with an agreed word list that will be used to write our own individual stories? What 50 words would we need to tell the stories of our own lives and experiences? How would that story go? (These words are all the vocabulary used in the 1960 Dr Seuss book *Green Eggs and Ham*. This book was written as a result of a bet between the author and his publishers that he could not write a story using only 50 words, after writing the 236 word *The Cat in the Cat*. As of 2019 *Green Eggs and Ham* has sold over 8 million copies worldwide.)

- **My class soap opera:** Learners are asked to consider a range of arts-based literacies in the development over time of a class soap opera. This project could take place altogether or span the academic year. Identifying as screen writers, producers, actors and stage directors learners have to attend to every aspect of the written, spoken and experienced words of their stories.

Writing our lives as storied works of art: Arts-based inquiries as a theoretical lens for exploring identity and affect in the work of Máire Zepf

Understanding reading, writing and literacy as cultural practices affords meaning and context to personal literacy and identity development as learners observe, interpret and imagine unique literary and literacy pathways within shared cultural experiences. Moving in focus from reading to writing literacy pathways through text, relationships between viewer (or reader), author and text become a central concern. Returning to Greene's description of experiencing the arts as a mysterious interpretive act (Greene, 2001) this chapter suggests that arts-based pedagogies that focus on the creative acts of storytelling and writing as live transactions could be employed to explore personal identity and literacy development in the context of culture in the classroom.

Hesford (1999) suggests that understanding writing as a tool for thinking requires that the writer becomes a reader of oneself, explaining that "the autobiographical act is not a mere act of retrieval of an already existing and complete self but rather a performative act through which the self is created and re-created in the process of the telling" (Hesford, 1999, p. 3). This process of active and reflective self-inquiry through making and experiencing stories about ourselves positions arts-based literacy practices within complex personal, social and cultural semantic webs.

Inquiry-based pedagogies for writing strategically to understand literacy and literature ask learners to collaboratively make meaning from genuine, personal curiosity and questioning and facilitate learner exploration of their own stories (and literacy and literary pathways within) and the stories and literacies all around them in the development of personal literacy and identity. As Eisner (2002) further suggests:

> the arts, as vehicles through which our inscriptions occur, enable us to inspect more carefully our own ideas…they speak back to us, and we become in their presence a part of a conversation that enables us to see what we have said.
>
> (Eisner, 2002, p. 11)

Understanding writing culturally as an affective as well as an academic experience an arts-based approach to writing in the classroom draws on additional literacies and ways of knowing about the world and ourselves that exist beyond language and the moment of the experience. Being able to turn a moment over in our stories and explore and later represent how we and/or our characters feel as a result involves a process of defamiliarisation of experience (explored in detail in part two of this text) that moves beyond a focus on curricular content to consider personal understandings of identity, self, community, culture and literacy in the classroom. Máire Zepf's Irish language verse novel Nóinín exemplifies in many ways these affective and identity aspects of literacy, learning and knowing inherent in authentic and arts-based meaningful strategic reading and writing practice.

FIVE MINUTES WITH MÁIRE ZEPF

How do you think learning through the arts can be encouraged and supported in the classroom?

Learning is about the arousal of curiosity, the critical questioning of arguments and approaches and the gentle teasing-open of cracks in mental doors that have been firmly slammed shut. Where teaching intersects with creativity, it requires a feather-light touch. Really, it is more about the development of a protective space inside which unknown ideas and approaches can grow, rather than any 'how to' guide. I am a huge fan of the Daniel Pennac 'Rights of the Reader' approach to reading. And when we dig a little into our own experiences as readers – our choices, rituals and habits, this self-awareness can inform a respectful relationship with young readers. My focus is on reading for pleasure, and there are simple ways to encourage this – from choosing your own books to an honest permission to hate a book. It involves setting aside snobberies about 'good' and 'bad' books and accepting that each reader's journey will be a different one. As a writer, I don't know how readers will engage with the text. That is their part in our author-reader collaboration!

As a child I loved Pat O'Shea's *The Hounds of the Morrigan* and still do. I still read children's books all the time. I have read and re-read that book so often that my copy is dog-eared and battered with use. It's funny – very funny – but it is also really beautiful and incredibly comforting. I think of it as a comfort-blanket in book form and it comes off the shelf when I am feeling stressed or afraid, as a happy place to escape into. School (the institution) can similarly be a sanctuary for many young people – a place of stability, clear rules and expectations, with a gleam of positivity and a backbone of moral conscience. The flipside of this, however, is that it can also jar with the teens' real experience, a dissonance that can make it seem false and contribute to the sense young people have of needing to mask their honest lived experiences, emotions and problems. There is integrity and health in going to the dark side, at least some of the time. An acknowledgement that life can be really hard and we can all struggle, is a place of bravery and strength. Teachers want to protect the young people, but the result is that they can feel ashamed to admit that they have difficulties.

I hope Nóinín's story will serve to open any reader's antennae to the possibility of 'this could happen to me'. Teens feel invincible and deeply dismissive of advice from adults on the digital arena in which they feel such ownership. An antidote to that might be to walk through this story as Nóinín and as Eimear and to feel how easily it could happen to any of us. I think I chose to write about it because I wanted to understand it better myself. I wanted to shake off that smug assumption of safety from which people witness another's victimhood. I firmly believe that we can't protect young people by keeping them away from digital danger. Instead we need to open up conversations about the protective nature of scepticism and the importance of tuning in to our gut feelings of 'something isn't right here'.

It was important to me from the very start of writing *Nóinín* that it wouldn't be a preachy book. It was part of its raison d'etre that we would step honestly into Nóinín's shoes, rather than stand in judgement of her. There are some really important and thorny issues raised in this book – about blame and shame and about the intergenerational clash of ideas, that may be powerful to open up wide in a classroom setting. The women in the book blame themselves about the tragedy, but Eimear is very certain that Nóinín's mum's instinct to victim-blame should no longer be tolerated. This is a generational shift that all readers will recognise, I think. Another area ripe for exploration in the classroom is teen friendship. Where are the lines between responsibility to protect a friend and their own autonomy to make decisions, even risky ones? This is a question young people face on a daily basis.

Could you tell us a little about your approach to writing, and the Irish verse novel in particular?

For me, the choosing of words, the 'art and craft of making text' is only the final stage in a long process. The ideas come first, the characters, the questions. Lots of this work is done without pen and paper. This is the staring-into-space stage of writing (and one that is often skimmed over in a school setting). Then comes the structural taming of the idea – the architecture of the story. And finally, when words get chosen, it's about trying to think myself directly into the emotional experience of my character. To feel the story in their skins and then to try to translate that so the reader can feel what I'm feeling. With a book like *Nóinín*, that is quite exhausting. Then I read aloud what I have written – hearing the words spoken sharpens my sense of what is working and what isn't. I often get myself completely stuck at every stage in the process. This is best fixed by leaving the work aside and coming back again another time to revisit. Often the problem becomes clear with a little distance.

All of my books started life in Irish, although some of them have been translated internationally (to eight languages now). Writing in Irish is instinctive for me, as someone raised in an Irish-speaking home. It is at the heart of my motivation to write – to be part of creative and expanding the canon of literature in the language I love. The identity of young Irish speakers is complex and fascinating. For those whose Irish comes only from a school context, the need for books that recognisably reflect contemporary young lives – socially and emotionally – through the medium of Irish is a stark one in order to nurture a holistic linguistic identity.

The verse novel is more than a hybrid of prose and poetry. It is a unique genre that stands very firmly on its own feet. It exists in a liminal flow between fractured prose and narrative poetry. I love the extra dimension it gives me – that as well as using meanings and sounds, I also have shape to play with the expression of thought. The long spaces, the tumble of words when a character is feeling disorientated, the stark repetitions of a brain in shock, for example. It also allows the reader a unique freedom to pace their own reading and to fill the space on the page with their own thoughts and experience. I chose to write *Nóinín* in verse because of how much I loved reading verse novels myself. I was also fascinated by their success with reluctant readers, unconfident readers and even hardened bibliophobes. There was some magic to the combination of light stripped-down text and narratives that I wanted to bring to the Irish language where there is little young adult fiction for older teens, and a tendency for older teens to read their fiction in English.

What advice would you have for aspiring young authors?

When you want to write a story, my advice is to try to delay the actual putting-words-down-on-paper part. Doodle and daydream first, observe the world around you like you are harvesting ingredients. Keep thinking and playing with your idea. It's really hard not to be impatient to rush to the writing stage, but the trick is to wait until you really can't bear to wait a minute longer to get it down. You'll find the words flow this way because you already know so much about your characters and story. The other tip I have for you is to make sure your story has a really bad problem. This is central to a good plot. Sounds a bit cruel, doesn't it? But you need to make something go wrong that is your main character's worst idea of hell!

Think about whose story is this? What do they want? Why can't they get it? (What is standing in their way?) And then, how will they overcome it? Try to be open-minded about your ideas and characters – let your mind switch the situations and places and different story possibilities to try them on for size. Stories usually grow and evolve rather than arrive fully-formed, so be prepared to muck around with it and experiment a little. Creativity is messy! Sometimes, I make Pinterest boards on themes, worlds or eras to inspire my imagination, or just doodle and scribble lots in a notebook to get going. There is no right and wrong, but the better you know your characters and world before you start choosing words, the better. Partly this is about observing your own real life and those around you, and partly it is about imagining yourself into the hearts and brains of your characters. Once you know how they feel, you'll be able to show your reader. I say 'show' because this is much more effective that 'telling' your reader. Rather than writing 'Marcus was angry', describe the clench of his teeth, the bulge of his eyes or the whiteness of his knuckles. Writers call this trick 'Show don't tell' and it is very powerful.

In your work with Quotidian you aim to move literature and poetry to public and community spaces in ways that engage every member of society as an audience. Have you any advice for teachers who might be thinking about extending their focus and work in literature beyond the classroom (or school)?

The central impetus behind all of our work at Quotidian is to break down some of the barriers that make literature feel inaccessible to people. Literature in general, and poetry in particular, can seem overly complex, elitist, abstract or high-brow, if your experience of them has only been via gatekeepers. The idea that literature is a code to be cracked, with correct and incorrect answers, can lead to a fear of making mistakes or having the 'wrong' response. Teachers are unused to seeing themselves as gatekeepers, and my experience is that the teachers I meet are just as likely to feel this discomfort as anyone else. Therefore, it can be a liberation to them too to be able to 'explore' literature and poetry in new ways with honest responses rather than learned interpretations.

At Quotidian, I work with poet Maria MacManus across a range of projects. Some of them bring poetry to new physical contexts (e.g., the city street, with 'Poetry Jukeboxes' and 'Lit Labels'). This is a simple, but surprisingly powerful tactic. Leaving the confines of a classroom to hear a poem, or going outside to write can fundamentally transform the experience. Going to a heritage or nature site to see/hear/smell/taste and touch with the alertness of a poet (taking notes if you like, even bringing armfuls of leaves, moss etc. back into the classroom if you can bear to) can lead to an experience of writing that closely mirrors

> the poet's own. Other projects we run aim to intersect literature through other art forms or community responses. Illustrating a poem, performing it as a group with actions, gesture and sound effects, or writing a poem in response to a piece of art can all open wide the children's innate creative responses. Poetry is all around us when we start enjoying language. In song lyrics and prayer, in nursery rhymes and picture books, in advertising and the back of shampoo bottles. Tuning the ear to its riches and its playfulness can be extraordinarily rewarding.
>
> *Could you suggest a sample creative writing activity for young authors who would like to experiment with free verse writing?*
> It often surprises me how differently thoughts come out in different languages. If you want to see what your Irish creative brain dreams up, my first piece of advice would be to not worry about spelling or grammar or any of those technical things. You can proof-read and polish those things when you have something you are happy with creatively. And if you don't know a word, put it there in English as a place-holder and fill it later. One of my favourite poetry prompts is to take a sound effect – like a crackling fire, a beeping machine or crashing waves – and to just start writing as you listen to it. Try not to think too much for this exercise, but just jump in feet first. And remember, with free verse, anything goes – put the words wherever they want to go. People are often surprised what bubbles to the surface when you use sounds as a prompt. It can awaken forgotten memories, spark a flight of fantasy, or a character's may just start talking to you from the page. If you like what has come out, you can work on it and sculpt it into shape. If not, just play the sound once more and jump in again.

In her interview Máire focuses closely on the reader-writer relationship and the curiosity, creativity, critical questioning and collaboration at its core. Writing Nóinín to understand her own story and themes emerging highlights the personal inquiry-based nature of the journey through text for both strategic readers and writers. Understanding writing strategically as storied inquiry into our own thoughts, experiences and literacies based on shared cultural and historical understandings learnt from the stories of others Máire highlights the importance of careful consideration of narration and perspective. Reading and writing from the first person perspective for Máire offers opportunities to enter different worlds at different points and walk a mile so to speak in the shoes of the characters within these textual worlds. Her conceptualisation of reading and writing as opportunities for growing ideas about our stories, ourselves and our worlds rather than just representing them extends strategic writing literacy focused pedagogies into inquiry- and arts-based spaces for learning and identity development.

Whitelaw's (2017) art as story aesthetic inquiry-based pedagogy offers a model for what this strategic writing might look like in classroom practice. Reporting on her own research (Whitelaw, 2012) explains how:

> through the positioning of art as story, students came to see their lives as works of art; they learned to resist single stories, cultivate an anti-deterministic stance, and build agentive identities. Students used art as a theoretical instrument for world sense making; they used art to theorize, inquire, and engage in the social imagination, positioning them as knowledge generators versus passive receivers. Using the relational space of art as a terrain for mapping diverse experience, students engaged in dialogue and came to understand compassion as a mode of critical inquiry and collective action.
>
> (Whitelaw, 2012, p. vi)

Whitelaw's study foregrounds the role of perception in arts and inquiry-based learning. Understanding perception as sensory-based she suggests that attention to the development of perception in learning affords exploration of related concepts such as awareness, insight, observation and acuity within an experiential approach to learning. Taking as text the students' own lives, Whitelaw asks what it would mean to consider the English classroom as a space where learners use art to strategically explore, understand and construct themselves as works of art and what opportunities do learners have to construct their own lives as stories. She defines stories as lived ways of shaping, exploring and reconstructing human experience in a variety of forms, encouraging "permeable boundaries among the arts, students' lives, and the world, creating powerful new relational spaces for inquiry in the classroom" (Whitelaw, 2017, p. 46).

This meaningful and identity driven focus on literacy and learning through story allows learners to invent, reinvent and experience their own stories and the stories of others in agentive spaces for learning. By positioning their own lives as important texts

Whitelaw argues that learners open opportunities for agency in learning and, echoing the words of Patricia Forde in her interview, begin to see stories everywhere. Through their perceptual development learners better understand and strategically connect different kinds of reading and different kinds of texts. Most importantly, Whitelaw argues that as a part of this process, learners and teachers blur preconceived boundaries between home and school reading, and literacy practices, and make new connections between art and literacy, in and out of school and curriculum content and meaningful aspects of their own lives.

Similarly, through arts-based pedagogies learners come to understand that they can construct themselves in many different ways and their identities are not fixed but emerge to be strategically written and rewritten in daily practice. Using art as a theoretical instrument of inquiry to understand rather than as an object to be known arts-based pedagogies "opened students' hearts and minds to each other's lived worlds and served as a site of dialogue across difference" (Whitelaw, 2012, p. 212).

Whitelaw suggests a starting point for teachers to be asking learners to think about their own lives and the lives of others as storied works of art and to consider the affordances of story as a means of understanding ourselves and others. Her inquiry oriented approach goes on to focus on a number of key inquiry and identity focused areas, namely inquiry in the world and the arts in students' lives; inquiry into each other and the relational contexts of art and story; inquiry into themselves and the arts of students' lives; and inquiry into form and meaning and epistemic possibilities through art as story.

Máire's discussion of Daniel Pennac's *Rights of the Reader* approach to reading provides a meaningful and culturally relevant framework for exploring reading and writing collaboratively and through inquiry with young people in the classroom. Just as Whitelaw suggests learners are encouraged from this perspective to look for and actively engage with stories that mean something to them and talk to and about their own life experiences.

The rights of the reader are the right not to read; the right to skip; the right not to finish a book; the right to read it again; the right to read anything; the right to mistake a book for real life; the right to read anywhere; the right to dip in; the right to read out loud; and the right to be quiet (Pennac, 2006). These reader rights provide a democratic, non-deterministic and identity affirming backdrop for reading and writing a variety of textual and cultural worlds in classroom practice.

Read alongside Máire's consideration of her own reading and writing practices these ten statements about reading could form the basis of a classroom inquiry collaborative project around understanding the rights, responsibilities and experiences of strategic writers as well as readers. Learners could consider, within the wider exploration of their own lives as storied works of art, the different kinds of literacies, form and representation these stories could employ. What rights and responsibilities matter for writing in and about our own worlds? These strategic writer statements could later become resources to scaffold classroom reading and writing practice. From within the protective and structured spaces offered by these statements of successful and strategic reading and writing practice learners can collaboratively experiment with, share and develop their own experiences, stories and identities in ways that draw reader and writer worlds closer together. Máire's text and interview also highlight the importance of spaces for all kinds of stories in this inquiry process, happy and sad, comforting and troubling, light and dark. The following extract written by Máire explains her own experiences engaging learners in creative writing practice away from the written page and traditional textual mode.

'WRITING' BEYOND THE BLANK PAGE, UPSIDE DOWN STORIES AND IMAGINATION WORKOUTS (WRITTEN BY MÁIRE ZEPF)

It came as a surprise to me when I first started running creative writing workshops in schools that children had so little confidence when it came to developing their imaginative ideas. My earliest workshops ran aground amidst a tsunami of questions about everything from which pen to use and which lines to write on, to questions of spelling, punctuation and requests for reassurance. Particularly those children who lacked confidence in their technical literacy abilities felt that stories weren't something 'they were good at' and this blocked their creative flow completely. As a writer well-versed in the messiness of idea development and first drafts, I was disheartened to see how little of the muckiness of creativity remained in the school setting.

For these reasons, I developed various workshops which worked away from the written page. Instead, I ran brainstorming sessions based on a variety of prompts that would allow us to fill the room with thoughts, bounce them off each other, invert, grow or explode them. The result was a creative buzz that was great fun. At the end, children would choose something from the collective idea cloud – an idea they enjoyed so much they felt compelled to write it. This was much more like what writing feels like to me.

There are many ways to do this, but here follows one example, from a project called 'Head Over Heels' that I ran in 25 primary schools in Northern Ireland as Children's Writing Fellow. The idea here was a simple one – that of 'Upside Down' stories, of reversals and flipping of known tropes. It is a simple trick and one that yields a flood of ideas, many of them very funny indeed.

I began workshops by explaining the concept, using the example of a princess. I asked the children to tell me (verbally) her most common attributes. What does she look like? Where does she live? What does she like? I encouraged them to give the most obvious answers they could think of. The list usually involved some of the following characteristics – beauty, wealth, femininity, pretty dresses, good manners, timidity etc. Then I would ask them to take one attribute and turn it upside down. What if she didn't wear pretty dresses, for example? What if she dressed like a punk? Or played football? Or refused to adhere to societal beauty norms? Generally, the room would explode with raised hands and wild ideas. Then we would look at another attribute in the same way, revealing bearded princesses, ninja princesses, grotesque, rebellious, skateboarding, mucky, rude and ambitious female characters, each with a fragment of a story already attached.

Next, I revealed my sack filled with objects. Each object represented a well-known storybook character. The children took turns to pull an object from the sack, taking time to identify its 'usual' attributes and then we begin our 'upside down' stories. All of this was done collectively. Objects included puppets of a dragon and a grandmother, the wand of a fairy, a Viking helmet, a baby's rattle, a robot etc. We would interrogate the identified characteristic of each. What if a dragon didn't breathe fire, but something else instead? What if it was not big but pet-sized, or teensy tiny? What if it didn't live apart from people but next door? The children were encouraged to piggyback on each other's ideas, to embellish, to further exaggerate. By the end of the hour's session, there was palpable creative electricity in the room. At this point, I would ask the children to take one idea from the idea cloud we had

> created. This would be their story. In reality, it was a fragment – a character or a setting, a vivid mental picture that they were excited to write. I have often since run similar 'imagination workouts' using one theme. Robots alone, or dragons, can easily fill an hour of intense and engaged brainstorming!

Máire's description of her own process as a writer exemplifies many of the features of a meaningful and inquiry-based approach to strategic writing in the classroom and the extract above further emphasises the possibilities for strategic creative writing pedagogies beyond the blank page and written word. Máire tells us that much of her own writing is done without pen and paper, involving what she terms "staring into space", but spaces that are imaginative and creative. When we think about writing practices in traditional classroom settings, it may be hard to imagine (in comparison with Máire's pedagogical approach illustrated above) where and when this time to doodle, day dream, observe and inquire takes place. Finally, and only after this process of imagination, Máire tells us that the words come in the form of thinking directly from and into the emotional experiences of her characters. Her approach to strategic writing centres clearly on the affective domain and reading aloud and taking distance from ideas are also central.

Thinking of Whitelaw's key areas for inquiry strategic explorations in these different areas allow time for learners and writers to encounter new texts, ideas and literacies, then return to the growing of their own stories. Máire's understanding that imagination and creativity have to come before the words is a central aspect of an arts-based pedagogical approach and her assertion that writers need time and space to "sculpt a story into shape" itself suggests the variety of literacies, practices, types and understanding of texts that come to bear on a strategic writer as we work to author a text.

Taking herself as an example of this she notes her motivation for writing as wanting to extend the Irish language culture and questions in her approach how thoughts and ideas appear and develop differently in different languages. Her use of the verse novel as form works to defamiliarise everyday thoughts and experiences in text and invites readers to focus in and beyond the moment in personal, emotional and experiential engagements with Nóinín's story. Further exemplification of this multimodal approach to storytelling through the arts is evident in Máire's text *An Féileacán agus an Rí* as Máire's following tweet hints at: "Please come and see our show! Did I say show? I meant our hearts and souls laid bare in dance and words and pictures. We hope you will love it as much as we do" (Zepf, 2020, tweet).

Máire's tweet announces an Irish and contemporary dance adaption of her new book *An Féileacán agus an Rí*, to include a blend of movement, dance styles, music, English and Irish language words, text and illustrations. Connecting with key themes from the previous chapter and understanding the unique opportunities for storytelling inherent in each cultural mode of artistic expression author Máire Zepf, dancer Clara Kerr and illustrator Shona Shirley MacDonald's work fuses together in a collaboration of intense feeling and heart. Moments from the adaptation, for example how for seven long years Éadaoin was blown as a butterfly in all directions by the wind, are not only heard but felt and experienced by viewers to this live multi-dimensional text.

A recording of the show is available to view on Máire's website and exploring this along with Máire's written text provides endless opportunities for discussions around storytelling, strategic reading and writing, arts-based literacies and languages for learning. It also questions and extends our understanding of text in ways that could be interrogated in detail in the classroom. Are both of the retelling of this myth stories? Texts? In what ways are they similar? In what ways are they different? How do Máire, Clara and Shona separately and later collaboratively tell the same story in different ways? What is lost and gained by engaging with this ancient story in this way? What literary and literacy story paths are identifiable? What are the implications for how we tell our own stories?

In a retelling of a story from the oldest existing Irish manuscript it would also be very difficult not to draw parallels from this experience to the oral and performative tradition of storytelling in Ireland and how this story may have been told through the centuries. Reading the words between dance movements and against the backdrop of Shona's illustrations this retelling of the ancient Irish myth derives its energy from the simultaneity and diversity of artistic, aesthetic and affective expression. It is also reminiscent of Máire's own experiences growing up in Ireland, where her father, like the wordsmith in Patricia's text, travelled around the Gaeltacht in Donegal calling on elderly people and collecting words so that they would never be forgotten, also translating and making up his own Irish texts when something was needed that didn't at that time exist.

> **STRATEGIC WRITING AS INQUIRY INTO OURSELVES: THE ARTS OF LEARNER LIVES**
>
> - **Multimodal Memoir Project**
>   The following assignment is adapted from the work of Kist and Semingson (2017).
>
>   In this personal inquiry-based multimodal memoir project learners are encouraged to think about the various texts of their lives that have had significant impact on their identity development and learning. Learners are asked to represent this personal inquiry journey in a mode or modes meaningful to them. Such texts may include books, films, television shows, music, newspapers, magazines, sports, restaurants, food, cars, fashion, architecture, and/or interior design (to name a few examples). Learners are encouraged to visit Google Images, Flickr, Yahoo Image Search, YouTube, etc., and find some non-copyrighted images or video clips related to the important texts of their lives. Digital storytelling and comic book online resources are suggested for the final presentation of the project. Learners are asked to draw out some individual and recurring themes running through their autobiographies and multimodal lives as possible literary or literacy pathways through their own experiences.
>
> **Nóinín *(Máire Zepf)***
>
> Máire's exploration of youth, friendship, love and online grooming in verse novel form draws attention to the power of the arts and free verse in particular to tell personal and cultural stories of shared experiences. The following activities are offered by author Máire Zepf.
>
> - **Cupán Tae agus Cupán Cainteach**: Learners read chapter six (Cupán Tae) alongside chapter fifty (Cupán Cainteach) and write their own poems about a cup of tea or coffee. These might be based on a memory of a particular time, place or person, or a case of unsayable words. Here anything goes – the cup of tea poem might be sci-fi or a political commentary, a love story or a descriptive piece. A task for the learner is to decide what they want their cup of tea poem to be, say and do. What could it mean and allow expression of in each of their own unique lives and experiences?

- **Poncaíocht**: Learners read chapter eighty-five (Poncaíocht) and then 'punctuate' a recent conversation they disagreed with. Play with the words on the page, in terms of size, emphasis, font, colour, possible images. How can you manipulate this text to explore different character perspectives and points of view? How can we act out these conversations in the classroom giving physical expression to the shape of the language on the page? Voice? Props? … How can we express and negotiate disagreements with friends and family to facilitate successful resolution? What do we need to think about? How can we step back from the conversation and see the arguments from multiple perspectives? Where is the line drawn between protecting a friend and personal autonomy and choice?
- **Féinín**: Learners read chapter twenty-one 'Féinín', and then take their own selfies and write about what they see and feel in those moments of self-portraiture. Learners could first be asked to personally respond to their photographs in prose form. Later learners could be asked to think about how they could respond to their photographs through poetry and other arts-based literacies and media for self-expression. What does the image itself say about ourselves?

Conclusion

This chapter explores how inquiry oriented arts-based pedagogies that focus closely on literacy aspects of strategic reading and writing across a wide variety of modes can be incorporated into classroom practice. Distinctive arts-based literacies centring on imagination, interpretation, curiosity, emotion, perception and compassion are discussed alongside a developing understanding of the complex personal and cultural relationships between reader, writer and text. Strategic reading and writing in culture are explored as both cultural practices and personal opportunities for identity development. Literacy is, from this perspective, reframed as a cognitive, psychological, linguistic, sociocultural and socio-political act that requires active and agentic engagement from learners, becoming akin to Silverstein's (1981) imagining of a kind of bridge that:

> will only take you halfway there, to those mysterious lands you long to see. Through gypsy camps and swirling Arab fair, and moonlit woods where unicorns run free. So come and walk awhile with me and share the twisting trails and wondrous

worlds I've known. But this bridge will only take you halfway there. The last few steps you have to take alone.

(Silverstein, 1981, p. 12)

Understanding stories as all around us, and that interrogation of these stories blur boundaries between in and out of school texts, reading, writing and literacy practices, this chapter explores inquiry-based pedagogies that ask learners to strategically read, write and inquire into their own lives and the lives of others as storied works of art. From this perspective knowledge, interpretation and imagination are deeply connected and intersect in momentary and experiential encounters between reader, writer and text where we can move beyond the moment itself to notice what we have not noticed before and know more than we can tell.

Knowing will be more valid – richer, deeper, more true to life and more useful if…our knowing is grounded in our experience, expressed through our art, understood through theories which make sense to us, and expressed in worthwhile action in our lives.

(Reason, 1998, p. 6)

Bibliography

Children's and young adult literature explored in this chapter

Forde, P. (2015). *The Wordsmith*. Ireland: Little Island.
Zepf, M. (2019). *Nóinín*. Ireland: Cois Life Teoranta.
Zepf, M. (2019). *An Féileacán agus an Rí*. Ireland: Futa Fata.
Zepf, M. Kerr, C. MacDonald, S. (2020). *An Féileacán agus an Rí* dance production. Available at https://www.mairezepf.com/single-post/2020/04/01/Féileacán-agus-an-R%C3%AD—the-dance-show.

Other possible texts for exploring literacy ideas and pedagogies highlighted in this chapter

Juby, S. (2015). *The Truth Commission*. USA: Viking Books.

This text is presented in the form of narrative nonfiction including footnotes, illustrations and notes from the characters themselves. As a project for her creative nonfiction module at arts school, Normandy Pale writes a chronicle of the Truth Commission, a group comprising of Normandy and two friends who seek truths from classmates and faculty about a number of known secrets.

Lach, W. (2006). *Can You Hear It?* USA: Harry N. Abrams.

In association with the Metropolitan Museum of Art, this text introduces readers to great music through great works of art, focusing on sensuous and aesthetic knowing and visual, aural and mental imagery.

Myers, W. D. (2010). *Autobiography of My Dead Brother*. USA: Harper Collins.

This text blends innovative first person narrative, realistic sketches, cartoons, comic panels, photos and graphic elements and has been likened to photo realism in its painting of a portrait of adolescent life.

Raczka, B. (2007). *Artful Reading*. USA: Millbrook Press.

This book presents paintings from art galleries around the world that depict readers with accompanying text including information on the painting and the enjoyment of reading different kinds of texts in many different times and places.

Tan, S. (2016). *The Singing Bones*. Australia: Walker Studio.

This book is a collection of 75 clay figurines inspired by Grimm's fairy tales accompanied by short excerpts from each story.

Chapter bibliography

Abbs, P. (1987). *Living Powers: The arts in education*. London: Falmer Press.
Alderson, J. C. (2000) *Assessing Reading*. Cambridge: C.U.P.
Barton, G. (2013). The arts and literacy: What does it mean to be arts literate? *International Journal of Education and the Arts, 14*(18), 1–21.
Boyd, J. (1999). Myths, misconceptions, problems and issues in arts education. Retrieved 30 August 2020 from https://pdfs.semanticscholar.org/47cd/710627155c750d0aaddb109216b60c64bb75.pdf?_ga=2.206897939.1060960218.1598400426-1848330292.1597960647.
Dowling Long, S. (2015). The Arts In and Out of School: Educational policy, provision and practice in Ireland today. *International Electronic Journal of Elementary Education, 8*(2), 267–286.
Eisner, E. (1985). Aesthetic modes of knowing. In E. Eisner (Ed.), *84th Yearbook of NSEE: Learning and Teaching the Ways of Knowing*. Chicago, IL: Chicago University Press.
Eisner, E. (2002). What can education glean from the arts about the practice of education? *Journal of Curriculum and Supervision, 18*(1), 4–16.
Geertz, C. (1973). *The Interpretations of Culture*. New York: Basic Books.
Goldberg, M. (2017). *Arts Integration: Teaching subject matter through the arts in multicultural settings*. New York, NY: Routledge.
Greene, M. (2001). *Variations on a Blue Guitar: The Lincoln Center Institute lectures on aesthetic education*. New York: Teachers College Press.

Greene, M. (1980). Aesthetics and the experience of the arts: Towards transformations. *The High School Journal, 63*(8), 316–322.

Gulla, A. (2018). Aesthetic inquiry: Teaching under the influence of Maxine Greene. *The High School Journal, 101*(2), 108–115.

Hall, K. (2003). *Listening to Stephen Read: Multiple perspectives on literacy.* UK: Open University Press.

Hesford, W. (1999). *Framing Identities: Autobiography and the politics of pedagogy.* Minneapolis: University of Minnesota Press.

Kist, W. with Semingson, P. (2017). The multimodal memoir project: Remembering key YA texts. *The Alan Review,* 44(1), 92–97.

Kress, G. (1997). *Before Writing: Rethinking the paths to literacy.* London: Routledge Publishers.

McArdle, F., Wright, S. (2014). First literacies: Art, creativity, play, constructive meaning-making. In Barton G. M. (Ed.). *Literacy in the Arts: Retheorising Learning and Teaching,* (pp. 21–38). Switzerland: Springer International Publishing.

McDermott, R. Varenne, H. (1995). Culture as disability. *Anthropology and Education Quarterly, 26*(3), 324–348.

Mercurio, M. L. Randall, R. (2016). Tributes beyond words: Art educators' use of textiles to memorialize the Triangle Shirtwaist Factory fire. *Journal for Learning Through the Arts, 12*(1), 1–16.

Pennac, D. (2006). *The Rights of the Reader.* UK: Walker Books.

Reason, P. Heron, J. (1998). A layperson's guide to cooperative inquiry. Available at https://wagner.nyu.edu/files/leadership/avina_heron_reason2.pdf.

Short, K. (2011). Reading literature in elementary classrooms. In Wolf, S. Coats, K. Enciso, P. Jenkins, C. (Eds.), *Handbook of Research on Children's and Young Adult Literature,* pp. 48–63. London: Routledge

Silverstein, S. (1981). *A Light in the Attic.* USA: Harper Collins.

Smyth, E. (2016). *Arts and Cultural Participation among Children and Young People: Insights from the growing up in Ireland study.* Dublin: The Arts Council.

Whitelaw, J. (2017). Arts-based literacy learning like "New School": (Re) Framing the arts in and of students' lives as story. *English Education, 50*(1), 42–71.

Whitelaw, J. (2012). Cultivating Aesthetic Practice for 21st Century Learning: *Arts-based literacy as critical inquiry.* PhD. US: University of Pennsylvania.

Wright, S. (2012). *Children, Meaning-making and the Arts* (2nd ed.). Frenchs Forest, Australia: Pearson education.

PART

Reading and writing widely for personal purposes

CHAPTER 3

Reading, writing and genre as personally resonant and sociocultural practices: Telling the human story of literacy as personal and social practice

About this chapter

This chapter shifts focus from a foregrounding of strategic reading and writing practices to learn about literacy and literature to Short's (2011) second purpose of children's and young adult literature for literacy development, reading (and writing) widely for personal purposes. To this end this chapter explores human aspects of literacy, namely how literacy can be understood as a process of learning through thinking and talking about ourselves and our experiences in diverse personal and social contexts. Understood in this way, the human practice of literacy becomes inseparable from our daily experiences, conversations and lives. Research, literature and children's and young adult literature authors explored here suggest the importance of voice, meaning, authenticity, continuity, connection, community, remembrance, personal resonance and identity in literacy learning.

Related pedagogies for exploring the human story of literacy in the classroom focus on empowering learners through dramatic, creative and innovative approaches to reading, writing, genre and text. Some pedagogical examples discussed in this chapter include pedagogies for interactive, dramatic, performative and meaningful reading aloud; authentic pluralistic language exploration; shared reading histories and genre studies; dialogical and defamiliarised relationships between differently narrated stories and life histories in identity and autobiography writing; and (non-traditional) texts as connecting readers, writers and their real and imagined worlds in particular ways to facilitate identity and literacy development in personal and social contexts.

Readers and writers emerge from this human story of literacy as co-makers of identity, text, meaning and worlds beyond paper as they connect the dots in experiences between characters in fiction and their own. As we explore these personal and social human journeys in literacy through non-traditional text, we remember that "fiction, in giving you a front row seat to another person's heart, allows you to be male, female, an armoured bear – but every child does urgently need to be able to see themselves somewhere" (Rundell, 2019, p. 58).

About the authors

Paul Fleischman

Paul Fleischman is an American author whose work deftly portrays the intricacies of the interrelationships between the written and the wider world. Many of his texts can be understood as collections of experiences exploring the diversity and commonality of the human condition, a theme which exemplifies our understanding of the human story of literacy as personal and social practice. Paul has described himself as a maker at heart and many of his texts embody this notion, taking on properties and evoking experiences beyond their written form.

Paul has received numerous awards including the Newbery Medal, Newbery Honour, Scott O'Dell Award for Historical Fiction, California Young Reader Medal, Boston Globe-Horn Book Award Honour, Pen Center USA Literary Award, Green Earth Book Award, Sigurd Olsen Nature Writing Award, Christopher Medal, Leo Politi Golden Author Award, Horace Mann Upstanders Lifetime Achievement Award, Golden Kite Honour, New York Times Outstanding Book Designation, Parents' Choice Award, ALA Notable Book Designation, Jane Addams Children's Book Award Honour; nominations including Hans Christian Anderson Award, National Book Award, ALA Best Books for Young Adults; and finalist placing for the Los Angeles Times Book Prize for his writing. For more information see http://www.paulfleischman.net.

Paul's stories connect inner experiences, feelings and lives with the lives of others through conversation, collaboration and dramatic performance. This chapter explores some of his texts and exemplifies his wider engagement with literacy, identity and learning themes in his writing. Texts explored include *The Matchbox Diary* – a found object memory diary autobiography; *Alphamaniacs* – a sideshow of mini biographies of the creators of "verbal wonders"; *Seek* – an autobiographical sound portrait of a life told through a symphony of voices; *Whirligig* – a flash forward novel that continuously whirls and moves in the surprising shapes of its name sake; *Zap* – a seven-in-one genre play extravaganza mixing the voices of Shakespeare, Chekhov, Beckett and others in a dramatic and interactive performance that leaps off the stage and into our imagination; *Joyful Noise: Poems in Two Voices* – poems to be experienced and read aloud by two speakers; *Eyes Wide Open: Going behind the Environmental Headlines* – an agentic tale of climate change for young people; and *Dateline: Troy* – a creative retelling of the Trojan war through newspaper collage.

Todd Hasak-Lowy

Todd Hasak-Lowy is an American author, translator and professor of literature at the School of the Art Institute of Chicago. Central to his craft is a profound understanding of the power of literature to cast light on unseen and inner aspects of experience. His narrators stand out in their ability to look inward and share the feelings and emotions of their experiences and those of the characters within their stories with readers, highlighting very strongly that not all stories are told the same way.

Todd publishes across a range of genres as his work considers creative opportunities for how we can tell stories in non-traditional ways. Todd has received numerous awards including the Risa Domb/Porjes Prize for Hebrew Translation, Eureka Excellence in Nonfiction Silver Award, Parents' Choice Gold Medal Award, Bank Street CBC Best Children's Book of the Year Award and finalist placing for the National Jewish Book Award and the Dorothy Canfield Fisher Book Award for his writing, collaboration and translations. For more information see https://www.toddhasaklowy.com/.

Todd's work focuses on the power of bringing external personal experiences inward in a study of the role of interiority, identity and the self in literacy and learning. *33 Minutes* tells the story in real-time and flashback of the breakdown of a friendship between two young boys. *Somewhere There Is Still a Sun*, a collaboration between Todd and Michael Gruenbaum, tells Michael's incredible story in first-person present narration of his time as a boy and teenager in Nazi occupied Czechoslovakia, the Jewish ghettos of Prague and finally the Terezin concentration camp. *We Are Power: How Nonviolent Activism Changes the World* is an empowering text for older readers, telling the story of how young people can peacefully make a change in the world.

Finally, *Me Being Me Is Exactly as Insane as You Being You* tells a story entirely in lists of one boy's life. Taking a diary like approach, this story narrates Darren's inner thoughts through an adaptation of free indirect speech, where the narrator uses Darren's words and perspective but without Darren necessarily being aware of the narration in any way. The form of this narrative develops through a series of lists made on just four significant days in his life, but the story told encompasses many of the significant events and experiences of Darren's entire life and exemplifies in great detail what a human story approach to literacy as personal and social practice looks like in real life.

Introduction

In his paper *The Skin We Ink: Tattoos, Literacy, and a New English Education*, Kirkland (2009) examines what he describes as the human story of literacy as personal and social practice. Presenting tattoos as literacy artefacts that allow young people alternative and meaningful ways to write the stories of their lives this paper extends our definitions of literacy beyond the "technical, prescribed, or academic functions that privilege and serve only specific forms of texts and groups of people" (Kirkland, 2009, p. 376). Reading one young man's (Derrick's) tattoos he suggests that engaging with literacy means not only using words but also imagining new possibilities for (self)expression. Emphasising the significance of new and emerging literacies for teaching and learning Kirkland reminds us that:

> while human beings – poets and writers – have long written with "an inexhaustible voice" and "a soul, a spirit capable of compassion and sacrifice and endurance," today's youth are doing so in new and diverse ways – on computer screens and on the walls of buildings, on paper and on flesh. Their expressions of human experience exist in multiple forms, which can present new challenges and possibilities for English education. Significantly, these new forms in which the human story is etched may raise important questions as to what counts as English teaching today.
> (Kirkland, 2009, p. 375)

Moving to Short's (2011) second purpose for children's and young adult literature in the context of literacy development, to read (and write) widely for personal purposes, this chapter explores the human story of literacy as personal and social practice. As Short (2011) explains, reading and writing widely for personal purposes involves "not only personal enjoyment of reading, but social opportunities to share and become interested in a wide range of genres, authors, styles and themes" (Short, 2011, p. 55). Echoing the advice of Patricia Forde in the previous chapter, learners should be encouraged to read across a wide range of different text types and genres as teachers come to understand that children's and young adult literature provides learners not only with a reason to learn to read but a reason to keep on reading and writing for the rest of their lives (Galda, 2001). In this way reading and writing widely is supported through classroom pedagogies that focus on independent reading and read alouds as learners explore through story and text personal purposes for reading within their own lives.

Imagining readers and writers as makers of worlds, this chapter understands literacy as embedded in and inseparable from the personal and social real life experiences of individuals. Working both within (to negotiate personal and emotional literacies) and without (to navigate shared and social literacies) the self, human aspects of literacy allow opportunities for young people to narrate their experiences, identities and selves using a multitude of authentic personal and borrowed voices. The works of the key children's and young adult literature authors employed throughout this chapter balance and complement each other in their exemplification of how we might, as teachers, engage young people in the human story of literacy as personal and social practice and focus on how and why we learn through telling our own life stories in a variety of different ways.

Understanding narrative and genre as frameworks for personal interpretation and social action within personally resonant and sociocultural reading and writing practices

Understanding Derrick's tattoos as literacy artefacts incorporating life struggles, stories and symbols and connecting personal stories to wider social ones exposes a sociocultural understanding of literacy as a human and personal practice at the heart of reading and writing widely for personal purposes. As Derrick himself explains, talking about one of his most personal and meaningful tattoos, "to a lot of people, this is just my brother's name on me, but I put it on me after he was killed" (Derrick in Kirkland, 2009, p. 385).

Derrick's tattoos are personal commentaries on a life lived in a search for meaning and belonging that comes from an innate desire to understand, dialogue with and reflect on our own experiences in the world. These stories told in ink are echoed elsewhere – for example the story told in a memorial tattoo for a young cousin extends to and from paper (Derrick's journal) and fabric (sport jersey number). In these moments and stories Derrick struggles to answer the world. This understanding of the relationship between the individual, meaning and the world as personal at heart draws on the work of Holland et al. (1998) who explain that:

> the self is a position from which meaning is made, a position that is "addressed" by and "answers" others and the "world" (the physical and cultural environment). In answering (which is the stuff of existence), the self "authors" the world – including itself and others.
>
> (Holland et al., 1998, p. 173)

This personal oriented understanding of meaning and identity (the self) in learning presents the relationship between self and world as a dialogical one that results in learning through improvisation as individuals search for new answers to old questions about what it feels like to be a learner in a particular context. Derrick's tattoo of his brother's name is both a deeply emotional testament to a past and a promised continuation of this past in the future as new stories that will be shared with others in a variety of diverse forms and in different ways. For Derrick each new story will build on his life experiences with his brother and will represent meaningful remembrance in a deeply personal literacy practice.

This idea of meaningful remembrance aligns closely with Kucirkova and Cremin's (2020) discussion of personal resonance in literature as the interaction between (fictional) text and the personal histories of its readers. Kuzmičová and Bálint (2019) suggest that when adults read for pleasure, they read widely for personal purposes by activating their life experiences in tandem with reading the experiences of characters in the text. They also draw in and on past, present and future selves and identities in their engagement with stories. These personal connections to text support reading, literacy and identity development.

Similarly, Cremin et al. (2014) reveal how teachers draw deeply on personal resonance, meaning and affect when discussing their own self-chosen currently reading adult books. In contrast, when discussing self-chosen children's books from their classrooms their textual choice was largely characterised by a professional focus, specific literacy objectives addressed in the book (character, plot, language) and a calculation of how much work could be generated from the text. This approach favours functional aspects of literacy but fails to draw out for young learners the importance of making meaningful personal connections with stories and text.

This meaningful personal connection becomes something transformative in an understanding of literacy for personal purpose as affording young people a "critical awareness of ways of knowing and believing about self that comes from thoughtful examination" (Gallego and Hollingsworth, 2000, p. 15). Symbolising his story through the artistic expression of tattooing on flesh, Derrick "participates in the human act of literacy that moves the personal closer to the transformative" (Kirkland, 2009, p. 386). In the act of inscription Derrick reflects on and is changed by his own stories as his personal inner experiences become public statements of learning and identity. These tattoos and the personal stories they embody will themselves become texts for others to read, engage with and respond to in personal and social human journeys in literacy.

In this way as well as telling his personally significant life stories, Derrick's tattoos take on social significance as they also tell the world about his emerging philosophy of life and developing identity. Viewed together by the world, each individual tattoo and story becomes something more than the sum of its parts, it becomes a person with a history and many potential future learning trajectories. This social dimension of personal literacy practice allows Derrick points of connection with the stories of others and highlights the potential humanity of literacy as a participatory practice of solidarity (Fisher, 2003). Derrick's skin and the tattooed stories etched on it become a public canvas on which he can experiment with the form and content of the stories he tells about himself and others, in the development of an identity which is simultaneously private and public, intensely personal, but only meaningful when read and shared in social contexts and with the experiences of others. This dynamic and relational understanding of literacy has many implications for how we, as teachers, ask our learners to share their life stories and experiences in reading and writing widely for personal purposes in the classroom.

Derrick's memorial tattoo dedicated to his brother Boss, depicting the name Boss and an image of a bulldog, "allows him to appropriate the name of Boss and revoice his brother beyond his name. The name and the bulldog characteristics that once belonged to Boss now belong to Derrick." (Kirkland, 2009, p. 388). This dynamic connection moving between self to others and back again places personal literacies in "the humanity of community – the reasons and willingness to attach and commune as branches on the same family tree" (Kirkland, 2009, p. 387) and encourages participation in cocreated traditions around words, sounds and power (Fisher, 2007). Understanding our classroom reading and writing literacy practices in this way affords teachers and learners the opportunity to participate in an authentic and meaningful community of learners through mutual engagement, joint enterprise and a shared repertoire (Wenger, 1999) of human and personal literacy practices, namely our telling of authentic stories of ourselves.

In the same way that Derrick's tattoos become identity artefacts as he shapes a self-capable of scripting new and non-traditional narratives of self, literacy and learning, so too paying careful attention to the content and form of literacy practices in the classroom through personal and identity affirming pedagogies and practice can support learners in experimenting with their own understandings of self, literacy and learning. Derrick's tattoos narrate human stories of place, belonging, struggle, culture and identity often devalued in school (Kinloch, 2007). Aligning with ideas explored in the previous chapter, Kirkland suggests that to address this English teachers should employ with their learners a study of humanity that exists off the page and demands new ways of reading, writing, seeing and being seen in the world. He suggests such a study should allow for learners a juxtaposition of individual identities and understandings of the world against multiple identities and understandings of the world in society.

Connecting Kirkland's understanding of literacy as personal and social practice to Short's (2011) reading and writing deeply for personal purposes as explored thus far reframes literacy as a dynamic and interactive space for personal learning and identity development. This chapter now moves to investigate what this understanding of literacy practice could look like in the classroom, beginning with a reconceptualization of narration and genre as usable resources and frameworks for exploring personal and social aspects of experience.

Understanding narration as a lens to view real and fictional worlds affords educators and learners opportunities to employ unexplored ways and genres for telling our stories to make all of our lives more visible. This understanding of narrative as a framework for interpreting personal life events and how we think about ourselves and others is explored in detail by Kucirkova and Cremin (2020). They explain how "stories make reality a mitigated reality, that is they act like a buffer between what we viscerally experience and what we tell others we have experienced; thus narratives act as a guide for locating ourself in relation to others (and ourselves)" (Kucirkova and Cremin, 2020, p. 33). Engaging with narrative as a meaning making tool, rather than something itself to be understood, affords learners opportunities to play or experiment with narrative and genre in ways that develop personal purposes and understanding of individual literacies and identities.

This personally resonant and sociocultural understanding of narrative as a meaning making framework suggests that we should also consider genre not in terms of rules for text but as frames for social action. As Bazerman explains:

> [genres] are environments for learning. They are locations within which meaning is constructed. Genres shape the thoughts we form

and the communications by which we interact. Genres are the familiar places we go to create intelligible communicative action with each other and the guideposts we use to explore the unfamiliar.

(Bazerman, 1997, p. 19)

He suggests that sharing with learners an understanding of genre as a place where meanings are made in an interaction between personal purpose and social audience frames classroom practices of reading and writing anew and allows teachers to open up fresh discursive landscapes for these practices including landscapes and roadmaps existing in the previous experiences of our learners. To support this understanding in our selection of classroom texts for reading as teachers, we should openly discuss and share genre selection with learners. Teachers should not introduce texts in the classroom:

as though all writing required the same stances, commitments, and goals; as though all texts shared pretty much the same forms and features; as though all literacy were the same. Nor should we ignore students' perceptions of where they are headed and whether they are much moved to go toward the places we point them toward.

(Bazerman, 1997, p. 22)

Thus, an explicit focus on genre and the many different ways within these genres that stories can be narrated demystifies the writing process for learners somewhat and asks them to consider what stories they would personally like to tell and in what ways. In this way genre study can itself be understood as an interactive tool and pedagogy for accessing the personal and social resources, genres, narrative voices and experiences learners bring with them to classroom practice, as well as introducing learners to new literacies and discourses. Careful consideration of genre in classroom practice may even allow learners to "become capable of remarkable performances as they speak to environments they grasp and they want to speak to" (Bazerman, 1997, p. 25).

Engaging with genre in this way helps teachers develop pedagogies to support a human understanding of literacy as storytelling in personal and social practice. As each genre represents an interaction involving a unique personal purpose and audience (Bentley, 2013) genre study engages learners in a study of personal intention in social context and asks not only why this story was told this way, but also what other opportunities for telling this and these kinds of stories exist for writers.

Bazerman's understanding of genre as a rich multidimensional resource for literacy and learning emphasises complexity rather than conformity as a problem in reading and writing widely for personal purposes practice for learners as in these practices they attempt to answer the world (Holland et al., 1998) and create a space for the personal literacies that they themselves value. Exploring genre can afford learners opportunities to move from an identity of a reader to that of a writer of their own stories as they see new possibilities for engaging in diverse human and classroom, personal and social literacy practice. As Bazerman explains:

> students are likely to learn how powerful a tool writing is to carry out specialized work and how empowered they are in entering focused, specialized discussions in appropriately forceful ways. With that knowledge they are more likely to respect alternative discourses and their own ability to enter those discourses when they are interested in doing so… It is only those who have never participated more than marginally who do not notice where they are, because they do not perceive why all that detailed attention is worth their effort. Once students feel part of the life in a genre, any genre that grabs their attention, the detailed and hard work of writing becomes compellingly real, for the work has a real payoff in engagement within activities the students find important.
>
> (Bazerman, 1997, p. 27)

Narrating inner stories and relational identities: Text as a complex and flexible personal meaning making machine and the work of Todd Hasak-Lowy

Understanding literacy as a human practice with deeply personal and social aspects has many implications for how teachers engage learners in reading practices in the classroom. Mackey (2016) illustrates very well the experience of reading from this perspective as a weaving of words and worlds in the creation of new and unique meanings through a reading of text as he explains:

> whether reading for the first time, or repeating an encounter with a text, we necessarily embed the textual experiences inside the events and understandings of our local life at the time. It is not an

optional extra; it is woven into the experience itself... We read our own worlds into the words of our books, and these worlds will not be subtracted from the understanding we develop from the texts.

(Mackey, 2016, p. 263)

This idea of readers as active makers of new meanings and worlds as they read widely for personal purposes is shared by the children's and young adult literature authors contributing to this chapter and exemplified in their texts.

FIVE MINUTES WITH TODD HASAK-LOWY

How do you think reading can be encouraged and supported in the classroom?

My approach to reading begins with a fundamental assertion of Reader Response Criticism that goes something like this: the meaning of a literary text emerges out of a dialogue between the reader and the text. The author, obviously, creates the text. And it may be that the author has all sorts of ideas about the meaning of their work. But ultimately the writer is absent when the reading (and responding, and teaching, and writing about the text) happens. The way the reader makes meaning is by deciding that some parts of the work matter more than others and then filling in the gaps that surround those parts. I was once taught that fiction provides an illusion of fullness. We read the work and it seems like we're getting everything, but of course we not. All you have to do is try to write a piece of fiction to see that you're always inescapably providing just a tiny fraction of the information you could about the world you're representing (especially when you add to the mix the interior world of your characters).

When I talk about being an "active reader" I'm talking about readers who realize they must speak for the text, must make the implicit explicit, and must, above all, realize that the meaning of the text isn't inserted by the author into the text. The text isn't a map with a buried treasure somewhere inside, it's a complex, flexible machine that can be used to make all sorts of meaning. As for the classroom, when I teach literature, I spend a lot of time focusing on very small amounts of text. I typically read the opening (or some rich early passage) and ask for responses from the students. There are times when I'll ask a question that helps them focus, but it's a question that is still pretty open ended (How is time organized here? How would you describe the perspective here?). I'm always trying to help my students see that if we slow down, we'll see just how much we can make the text say.

What is important to you as you write fiction?

I'm often trying to figure out what fiction can offer that other forms/media can't. One of the answers I often fall back on is that fiction is incredibly good (especially when compared to TV and film) to represent the interiority of its characters. And our inner lives are infinitely complex. Even just a moment of them are. When I'm writing I'm invariably locating things deep inside someone, even when there is meaningful external action taking place. To me, external events really only matter when we are experiencing them through a character. Most of our students consume stories through screens, through TV and film. There are plenty of great TV shows and films, and these stories are typically more subjective than we may realize, but still, they typically privilege external events and are pretty superficial when it comes to communicating inner life. In this regard, I think it's necessary to help students see how a literary work is digging deep into a character's consciousness (some of this requires giving them the technical vocabulary to describe this – teaching them how to use a term like "free indirect style" can prove worthwhile, for example). It can be useful to give them a chance to discover how a crucial "event" in a work can be entirely internal. It can be useful to ask them how, for instance, memory is operating in a narrative.

Short, creative writing assignments with students can help them discover some of this for themselves. Have them describe just a few minutes from earlier in the day, and tell them to try to get on the page everything that was happening in their heads when they, for instance, were making their way to school. To me, experience or life or whatever you want to call it is like an iceberg. Ten percent is visible above the surface. That's external reality. The rest, the vast majority, is between our ears, invisible to everyone but the individual. And there are even parts of that we can't really see. That's why "close" third-person can prove so useful. My narrator in *Me Being Me* is both Darren and not Darren, because there's so much Darren can't fully see – or at least can't put into words. But his story is interesting ultimately because of his inner story, at least in my opinion.

I often tell people that what *Me Being Me* is really about is that moment when you realize that all those people in your life you thought were stable/fixed/unchanging and (or and/or) reliable aren't. Or can't be. Or won't be. And that realization is when you become an adult. On some levels it's a sad moment, because there's so much loss in that realization. It's scary, because you come to see how alone you are at a certain level. On top of that, this tends to happen (or at least it happens in Darren's case) during a time when he's changing radically. Some of this change is physical, and that really matters. But some of it is simply being in that liminal territory known as adolescence.

How do you think these kinds of inner stories could be explored in the classroom with young people?

Me Being Me tries to represent multiple aspects of Darren's life. Some are big and serious and some are small and ridiculous. But they're all him. Ultimately, they're inseparable. I suppose an effective teacher and an effective pedagogy has to address the fullness of the students. Not explicitly, not directly, but somehow you've got to relate to them as the full humans that they are. Literature can be handy in this regard, since it's less threatening to talk about Darren's sex life than their own. But learning is elusive. It's hard to know when, where and how exactly learning happens, at least if we're after something bigger and deeper than the standard "I will now convey my knowledge to you" model.

There are conversations happening in class, and the student, by listening and contributing, comes to make new connections, thinks new thoughts, articulates something (whether aloud or in their notes or even just in their heads) that they've never articulated as such before. In this regard, you need to create a classroom in which students are truly connecting and communicating with each other. But before you can do any of that you have to establish the atmosphere in the class. Students have to believe that it's a safe place, where they'll be heard and seen and not judged too harshly for saying something that might not be the smartest thing. I find it useful to pull back the curtain pretty regularly, to be utterly frank with them about, for instance, why we even have discussions in class, about why I want them to talk.

I like to teach my students an idea called "relational identity". It's theory formulated by the scholar of autobiography, Paul John Eakin, according to which all identity is relational. In other words, Eakin argues that individuals are not autonomous or truly separate from others. Rather our identities exist solely in our connections to these people. I illustrate this, literally, with all sorts of clumsy diagrams that attempt to show how individuals exist not as points in a network, but rather along the various connections between their node and the nodes we label as other people. I also try to explain this theory by asking them to consider that when we say something like, "Ever since she died I feel as if part of me is gone", we are describing something very literal and very real. Part of us is truly gone. My students don't necessarily agree with this theory, but it gets them thinking. I suspect teaching this theory while teaching *Me Being Me* would produce some interesting results. Because what happens to someone whose identity is tied up in all these other people's identities when those identities are in such flux?

In almost every class of mine, at some point I also teach a short excerpt from Viktor Scklovsky's essay "Art as Technique", which is the one that introduces the notion of defamiliarisation. Honestly, if I could only teach one thing to my students, it would be that. It is such a profound concept, one that can be applied in so many ways. One of them, of course, is that we can defamiliarise not just content but form as well. One thing a teacher can do with students here is have them defamiliarise something in writing. Let them try it out and see what it feels like. For some, this can be enough. But the larger objective can be to get them to think and think deeply about the problem that defamiliarisation is an answer to. The problem is not really seeing things, is taking things for granted. And there are certainly many things in our classrooms and pedagogies that we no longer really see. Once we're introduced to the concept of defamiliarisation, we can read differently, especially on the micro, line-to-line level. We will become better close readers, as we'll have now been trained to notice how a given writer helps us see common things in a strange, new light. We notice not just what the narrator tells us, but how. If a teacher wants to really push this and take some chances, well, you can turn the concept onto the class itself. What can we defamiliarise when it comes to this thing called education or learning?

The writer John Barth once said that every writer is showing up to a party that's been going on for at least 3,000 years. In other words, it's really hard to be truly original, so much has already happened at the party. But when I'm writing I'm trying to avoid conventions and (especially) clichés. There's just nothing very interesting about them. At the same time, I'm telling a story that in some ways is a story told before (there are only so many *kinds* of stories). *Me Being Me* is in part a romance, and Darren and Zoey's story travels through some familiar territory. So I tried to get my reader to experience these stations in a new way. There's a list about their knees touching that felt like a new way to represent an early moment of physical contact between them. It could be fun to brainstorm with students original ways to gain access to well-trodden territory.

Narration becomes of key importance when we understand that there are only so many kinds of stories. Can you tell us about your narration in Me Being Me?

Me Being Me is narrated using a form of free indirect speech. Free indirect speech narratives are based on an impossible alchemy. The narrator is, at once, two different entities: a character and an outside narrator. And often it's impossible to trace out the border between them, to know, for instance, when a word "belongs" to a character and when to the narrator. The distance between narrator and character can change constantly, making this kind of knowing that much harder yet. You choose a mode of narration because it helps you find access to the words that will allow you to create the world you're trying to create. To write this book I had to be very much Darren and very much not Darren at the same time. Reading and writing stories gives us this chance to be both ourselves and someone else; to occupy two subject positions simultaneously. Film just doesn't really do that, at least not in the same way. And free indirect speech is the representation of this already, of a voice (or perspective, or, simply, a narration) that is two people (or two sensibilities) combined. The closeness between Darren and the narrator of *Me Being Me* suggests the fact that the other agent responsible for his narration is, in some weird sense, serving Darren. He is, put differently, translating Darren to and for the reader. He is making Darren available to the reader in ways that Darren can't and wouldn't. Darren would be too self-conscious to narrate, at least like this. But this other entity can be brutally, even courageously, honest for him. And maybe there's a good exercise in there for students.

What were your favourite childhood books, and what advice do you have for young authors?

Two favourite books come to mind. S. E. Hinton's *The Outsiders*. That book was hugely important to me in middle school, which were the worst years of my life. I think I liked it because it represented alienation so convincingly. And also because the narrator's voice was so compelling. I also liked a much more obscure book: *The 100: A List of the Most Influential Persons in History* by Michael H. Hart. I loved this

> book. It's a kind of ridiculous project (how is one to decide the relative influence of Jesus versus Isaac Newton?), but I found it irresistible. I've always loved lists and rankings and the order they promise. My advice to young authors is three-fold: 1) Read a ton. Read lots of what you like and a little of what you don't. You just need to put a lot of words into your head before good words will come out of you. 2) Read as a writer. By which I mean: when you like something, ask yourself why. Reverse engineer the stories you read. 3) Write what you want to read. Writing is a silly way to try and get rich or famous, so write assuming that you'll remain somewhere between pretty and completely obscure. Write in such a way that the writing itself is enjoyable.
>
> *Could you share with us the title of a list not included in* Me Being Me *that could form the basis for a classroom creative writing exercise?*
> 7 Moments in Darren's Life He'd Revisit If He Had a Time Machine, Including 3 He'd Revisit So He Could Live Them in a Radically Different Manner.

The form of Todd's novel *Me Being Me Is Exactly as Insane as You Being You*, told entirely in lists, challenges readers to be active meaning makers and fill in the gaps in text in imaginative and creative ways, drawing as much on our own personal life experiences as what we know about Darren. In a text that obscures as much as it brings to light, Todd asks readers to actively connect through personal resonances with Darren's experiences to make our own meanings from the story.

His conceptualisation of a text as a complex, flexible machine for diverse meaning making is a creative and innovative entry point for teachers to think about how we can define and use texts in classroom practice. It imagines a community of practice where learners can tinker and personally experiment with textual content and form, pushing buttons and spinning wheels with as of yet unknown consequence and reaction. Developing this metaphor could also suggest that as we operate, dismantle and rebuild our textual machines in classroom practice, we learn something new about each individual part (word, punctuation, meaning, technique) and the whole (text) in our personal and social interactions with and around it.

Understanding this kind of meaningful personal interpretation and interaction to be at the heart of the reading process Todd highlights an illusion of fullness present in fiction, whereby as readers, authors or teachers we think we can capture alone everything important to the story experience. Conversely, for Todd meaning is shared and made through dialogue between readers and texts. Offering examples from his own classroom practice he foregrounds the importance of deep and dialogical personal engagement with small pieces of text. For Todd the illusion of fullness in fiction is countered by the very real fullness of readers in terms of their own life experiences. This is where the magic happens, so to speak, as in the interaction between reader and text, meaning is made as the personally resonant parts of the stories we read about others, just like Derrick's tattoos of people important to him, become something of our own.

Darren's story reminds us that for young people all actions and interactions, including those related to reading and writing widely for personal purpose in the classroom, tell our own personal stories of identity, complex and complicated stories of who we are and who we would like to be. This may explain why, at times, some learners may not be willing to engage in particular activities in classroom practice, as putting forward opinions, ideas or writing means putting forward a part of themselves. The complexity of adolescent identity and understanding who we are comes into focus from the first few pages of the novel as the narrator tells us how Darren came to be named Darren in the first place. Evoking human emotions we are all familiar with the narrator who explains how Darren's name, one of our strongest beginning markers of identity, ended up being some sort of compromise between his parents… meaning that "Darren" was nobody's first choice.

At the heart of Todd's writing is a profound understanding of the infinitely complex stories of our personal inner lives and identities. Exemplifying the human story of literacy his novel lays bare the personal and social aspects of literacy illustrated throughout this chapter as meaning is transacted between real and written worlds for Darren, as both worlds are populated by the people and things that mean most to him. Reading this text, itself in many ways a study in identity, adolescent learners can come to better understand how they might personally reflect on their own experiences and feelings.

This complex understanding of learning as negotiating identity and mediating meaningful literacies and experiences in daily practice as something that we all engage in without full view offers a powerful example of the transformative aspects of developing literacy as a human practice. Helping learners see the complexity of understanding our own lives Darren's story narration opens up opportunities for classroom explorations and discussions of the kinds of reflection and action required by learners to transform their understandings of self, literacy and identity. For Todd the teaching of and experimentation with technical skills and terms for literacy, such as free indirect speech narration, for example, shares with learners a language and a tool for reading and writing their own stories and the stories of others (see Wood, 2009, for more detail here).

Focusing on personal aspects of meaning and learning Todd opens up a myriad of possibilities for personally focused reading and writing pedagogies that ask learners to think about life and world events first from the personal perspectives of their own inner thoughts and feelings. Understanding the interrelatedness of our identities and the identity of others would provide an interesting context for a discussion of adolescence as a journey in the context of learner real life and Darren's fictive experiences in the novel. Encouraging learners to also experiment with different styles of narration, and in particular free indirect speech, and talk about and share their experiments opens up new shared ways of talking and thinking about ourselves in the classroom.

Todd connects carefully self-reflection and transformation with the complexity of narration and narrators in children's and young adult literature texts in his novel *Me Being Me Is Exactly as Insane as You Being You*. Explaining his approach to writing this diary list novel, Todd tells us that he wanted to defamiliarise the form of the Young Adult novel itself, the way others have defamiliarised content and story within. Drawing on the work of Viktor Schklovsky and his assertion that defamiliarisation is, more or less, the point of all art as art makes language strange, as well as the world that the language presents (Schklovsky, 1917), the unusual narration of Darren's experiences calls readers to question how we ourselves see the world and understand our own experiences. Lists (such as for example, 4 Emotions Darren Identifies in the Sound of His Mother's Footsteps, Which Are Clearly Approaching; 4 Physical Distances Separating Darren and His Dad during the Three Minutes Immediately Before, During, and After the Moment in Which Darren Finally Learns Why His Dad Is Here This Morning; 10 Subjects Darren and His Dad Do Not Discuss during Their Drive to School; 6 Features of Darren's Seat That Could Be Improved and in Fact Should Be Addressed by the Good People at Superbus; 6 Instances of Physical Contact Involving Darren and Zoey That

Take Place between Battle Creek and Ann Arbor) force us to see ourselves and the world in new and strange ways we would never have thought possible and opens up new possibilities for our own personal narration, writing and self-expression.

This nuanced and personal approach to reading also has important implications for how it becomes possible for us to tell our life stories. Todd suggests that encouraging learners to experiment with defamiliarisation in their own writing is essential for helping them to understand how narrators tell their stories in a variety of different ways. Readers of *Me Being Me Is Exactly as Insane as You Being You* will find his suggested creative writing activity fascinating while non-readers of the novel can complete the exercise based on their own lives and with themselves (or perhaps a version of themselves?) as narrator.

Todd's defamiliarisation approach to writing creates for learners new writing (literary and literacy) problems to be solved. These writing problems are also problems for personal identity development and how we see ourselves and our engagement with literacy and learning inside and outside of the classroom. The following provides some beginning ideas for developing pedagogies and activities to explore voice, genre and narration in the work of Todd Hasak-Lowy.

VOICE AND NARRATION IN CHILDREN'S AND YOUNG ADULT LITERATURE: ENGAGING WITH LITERACY AS PERSONAL AND SOCIAL PRACTICE

- **Reading a history of people to build books and stories in common:** Teachers could use the six case studies of nonviolent activists and their movements (Gandhi, Alice Paul, Martin Luther King Jr., Cesar Chavez, Vácalv Havel and Greta Thunberg) presented in *We Are Power: How Nonviolent Activism Changes the World* (Todd Hasak-Lowy) to engage learners in histories that help them understand their world and their position within it, including the power they hold to change these positions and worlds through agentive and nonviolent action. Divide the class into six groups, with learners self-selecting which case study and story interests them. Each group is responsible for reading, researching (including identifying other texts and stories), making personal connections with and finally presenting and sharing their learning about the worlds and experiences each case study represents with the other class

groups. Learners can complete individual or shared reader's notebooks to document their learning process.
- **Addressing the world with new shared understanding:** This shared learning can be developed in a full class activism project based on a particular class, school or local concern.
- **Biography as history, primary sources and authentic texts:** Teachers can use the authentic and emotive story told in *Somewhere There Is Still a Sun* (Michael Gruenbaum and Todd Hasak-Lowy) to nurture compassionate and human literacies in cross curricular classroom activities and encourage learners to understand their own life experiences and the world in different ways. The archival and primary documents within the text support discussion on and exploration of primary sources and authentic text and meaning in history, learning, media and beyond. Supporting philosophical discussions around the nature of truth, humanity, courage and justice, this text suggests young people should consider more critically personal and received interpretations of meaning made in real and fictional worlds.
- **Primary sources and authentic documents in my life:** Encouraging personal connections with history learners can consider and collect documents and other artefacts that represent primary source documents of their own lives. These may include text messages, emails, vlogs and so on. How do these texts represent each learner? What do they say about us individually and as a class? How do they compare to the documents in our key text? How might we use these as resources for writing, recording and autobiography?
- **Collaborative writing practice:** Mirroring the collaborative writing process of *Somewhere There Is Still a Sun*, learners could work in pairs to collaboratively write a story of each other's experience based on this shared pool of primary sources and documents, thinking about how they can understand and represent their experiences and stories together in new ways.
- **Translation:** The theme of translation in writing could also be broached here with learners, of particular significance when English as an Additional Language (EAL) students are a part of the class group.
- **Time capsule writing:** Focusing on the immediacy and real-time telling of its story *33 Minutes* (Todd Hasak-Lowy) can be used by teachers as a model for similar writing projects with learners. Think about how you could record one day or part of a day of your life in and out of school for a time capsule or class project. What would we need to record? Experiences? Feelings? Conversations? Sounds? Moods? Relationships? How might we do this? In

text? Drawings? Maps of our learning and social experiences in school? Using cameras and phones? How would we include teachers, parents and siblings? How would we present our experiences as stories to the world?
- **Defamiliarising experience:** Choose one hour of your life in the last 24 hours. How can you represent your thoughts, feelings and experiences at this time in writing? What story can you tell (making dinner or arguing with a friend)? How can you tell this story in a different way (in the form of a recipe or using only direct speech)? Could we tell a story using the sign systems and language associated with our favourite game, sport or hobby?
- **Voicing experience:** How could we use free indirect speech to narrate a story about a significant moment in our own lives? What would we have to say to and/or about ourselves in these moments? How would we represent this in writing? What do we learn from writing, sharing and talking about these inner stories of identity with others in the classroom?

Genre and (auto)biography as personal learning artefacts for making the familiar strange in the scripts and stories of Paul Fleischman

Creating opportunities for the open sharing of personal literacies, inner thoughts and experiences is difficult in the classroom and requires first a safe and supportive learning environment centred on authentic, meaningful, shared and public communication and engagement. Building towards strong connections between personal and social aspects of literacy, author Paul Fleischman conceptualises reading as an authentic, interactive and empowering practice for young people. A focus on the lyrical quality of words and understanding language itself as a kind of music is central to his writing where he explores the rhythm and flow of life as a continuous and reverberating whirling.

FIVE MINUTES WITH PAUL FLEISCHMAN

How do you think reading can be encouraged and supported in the classroom?

Adults invest time in learning something new if they see a benefit. Kids are no different. So it seems to me that the best way to create readers is to show kids from the start what reading can do for them. It can answer their questions, enthral them with stories, take them into the past and the future, and connect them with others. This last has been my focus, the result of growing up with the radio on, taking part in classroom reader's theatre and hearing my father read his books aloud as they were written.

Once you're a reader, you can engage with a listener, be it a library pet, a younger sibling or student in a lower grade. That synergy is exciting. It's the same experience that chamber musicians have, creating something that's more than the sum of its parts. My poetry for two and four voices was written to pass that experience on. *Bull Run*, *Seedfolks* and *Seek* were likewise written with classroom performance in mind. When I see students who aren't a class's strongest readers clamouring to be the first to perform the *Joyful Noise* poems, I see my theory being confirmed. Those kids are hungry to put language to a use other than phonics worksheets and spelling tests. Maybe they're especially attuned to sound. Perhaps they have untapped social skills, always aware of how their co-performers are doing. Maybe they have a strong need to be heard by the world. The more types of language experiences we expose our kids to – from letter-writing to word games to fully staged plays – the more likely they'll be hooked.

(Auto)biography forms the basis of a number of your stories where memory is recounted through a variety of forms, styles and media. What advice would you have for teachers who want to support young people to write about their own life experiences more creatively?

If I were a teacher, I might start with paper, showing off its different weights and finishes and showing students how to create their own books. Tactile qualities are as much a lure here as with manipulatives in math. So is the lure of smallness. It's powerful to commit your thoughts to paper, but privacy might be important; something easy to hide could be a plus. I'd also show examples of other note-takers' work, ancient as well as closer at hand, making the point that thoughts committed to paper are likely to far outlast anything stored on a hard drive.

There are many worlds beyond paper, of course. Sound recording is easily accomplished on a smart phone and can do things the pencil can't. What about an aural journal composed of everyday sounds, from the electric toothbrush to school bus chatter to TV news? Or each day presenting one sound followed by explication? Or describing the people around one through sound profiles? For those, like me, who see the

> world as a musical score, recording and overdubbing and editing would hold huge appeal.
>
> *Have you any ideas for particular class projects teachers could plan for engaging their learners in meaningful writing practices in the classroom?*
>
> A diary of objects would make a great project, especially for kids, like the one in *The Matchbox Diary*, who can't yet read and write. This could also be accomplished through photos, which are easier to gather into a collection, though there's a power and resonance in physical objects that's hard to top. Perhaps this is why videos, which can combine words, images, and sounds and should logically be the most powerful medium, don't always feel that way. In the same way that many photographers prefer black-and-white to colour, there might be power in narrowing our focus. Maybe it's that we have to bring more imagination to an object or a word than a video. What's unquestioned is that giving students multiple ways to record their lives can only help teachers' chances of success.

Thinking about reading in terms of what it can do for learners aligns very closely with reading widely for personal purposes and Holland et al.'s (1998) understanding of the self as a position through which answering the world authors the world, self and learning anew. For Paul reading is a practice of and for connection, a relationship between the reader and the world, that can be fully actualised in dialogue with, through and about text. His approach to reading as a social and shared performance relationship between speakers and listeners balances and complements Todd's focus on interiority and personal meaning in reading practice.

Understanding the human story of literacy as personal and social practice we, as teachers, have to open up the world of reading to young people so that it can be experienced in a wide variety of ways and textual forms. Connecting to contemporary issues for young people both Paul (*Eyes Wide Open: What's Behind the Environmental Headlines*) and Todd (*We Are Power: How Nonviolent Activism Changes the World*) suggest ways that young people can agentively and reflectively engage with societal issues to develop deeper understandings of their identities and positions in the world beyond the classroom. Through seeing things in different ways they can answer the world (Holland et al., 1998) in a way that, rather than allowing them to see things as they really are, allows young people multiple lenses for reflection on the pluralities of experience that exist for themselves and in the world.

Understanding reading as a social practice, Paul's work encourages authentic language exploration as he reminds readers that just like writing reading can allow readers to communicate, voice, experience and embody learning in new ways. Starting from their own familiar personal experiences and life stories through performative reading aloud pedagogies, learners can interact with others who explore similar experiences but who have started from somewhere else. This interactive and socially oriented approach to reading aloud differs from more traditional read aloud approaches as it opens up real and fictional worlds for exploration and questioning safeguarding against reading aloud as described by Meek (1992) as a process whereby:

> most adults who read to children keep the reading whole; they go to the end of the story... As a result, children get the story as something entire, the world in a book...and the listeners are kept inside the telling or the reading for its duration.
>
> (Meek, 1992, p. 177)

Paul's approach to text, genre, reading and writing is a playful one and, similar to Todd, encourages learners to tinker with text in a variety of forms. As active meaning makers in Paul's texts, readers do not spectate but personally and uniquely co-create story worlds based on their shared past and present experiences and those explored in the text in interactive reading communities of practice. Inclusive reading aloud practices work to strengthen reading communities of practice by developing what Cremin et al. (2014) term a shared reading history of 'books in common'.

These common stories allow learners a shared language, akin to Wenger's shared repertoire and Fisher's co-created traditions around words, sounds and power to talk about and experiment from their own personal life stories and develop human aspects of their own literacy practice. This practice can be experimented with to develop pedagogies and activities that build on community and commonality as exemplified in the previously suggested activities for Todd's texts, in particular the activity that focuses on reading a history of people to build books and stories in common. As Kucirkova and Cremin explain "in relaxed informal spaces, reading aloud, potentially a richly resonant and affective encounter, can help develop young people's awareness of themselves, of others and the wider world" (Kucirkova and Cremin, 2020, p. 41).

Paul's *Joyful Noise: Poems in Two Voices* is a collection of poetry written to be read aloud by two people, sometimes alternating parts and sometimes simultaneously, simulating the sounds of the insect world. Read aloud these poems become shared experiences in the plurality of language, sound and storytelling and reading itself becomes a tool for personal sensuous expression. This use of multiple voices to create new meanings and experiences features in a number of Paul's works for younger and older audiences. *Whirligig* for example, uses flash forward rather than flashback to tell the personal and human story of one young teenager seeking redemption for a desperate act. A number of narrators voice Brent's story, making it their own and connecting with the reader in such a way that Brent's story becomes a story about all of us and our human and personal struggles and stories of literacy and identity. Fitting in, growing up, suicide, depressions, death, loss, grief, family, culture, hope, community, belonging, cancer, heritage and holocaust are only some of the human struggles and stories voiced in the text.

READER'S THEATRE AND WRITER NOTEBOOKS: LISTENERS AS CO-NARRATORS OF THE STORY

- **Read aloud performances and reader's theatre**: Many of Paul's stories are written to emphasise read aloud, reader's theatre and performative approaches to text (for example *Joyful Noise: Poems in Two Voices, Seedfolks, Zap* and *Seek*) and Paul has included within some texts advice for how they can be experienced through performance. Engaging with these texts and reading through reader's theatre allows learners to develop vocabulary, comprehension, fluency, accuracy and confidence in repeated read aloud practices. Related activities for learners as they engage in reading as performance could encourage dialogical and sensuous exploration of the worlds, characters, voices and noises in these stories.
- **Embodiment and dramatic roleplay**: Readers might like to further experiment with a variety of diverse drama roles and activities as they read these texts. Learners can, for example, imagine themselves as directors, prop and set designers, sound and special effects managers, and as they read these texts, authentically engage in activities and experiences

> that ask them to do precisely what directors, prop and set designers do in the translation of a text to a physical, visual, oral and aural experience, keeping a reader/writer notebook that documents their shared journey of collaboratively recreating their texts.

Returning to Bazerman (1997), who tells us that"

> Learning to write is hard work, requiring addressing ever more difficult writing problems, so that if we want students to learn to write we must locate the kinds of writing they will want to work at, the kinds of writing problems they will want to solve.
> (Bazerman, 1997, p. 26)

Understanding literacy as something personal and so inseparable from our own life experiences (the human aspect of literacy) affords teachers opportunities to draw on identity related themes and "problems" to engage learners with writing in the classroom. Remembering Derrick's tattoos as alternative literacy texts suggests teachers should consider how learners can tell their literacy stories in the classroom, more specifically the many different shapes, forms and genres this exploration of self can take. Blending these ideas together through the genre of autobiography, for example, can allow multiple opportunities for meaningful and authentic writing in the classroom. Cummins and Early (2011) explore the use of what they term identity texts in multilingual classrooms, multimodal identity driven texts created by learners and shared with multiple audiences, to develop meaningful and identity affirming points of connection between teacher and learner home, school and life worlds. Similar to Derrick's tattoos these identity or autobiographical texts become powerful personal artefacts of and for learning as they require learners to make deep, personal and meaningful connections between their own lives and classroom content and practice.

(Auto)biography forms the basis of a number of Paul's stories where memory is recorded through a variety of forms, style and media. His innovative and engaging approaches to telling stories about ourselves, some examples of which are discussed here, can be used with learners of all ages (using genre or author study as an overall approach) to encourage a personal consideration of the many ways we can talk about and reflect on ourselves and identity with the world. *Alphamaniacs,* Paul's most recent publication, offers 26 unique examples in the shape of personal biographical stories, of individuals who have played and tinkered with language to build verbal wonders to tell their own life stories and the stories of others. From the retelling of well-known stories in number plates, to novels written without the letter e, to writing diaries amassing 3 million words a year, the stories about language shared in this book provide inspiration for a multitude of creative and innovative writing activities for young and older learners.

Paul suggests that an interesting pedagogical approach for teaching writing might begin with an exploration of literacy and writing as a three-dimensional entity, helping learners to visualise, touch and feel story worlds. Beginning with personal literacy journeys in traditional paper and ink Paul suggests how teachers and learners can think about and engage with this medium in new ways. Touch, shape, size, secrecy and personal and/or social purpose all take on an importance not always thought about by learners in the classroom. Writer as a maker (or books, worlds and stories) returns as a theme here and asks learners to consider their writing in classroom, personal, local and historic settings. Understanding the form as a part of the story itself provides rich opportunities for teachers to engage learners in meaningful and authentic identity affirming and focused writing practices and opens up new media and forms for the telling of stories.

In this way Paul suggests that how the learner sees the world has deep implications for their telling of stories. Taking his own life experience and writing as an example, he explains "none of those books would have been written had I not lived in that house" (Fleischman, 1999, p. 105). The centrality of story, music, radio, sound and reading aloud in his childhood all play a role in the way he now thinks about and tells his own stories. This life history influence is evident in particular in his text *Seek,* which tells the story of a teenage boy who receives an assignment in school to write his own autobiography. To do so he decides that he will listen back on his life and the voices and sounds of his experiences. Told in a collage of voices and reminiscent of Derrick's tattoos, Rob's story becomes the story of others as well as his own as he is joined in his narrative by the people and things that mean the most to him.

The opening line of Paul's *The Matchbox Diary* (Fleischman, 2013, p. 1) is "Pick whatever you like the most. Then I'll tell you its story." This invitation from a great-grandfather to his great-granddaughter begins a narrative that tells a story of growing up, emigration and experimentation with literacy practices to record a life story in innovative and creative ways. Pulling an old cigar box filled with matchboxes from a shelf reveals a found object diary of the old man's life. Begun when he was not yet able to write but wanted very much to record his experiences, each matchbox contains an item or photo representing a significant moment and story in his life. Literacy, identity and self-expression are all explicit themes in this book and can engage writers of all ages in thinking about new ways to record their own life experiences. This book also offers English as an Additional Language learners rich and meaningful opportunities for thinking about their experiences and how they can record and communicate these experiences in an answering of the world that will simultaneously help them recreate their own worlds and experiences (Holland et al., 1998).

Paul's playful approach to genre is exemplified in *Zap,* a text that immediately and intimately addresses its readers through the shape of the house manager of a small theatre company competing with the success of television who comes on stage and introduces the night's play. The audience of readers are encouraged to use the remote controls found under their seats to switch between seven dramatic performances, including parodies of the works of Anton Chekhov, Agatha Christie, Tennessee Williams, Samuel Beckett, Neil Simon and performance art alongside William Shakespeare's Richard III. This interaction between readers and characters continues throughout the text as the audience is spoken and gestured to, taken on as a confidant and ultimately becomes a part of the performance itself.

To fully understand the parodies an understanding of the parodied drama genres is of course necessary, however, as a text itself *Zap* offers learners a wonderful and entertaining introduction to challenging dramatic genres and playwrights as well as encouraging learners to experiment themselves with genre and form in their writing. This text, alongside *Dateline: Troy* and a number of Paul's other performance oriented works (including *Seedfolks, Bull Run* and *Seek*) provide teachers and learners with rich opportunities for engaging with a human understanding of literacy in personal and social practices through a multiliteracies approach to genre study and authentic language use in the classroom.

> **EXPERIMENTS IN GENRE AND AUTHENTIC LANGUAGE: SOCIOCULTURAL FRAMEWORKS FOR PERSONAL AND SOCIAL LITERACY PRACTICE**
>
> - **Experiments in Genre: The Unfamiliar Genre Research Project (Andrew-Vaughan and Fleischer, 2006):** This research and workshop centred project-based learning approach incorporates a number of elements and asks learners to find a genre that excites, challenges or intimidates them. Learners begin by identifying and then reading in an unfamiliar genre, collecting sample passages that appeal to them. At the same time they reflect on their experiences in a reflective journal they must write in each time they work on the project. Parent, peer and teacher conference support writing experimentation and the drafting of a piece of work by learners in the chosen genre. At the end of the project learners will write a reflective letter on what they have learnt about reading, writing, learning and genre as a result of completing this project as well as a letter to their parents sharing learning and experiences with family. All elements of the project are presented in the form of a research binder and shared with the class. The work of the children's and young adult literature authors explored in this chapter can be used as a set of mentor texts to support learners in the study of genre within this project or as standalone activities.
> - **Introducing genre:** Read the house manager's introduction to the audience at the beginning of the play in *Zap*. Why might a theatre company be taking this approach? Why do they want to compete with other forms of media and storytelling? How can they do this? What different ways can we tell our stories? Collect one sentence from each student written in a genre of their choice in a hat and draw each one individually and discuss as a class group.
> - **Modelling and supporting writing in particular genres:** Take any moment in *Zap* where the audience uses the remote control to switch stories. Why might the audience have switched stories at this point? Would you? Why? Write/improvise/perform the next part of the play as if the audience had not switched stories. How have you located your continuation of the story in the given genre?
> - **Combining and subverting genres in writing:** Take any moment in *Zap* where different genres, the audience and the real world

> collide on and off stage. What happens in these moments that mark them as different from other parts of the text? Can we identify any features of parody? How can we combine different genres in our writing in interesting ways (horror romance for example)? How can we subvert a familiar genre: e.g., can we write a murder mystery without a murder? What about form: e.g., can we tell a fantasy story in meeting minutes?
> - **Creating new genres in real worlds:** Thinking about a typical day, what kinds of texts, conversations and activities do we engage in? What are the similarities and differences between these? How could we write about these experiences: e.g., is my life a horror story? What features of genre can I use to write about my experiences, and what new features do my experiences add to the genre?

This chapter explores some of the ways a familiarity with identity affirming and non-traditional texts provides teachers and learners with new ways for thinking about and engaging with human and personal aspects of literacy in the meaningful practice of tell our own life stories. As we experiment with new stories and forms, Paul suggests that it may be beneficial to break this exploration down into smaller key moments and aspects of experience to allow deeper reflection and possible identity development and transformation.

Paul's *No Map, Great Trip: A Young Writer's Road to Page One* is a memoir and travelogue reflection that offers creative ideas, prompts and tips for young people who want to write. Talking about his publication on an online writing forum, Paul offers some lovely examples of creative writing activities for young people, including asking learners to draw a new continent (world making by naming countries, cities, geographical locations); turn their initials into a logo (drawing on personal identity and experiences, and coming up with a number of versions); build a found sculpture (thinking carefully about you can alter what you find to make a story); and think about plot differently by asking learners to pick three common objects and invent a game using them (Fleischman, retrieved 2020). These creative and innovative approaches to narration and writing alongside the ideas for personally and socially relevant pedagogies highlighted throughout this chapter encourage teachers to think about reading, writing, genre and narration in new ways as we move beyond the traditional text in our exploration of literacy practice in the classroom.

> **NARRATING (AUTO)BIOGRAPHY AND LIFE STORIES TO INTERPRET EXPERIENCE THROUGH A FOCUS ON THE HUMAN ASPECTS OF LITERACY**
>
> - **Physical, tactile and spatial storytelling:** Choose an item and tell its story (perhaps from a particular perspective). For example, you might tell the story of a day in the life of your classroom's whiteboard (or a kitchen cup, stone on the road). What might it think about the general goings on and life around it? How might it understand its own purpose in life and the actions of others?
> - **Telling our own stories in identity texts:** Make your own matchbox diaries limiting your story to five items. What items will you choose and why? How will you represent these items in your autobiographical text (physically, visually, in text)? What other alternatives to matchboxes could we use today to tell our life stories?
> - **Intergenerational stories and oral histories:** Interview a member of your family about their life. What are the most significant moments, relationships, objects and learning for them? Choose one of these and write its story.
> - **Writing multiple nonlinear narratives:** *Whirligig* offers us not just one story, but many stories in a nonlinear narrative about connection and disconnection as a part of the human experience. Outside of the space and time of the limited omniscient third-person narration of Brent's journey to redemption individual first person narrators tell in alternate chapters their own stories connected through the metaphor of the whirligigs. Focusing on narrative as a meaning making tool for writers, learners could consider why Paul has written his story in this way. A plurality of voice and time exists simultaneously for readers in a way that confounds logic and experience. How can we experiment with multiple and/or nonlinear narratives in our writing?
> - **Alternate realities for our stories:** Taking the narration of Anthony as an example, teachers could encourage learners to reflect on and imagine alternate realities in their reading and writing practice. Asking questions about our experiences is essential for the development of critical literacy. Public and private, real and imagined come together in this chapter to ask readers to think about the differences between an event and the experience of that event, what happens and how it makes

us feel. Can you write a story that incorporates alternate realities and points of view?
- **Entering the world of Whirligig:** Imagining yourself in the world of the text what might the whirligig symbolise and push you to think about based on your own life experiences?

Conclusion

This chapter explores literacy as a human practice that plays out in personal and social contexts as we tell stories about ourselves. Readers and writers are positioned as makers of text, meaning, identity, literacy and learning as we engage in exploration of literary and literacy pathways in traditional and non-traditional stories. Understanding literacy as a human practice in personal and social contexts this exploration of text becomes, through reflection, transformation and experimentation, an exploration of our own identities and lives. Reading and writing widely for personal purposes in shared human stories and struggles, we learn simultaneously about others, the world and ourselves. As Moore explains, "narrative is a strategy for placing us within a historically constituted world... If narrative makes the world more intelligible it also makes ourselves more intelligible" (Moore, 1994, p. 119).

Developing pedagogies for telling the human story of literacy in classroom practice encourages empathy, respect and understanding towards our life stories and the stories of others. Such pedagogies also support the study of our own learning biographies as well as the learning biographies of our learners to engage young people in meaningful, authentic and identity affirming talk, tasks and texts for literacy learning.

> Suddenly, everyone's opening up journals. We're supposed to write about our summers. Great. My summer was like being sick to your stomach. First, you feel worse and worse. Then you think you might have to throw up. Then you know you have to. Then you do. I write "I had a wonderful summer." There's no way I'm going to tell her the truth.
>
> (Anthony, in Fleischman, 1998, p. 76)

Bibliography

Children's and young adult literature explored in this chapter

Fleischman, P. (2020). *Alphamaniacs*. USA: Candlewick Press.
Fleischman, P. (2019). *No Map Great Trip: A young writer's road to page one*. USA: Greenwillow Books.
Fleischman, P. (2015). *Eyes Wide Open: What's behind the environmental headlines*. USA: Candlewick Press.
Fleischman, P. (2013). *The Matchbox Diary*. USA: Candlewick Press.
Fleischman, P. (2005). *Zap*. USA: Candlewick Press.
Fleischman, P. (2001). *Seek*. Chicago: Cricket Books.
Fleischman, P. (1998). *Whirligig*. New York: Holt Publishing.
Fleischman, P. (1997). *Seedfolks*. New York: Harper Collins.
Fleischman, P. (1996). *Dateline: Troy*. Cambridge: Candlewick Press.
Fleischman. P. (1993). *Bull Run*. New York: Harper Collins.
Fleischman, P. (1988). *Joyful Noise: Poems for Two Voices*. New York: Harper Collins.
Gruenbaum, M. Hasak-Lowy, T. (2017). *Somewhere There Is Still a Sun*. USA: Aladdin.
Hasak-Lowy, T. (2020). *We Are Power: How nonviolent activism changes the world*. USA: Abrams.
Hasak-Lowy, T. (2015). *Me Being Me Is Exactly As Insane As You Being You*. USA: Simon Pulse.
Hasak-Lowy, T. (2013). *33 Minutes*. USA: Abrams.

Other possible texts for exploring literacy ideas and pedagogies highlighted in this chapter

Cashore, K. (2017). *Jane, Unlimited*. USA: Penguin Random House.

An ambitious puzzle adventure, this text asks readers to choose their own paths through Jane's experiences on a trip to an island with her friend. Each choice will take Jane into a different type of novel – mystery, horror, space opera, spy thriller and fantasy.

Kristoff, J. (2015). *Illuminae*. USA: Penguin Random House.

This dossier of hacked documents (including emails, instant messages, medical reports, schematics, military files) is the first in a sci-fi space opera series charting the relationship between Kady and Ezra, beginning with their break up.

Myers, W. D. (2000). *Monster*. USA: Harper Collins.

Steve, a 16-year-old amateur film maker is on trial for murder, and in an attempt to cope with his experiences he decides he will make a film documenting his experience. The text is laid out entirely as a screenplay including, instructions for camera work, lighting (also adapted in graphic novel form, 2015).

Chapter Bibliography

Bazerman, C. (1997). The life of genre and life in the classroom, *Genre and Writing* (pp. 19–26). USA: Boynton/Cook.

Bentley, E. (2013). Supernovas and superheroes: Examining unfamiliar genres and teachers' pedagogical content knowledge, *English Education*, 45(3), 218–246.

Cremin, T. Mottram, M. Powell, S. Collins, R. Stafford, K. (2014) *Building Communities of Engaged Readers: Reading for pleasure.* London: Routledge.

Cummins J., Early M. (Eds) (2011). *Identity Texts: The collaborative creation of power in multilingual schools.* Stoke-on-Trent: Trentham Books.

Fisher, M. T. (2007). *Writing inRrhythm: Spoken word poetry in urban classrooms.* New York: Teachers College.

Fisher, M. T. (2003). Open mics and open minds: Spoken word poetry in African diaspora participatory literacy communities, *Harvard Educational Review*, 73(3), 362–389.

Fleischer, C. (2006). Researching Writing: The unfamiliar genre research project, *The English Journal*, 95(4), 36–42.

Fleischman, P. (2020). Interview.

Fleischman, P. Retrieved (2020). https://medium.com/@hccb/writing-tips-young-authors-b2432d337d97.

Fleischman, P. (1999). The accidental artist, *School Library Journal*, 105.

Galda, L. (2001). High stakes reading: Articulating the place of children's literature in the curriculum. *The New Advocate*, 14(3), p. 223–228.

Gallego, M. A., & Hollingsworth, S. (2000). Introduction: The idea of multiple literacies, *What Counts as Literacy: Challenging the school standard* (pp. 1–23). New York: Teachers College.

Hasak-Lowy, T. (2020). Interview.

Holland, D. Lachicotte, W. Skinner, D. Cain, C. (1998) *Identity and Agency in Cultural Worlds.* Cambridge MA: Harvard University Press.

Kinloch, V. (2007). The White-ification of the Hood: Power, politics, and youth performing narratives of community, *Language Arts*, 85(1), 61–68.

Kirkland, D. (2009). The Skin We Ink: Tattoos, literacy, and a new English education, *English Education*, 41(4), 375–395.

Kucirkova, N. Cremin, T. (2020). *Children Reading for Pleasure in the Digital Age: Mapping reader engagement.* London: Sage.

Kuzmičová, A. Bálint, K. (2019). Personal relevance in story reading: A research review, *Poetics Today*, 40(3), 429–451.

Mackey, M. (2016). *One Child Reading: My auto-bibliography.* Edmonton: University of Alberta Press.

Meek, M. (1992). in Kucirkova, N. Cremin, T. (2020) *Children Reading for Pleasure in the Digital Age: Mapping reader engagement.* London: Sage.

Moore, H. (1994). in Lawler, S. *Mothering the Self: Mothers, daughters, subjects.* London: Routledge.

Rundell, K. (2019). *Why You Should Read Children's Books Even Though You Are So Old and Wise.* London: Bloomsbury.

Schklovsky, V. (1917). Art as technique. In Lemon L. T. Reis, M. J. Eds. and trans., *Russian Formalist Criticism: Four essays*. (1960). Lincoln: University of Nebraska Press.

Short, K. (2011). Reading literature in elementary classrooms. In Wolf, S. Coats, K. Enciso, P. Jenkins, C. (Eds.), *Handbook of Research on Children's and Young Adult Literature* (pp. 48–63). London: Routledge

Wenger, E. (1999). *Communities of Practice: Learning, meaning and identity*. Cambridge: Cambridge University Press.

Wood. J. (2009). *How Fiction Works*. USA: Vintage Publishing.

CHAPTER 4

Reading and writing for pleasure in reciprocal and affinity-based story communities: Exploring digital literacies, humour and authentic spaces for the sharing of stories

About this chapter

Building on the previous chapter's focus on reading and writing widely for personal purposes (Short, 2011), this chapter explores digital literacy alongside pedagogies for reading and writing for pleasure in a variety of personal and social affinity spaces and varied contexts for learning. Understanding literacy and learning as personally resonant (as outlined in detail in the previous chapter), this chapter shifts literacy exploration from traditional classroom practice to social, authentic and personally meaningful affinity-based communities in real and virtual worlds. Through the research literature discussed, pedagogies for reading and writing for pleasure supporting literacy development emerge with a specific focus on authentic personal and social contexts and spaces for learning both in and beyond traditional classroom settings. The children's and young adult literature authors and texts featured in this chapter exemplify ways in which teachers can apply understandings and experiences of fan fiction, remixing and parody in particular as pedagogical approaches to connect with learner lives in new ways through engagement with collaborative dialogue in shared spaces, meaningful texts and authentic audiences for reading and writing widely for personal purposes.

About the authors

Joan Holub

Joan is an American *New York Times* bestselling children's and young adult literature author who has also worked as an art director and illustrator. She has written over 150 children's books and won numerous awards including the American Booksellers Association Best Books for Children, the Kirkus Reviews Best Children's Books of the Year, the Bank Street Best Children's Book of the Year and a Chronicle Books Author Appreciation Award.

Joan's books appeal to a variety of ages and interests and are both entertaining and educational. *Zero the Hero* is a maths-centric picture book pitting Zero and his friends against sneaky Roman numerals. *Little Red Writing* remixes traditional fairy tales while helping young readers develop their own writing skills. *Mighty Dads* sees older construction vehicles teaching their young construction vehicle children growing up skills. Her *Adventure Dolls* (aka *Doll Hospital* series) offers a doll's-eye-view of history. With Suzanne Williams she has written a number of book series including *Goddess Girls*, which tells the story of Greek Goddesses enrolled as students at the fictional Mount Olympus Academy; *Heroes in Training*, an adventure series about young Olympians; and *Grimmtastic Girls*, where each book focuses on a female fairy tale character attending

Grimm Academy, a fictional co-educational school. For more information see www.joanholub.com.

KJ Shapiro

KJ is an American psychologist, children's literature author and avid poetry lover since her own childhood. She is a member of the Society of Children's Book Writers and Illustrators. Her work has won a number of awards including the Bank Street Books Best Children's Book of the Year and Cincinnati's Librarian's Choice Award.

KJ's work parodies centuries of classical poetry and is meant to be read aloud in a celebration of humour, rhythm and rhyme. *Because I Could Not Stop My Bike and Other Poems* presents a series of poem parodies based on English and American poetry. *I Must Go Down to the Beach Again and Other Poems* spans five centuries of poetic and artistic expression including citations and endnotes of the original works. In her introduction to her work, KJ writes that though parodies are often written to make fun of something, these poems spring from deep respect, and this is very clear in her treatment and presentation of her parody poetry. For more information see www.kjshapiro.com.

Introduction

Engaging learners in reading and writing widely for personal purposes necessitates that teachers encourage learners to read for pleasure inside and outside of the classroom a range of different and varied texts. This chapter explores ways in which teachers and learners can engage with reading and writing widely for pleasure in a variety of different kinds of contexts, spaces and communities in and beyond traditional classroom practice, beginning with Gottschall's (2012) assertion that:

> fiction is a powerful and ancient virtual reality technology that simulates the big dilemmas of human life. When we pick up a book or turn on the TV – whoosh! – we are teleported into a parallel universe. We identify so closely with the struggles of the protagonists that we don't just sympathize with them; we strongly empathize with them. We feel their happiness and desire and fear; our brains rev up as though what is happening to them is actually happening to us.
>
> (Gottschall, 2012, p. 67)

In their exploration of reading for pleasure in the digital age, Kucirkova and Cremin (2020) take as a central focus the "fiction effect", highlighted by (Jerrim and Moss, 2018) in a 35-country Organisation for Economic Co-operation and Development (OECD) study with 250,000 teenage participants. This study evidenced that young people who read fiction frequently had significantly stronger reading skills than their peers. The same has not been found to be true for reading frequency of other text types (magazines, nonfiction, newspapers and comics), leading researchers to conclude that encouraging young people to read fiction for pleasure may be particularly beneficial for their reading and literacy skills.

Supporting an emphasis on fiction in reading development, Kucirkova and Cremin further explain how a "focus on the interrelationship between a personal and collective response to reading offers a rich conceptual space from which to explore the experience of reading for pleasure in the twenty-first century" (Kucirkova and Cremin, 2020, p. 6), understanding reading as a lived and shared experience taking place in a wide variety of contexts (home, classroom, online) for (young) people. This lived experience is not necessarily a dichotomy for learners, as is sometimes suggested in literature and research, as paper and screen explorations of stories occur simultaneously and complementarily in daily life.

Rather than focusing on particular text types (eBooks, printed novel, story apps), Kucirkova and Cremin (2020) argue that it may be more beneficial for teachers and researchers to carefully consider place, space and purpose when it comes to reading for pleasure. Their work highlights a shared social space for reading between children, teacher, parent and community reading lives as a focus for supporting young readers and creating spaces for reading reciprocity in communities of practice. Understanding fiction as a powerful and ancient virtual reality technology, this chapter aims to apply these key understandings of reading fiction for pleasure experiences to develop a range of pedagogies for reading and writing widely for pleasure in and beyond the classroom.

Affinity spaces for reading and writing for pleasure: Digital literacy in reciprocal reading and writing communities

Reading for pleasure, independent reading and recreational reading are all terms that highlight the powerful relationships between personal purpose, engagement, interest, desire, identity, choice, motivation and attainment in reading. Applying these central reading for pleasure concepts to the development of classroom pedagogies encourages teachers to focus on learner led engagement around identity affirming and personally selected texts in formal and informal social spaces. Building pedagogies around reading for pleasure Kucirkova and Cremin (2020) remind us that:

> reciprocal reading for pleasure is a dialogic process during which readers transform the meanings of texts through the volitional exchange of ideas and perspectives and find satisfaction in so doing… In reciprocal reading for pleasure there is no unidirectional transfer of knowledge from a text or from any given reader of it, but rather the ongoing sharing and pollination of ideas, the generation of new perspectives and the renegotiation of old views. These processes can give rise to knowledge transformation and are likely to be nurtured most effectively in reading communities.
> (Kucirkova and Cremin, 2020, p. 94)

Cremin et al. (2009; 2014) identify four particular key practices for teachers in the development of effective and evidence-based reading for pleasure pedagogies, including creating a social reading environment; setting time aside for independent choice led reading and reading aloud; making opportunities for informal book talk and inside text talk (classroom discussion and more informal interactions that afford learners opportunities to draw on and extend their shared knowledge of individual texts); and sharing recommendations for reading through reciprocal and interactive reader relationships developed in reading communities. These key personally and socially focused practices suggest ways in which teachers may create and develop reading and writing for pleasure communities and provide concrete tasks and approaches for beginning to explore reading widely for pleasure in the classroom.

As highlighted in the previous chapter, reading aloud as a particular focus is a central aspect of reading widely for pleasure pedagogy as it supports readers and offers opportunities for learners to access socially texts they cannot or have not yet read for themselves. The music and sounds experienced when listening to stories read aloud support engagement, concentration, comprehension and interaction yet in traditional classroom practice reading aloud focuses primarily on the development of reading skills, comprehension and content and is not necessarily concerned with encouraging independent and choice led reading.

Adapting the focus and purpose of read aloud in the classroom opens new opportunities for deeper and more meaningful engagement with a wider range of texts and genres while the fiction effect suggests that reading skills continue to develop over time. Additionally, Read aloud plus activities in informal and social spaces offer learners tasks before, during and after read aloud that focus on shared enjoyment and, are themselves, rich resources for conversations and for developing social relationships between readers (Cremin, 2018).

Central to these key practices for reading for pleasure pedagogy is the development of an authentic reading community of practice where meanings, perspectives and experiences can be shared, explored dialogically and extended, reflecting the lived experience of engaging with text. Kucirkova and Cremin (2020) suggest that within these reading for pleasure communities reciprocal understanding develops over time through dialogue in inter-thinking (or thinking together), whereby in physical and virtual contexts learners use dialogue and actions to exchange ideas and develop their individual and collective understandings. Important for teachers is the understanding that these reading for pleasure communities, or affinity spaces, exist in a variety of different contexts. As a consequence teachers can use physical and virtual contexts to support reading for pleasure and critical literacy for learners in many different but complementary ways, taking more opportunities to consider in our planning, pedagogy and practice, the spaces, places and purposes we curate for reading and writing.

The concept of an affinity space as a space or a series of spaces where people affiliate with others in joint activities based primarily on shared activities, interests and goals rather than shared race, class, culture or gender, provides a conceptual framework for the development of reading widely for pleasure communities within and beyond the classroom. Traditional definitions of affinity spaces refer to online and virtual communities but the concept can also be employed to organise classroom activities and engagements around children's and young adult literature, reading and writing in ways that reflect online features and definitions of affinity spaces.

Gee (2012) outlines a number of features of affinity spaces, including an understanding that an affinity space is a space for informal learning; the affinity comes from the spaces and the shared tasks, the people differ; experts and novices work side by side together; content, interactions and dialogue are fluid and emergent and the development of the practice is learner led; a variety of different types of knowledge and experiences are valued; participation in the group takes many forms; as ultimately affinity spaces will change over time with their users. Applying these features of affinity spaces to develop meaningful and engaging reading and writing widely for pleasure pedagogies in the classroom and beyond ensures a both a personal and dialogic authentic space and audience for authorship, ownership and engagement with reading, writing and literacy.

As teachers consider the spaces available inside and outside of the classroom for affinity-based engagements we can consider how we can adapt physical contexts (for example, creating an author's corner, time for reading with blinds drawn in front of a projected fire) and engage in online communities (author websites, online competitions, fan fiction) to allow new opportunities for different kinds of dialogue, inter-thinking, actions and interactions around reading and writing widely practice.

A focus on reading widely for pleasure pedagogies in affinity-based spaces as previously outlined necessitates a broadening of our definitions of text in classroom practice to encompass the wide range of reading choices available to learners. This more inclusive but expansive understanding of text and reader experiences facilitates authentic engagement in reading and writing but calls for pedagogical practices that focus explicitly on digital literacy in its broadest sense and the supporting and safeguarding of learners in these less familiar contexts for learning.

Digital literacy extends beyond traditional understandings of literacy as reading, writing, speaking and listening to encompass cognitive authority, safety and privacy, and creative, ethical and responsible use of digital media (Meyers, Erickson and Small, 2013). Eshet-Alakalai and Amichai-Hamburger (2004) identify a range of particular skills related to digital literacy including photo-visual skills (reading and understanding on screen instructions and information), reproduction skills (using digital media and resources to create something new), branching skills (understanding and constructing knowledge based on hypertextual, nonlinear and asynchronous cues), information skills (assessing information quality, reliability and validity) and socio-emotional skills (understanding the rules of participation in online spaces). Engaging with digital literacy in the classroom provides teachers and learners with rich and authentic resources, audiences and avenues for communication but to ensure learners engage safely in these online spaces careful attention is required to the development of the aforementioned digital literacy skills and related deeper understandings of the similarities and differences between real life and online life experiences.

Milovanovic and Maksimović (2020) outline a digitally literate person as being able to perform digital activities in concrete contexts of people's lives such as in learning, work, leisure and other aspects of daily life. They further define digital literacy itself as varied and uniquely developing for each individual according to the situation of each person, their life and digital literacy needs, highlighting also its relatedness to other literacies and the importance of an ability to reflect on the development of digital literacy itself.

They share a number of instructional practices for engaging learners in digital literacy in the classroom which include keeping a media use diary to reflect on digital decision making and media use; focusing on information search and evaluation strategies and skills that engage learners in discussion about the finding, evaluating and sharing content from a variety of sources to help learners make better choices about the quality and relevance of information; engaging learners in active interpretation of texts to explore new ideas, perspectives and knowledge while we read, view and listen to content; developing tasks requiring a close analysis of the nature of content and encouraging learners to use critical questioning to examine intent; asking learners to compare different texts about the same topic to develop critical thinking skills; incorporating simulation and role-playing activities to promote imagination, decision making skills and reflective thinking about choice and consequences; and finally drawing attention to multimedia composition and the understanding that every communication carries particular meaning according to the particular goals or intentions of the author/society/context in which it has been created. The pedagogies and sample activities suggested throughout this chapter offer many opportunities for teachers to engage learners meaningfully and reflectively with these instructional strategies and all key aspects of digital literacy suggested in this chapter thus far.

From readers to writers: Exploring the stories of Joan Holub through fan fiction and remix in virtual and physical affinity spaces

Curwood (2013) explores how fan fiction and remix offer a way into literature and opportunities for authentic personal responses in her ethnographic study of teenagers in the United States, Canada and Australia engaged with *The Hunger Games* in online fan fiction affinity spaces. Cassie, a young learner in Curwood's research project, for example, rewrites in the following extract familiar characters and known worlds in unique and imaginative ways.

> You and Harry are now the last two standing. You decide to walk where you think he will be: the camp where he allied with and then abandoned you. For better or for worse, you must now face him and put an end to these Games. You must fight Harry Potter. Harry Potter. The Boy Who Lived. The Chosen One. Your friend. Your mentor. Your idol. *Was your idol*, you think bitterly. Over the course of these Games, you have seen a different side of Harry. You would have never expected him to need saving… or abandon a friend. You reach the camp, and find Harry standing there. He is bloody and burned, but his wand isn't drawn. More than anything else, he just looks tired.
>
> (Cassie in Curwood, 2013, p. 88)

Curwood's work supports other similar research in this area, evidencing how fan fiction and online fandom and game affinity spaces can promote collaborative writing and roleplay across a range of real life and virtual spaces (Thomas, 2007); offer opportunities for writers to authentically engage with a wide variety of hybrid worlds, modes, genres and experiences (Magnifico, 2012); provide mentor texts and multimodal representations of worlds to inspire reading and writing engagement (Lammers, 2012); extend more participatory, collaborative, and distributed literature engagements to readers and writers as they develop writing skills through peer review and interaction with a global audience (Black, 2008); serve as important resources for teachers and learning to reposition some adolescents as capable literacy learners (Chandler-Olcott and Mahar, 2003); and finally facilitate learners in the making of personal and intertextual connections with literature (Bean and Moni, 2003). In these unique and highly interactive shared spaces for literacy and learning all these practices ultimately blur "any clear cut distinction between media producer and media spectator, since any spectator may potentially participate in the creation of new artworks" (Jenkins, 1992, p. 247).

In the above excerpt Cassie, a teenage girl, writes anew online the story of Harry Potter in the different yet strangely familiar world of *The Hunger Games*. Her words exemplify many of the unique aspects of fan fiction, namely that it is text written for young people by young people; that the expansiveness of fan imagination allows young people to use characters, settings and themes from literature meaningfully in creative composition; and that it allows young writers to experiment with a variety of modes and genres in ways that involve public dissemination, possible collaboration and interaction, and an authentic audience.

Through Cassie's engagements in fan fiction, Curwood (2013) suggests that she has been able to express a fan and writer identity; read and write for pleasure; experiment with becoming an author; explore new ways of conveying narratives; develop social relationships; move between media; compete; and retell a favourite story. In terms of identity, language and literacy, what Cassie has learnt seems to be immense. In this space she is an author for a real audience, and at the same time an editor, proofreader and collaborator as she engages about her work and the work of others in online chats, messages, boards, etc.

Cassie's experience takes place in an online affinity space through a fan fiction website, and her rich learning and literacy experiences as she enjoys her engagement in this online reading and writing community reminds teachers of the opportunities for encouraging students to engage with fan websites to develop their literacy practice in personally and socially focused ways. Learners are no longer limited to writing solely for their teachers alone in school settings. Rather new technologies and literacies shift reading and writing from individualised and author centric to collaborative, participatory and distributed practices where time and space function differently (Lankshear and Knobel, 2007).

Teachers could also look to local/school level intranet/password protected websites and online spaces to curate our own online reading and writing fandoms and communities, incorporating parental and community links as appropriate. Finally, as previously suggested teachers can also think about how we can develop fan cultures in our own physical classroom settings, designing opportunities for and with learners to engage with reading and writing widely for personal purposes as they might in these personal and authentic online spaces.

Curwood (2013) further explains the reading and writing practices inherent in engaging with fan fiction as based on remix culture, a practice of taking cultural artifacts and combining them in new and creative ways. She suggests that the remixing of worlds, authors and texts that writers engage in is itself a skill and should be included in reading and writing pedagogy. Mentor and exemplar texts are essential for related pedagogies as learners experience these texts they become themselves active producers of language, learning and knowledge. Additionally, engaging with fan fiction and remixing in the ways outlined here can afford learners new opportunities to read and respond to literature and text as well as immerse and/or write themselves in(to) new worlds.

Developing remix cultures in the classroom also opens up this space for explorations of a wide variety of personally resonant worlds, texts (including film, TV, song, computer games), and reading experiences beyond those selected by the teacher as learners collaboratively introduce, remix and reinvent with meaningful and personal purpose the spaces and places they are most comfortable and familiar with. Seeing a space in the classroom for texts and literacies personally valued is an empowering and identity affirming experience for learners central to authentic reading widely for pleasure and personal purposes classroom pedagogies and can develop critical, reading and writing literacy skills (McWilliams et al., 2011).

Su-Jeong Wee et al. (2019) evidence how parody study offers opportunities to encourage learners speak in, through, about and at texts in the classroom. Through parody learners engage in literacy development as they deconstruct and reconstruct stories from new and developed perspectives. Parody, as a form of remix, supports learners in particular in their considerations of content, theme, character, style, setting, as well as highlighting a particular focus on humour and language choice. Fairy tales and poetry, as we will see in our first author interview and later in this chapter, are modes particularly well-suited to remix and parody as they are made from perspectives and language that while at first glance may appear simple and straightforward, are in fact incredibly ambiguous and complex.

FIVE MINUTES WITH JOAN HOLUB

How do you think we can use reading for pleasure in the classroom to encourage and support learning?

Children's literature can be both entertainment and a tool for learning and literacy. My number one task as an author is to engage the reader with a strong plot and intriguing characters that make readers *want* to read my book(s) for pleasure. Learning can be imbued along the way. A teaching aspect should not and will not detract from the fun as long as that teaching is blended into a plot-driven storyline that engages and holds a reader's interest on its own.

Many of my main characters go on two concurrent journeys within a book. Two story threads are woven together from beginning to end of the text. One thread follows a personal journey in which the character learns something about themselves. Little Red Writing learns that she is brave. Zero the Hero learns that he's a hero, not a villain. The ancillary journey is an active plot-driven one in which the main character makes physical progress toward a story goal. This physical journey moves the plot forward, pulling the reader along with burning questions to be answered: How will this story turn out? Will the character succeed at her/his goal? Little Red Writing achieves her goal of writing a story and also defeats the Wolf-3000 pencil sharpener to save her school. Readers learn about parts of speech and how to write a book along the way. Zero the Hero and his friends defeat the Roman Numerals and readers learn age-appropriate information about math and numbers along the way. An innate understanding of musical and rhyming rhythm is ingrained in all of us and thus can facilitate literacy and learning. The rhythm and tempo of well-written rhyme in a story is similar to that of a song, as both have meter and pattern. I believe that communication via rhyme, both in written word or music, can lead to better retention of learning concepts.

What do you think about as you plan and write a story?

My standalone books and book series often begin with a title that intrigues me. For instance, I was drawn to the title *Goddess Girls*, because of the "G" alliteration and because I enjoyed mythology in elementary school. First, I considered what a series with that title could be about. I like writing about strong, smart girls as role models, which triggered the idea for an action-oriented girl-empowering series about (approximately) 12-year-old goddesses and gods attending Mount Olympus Academy (a middle school) where Zeus is the principal and teachers include Mr. Cyclops, who teaches Hero-ology class. As a young reader, I was fascinated by Greek mythology. Now, as an author, I relish the prospect of rewriting these original myths with a middle-school twist (and humour), starring Athena, Persephone, and other young immortals, as well as mortal characters such as Pandora and Medusa. The goddess girls that star in each book solve their own problems and the problems of others in parodies of the original myths. Middle school is familiar ground for young readers, which lends the Mount Olympus Academy setting a relatable foundation on which I build the Goddess Girls stories with co-author Suzanne Williams.

Why are fairy tale and myth central to your storytelling and how could teachers draw on these themes in the classroom?

World-building that draws on already-familiar historical references can more quickly establish a realm in which to engage readers. We find literary value in our joint human history and mythologies, which have withstood the test of time and remain influential in sports, advertising, branding products, etc. The Olympic Games, Nike, Titans, Amazon, and Pandora, are just some of the well-known names derived from these sources. Mythologies and fairy tales represent a familiar structure that is quickly and easily understood by readers. Authors can draw on these as pedagogical patterns, as co-author Suzanne Williams and I do in our *Goddess Girls, Heroes in Training, Little Goddess Girls, Thunder Girls,* and *Grimmtastic Girls,* series. (The first three are based on Greek myths, the fourth on Norwegian myths, and the fifth is based on Grimm Fairy Tales.)

In myth-based series, such as *Goddess Girls* and *Heroes-in-Training,* historical references are made relevant to a young reader's experience – what they know, see, feel, hear, live. Myth and fairy tale take-offs can instruct them on life lessons, yet it's important to strive to do this in a way that's current and relatable to a young reader's world view. Greek myths are not inherently funny. But add humour, friendship-drama and a fresh take on the characters who solve their own problems – huge problems such as fighting off evil beasts or difficult ones such as trying to decide if they like a boy – and readers can relate these myths to their own lives and understand that they are not alone in what they experience. When students encounter super-powerful immortals who have similar problems to their own reading can be an empowering, satisfying experience.

Originally, the myths from these stories were cautionary tales concocted by ancient peoples to help make sense of the confusing physical world around them. They didn't understand the science of thunder and lightning and so they created the myth that Zeus hurled thunderbolts when he was angry. As a creative lesson, teachers could ask young readers to create an imaginative mythology around what they know of their school, using fanciful explanations of things that happen. In humorous or fanciful ways, describe the jobs of the adults, including principal, cafeteria workers, custodian and various teachers. Create a fanciful mythology to explain school life and make sense of the rules and student cliques and organizations at their school. Or challenge young readers to take a traditional tale or myth and give it a new spin to create their own story. Ask them to put two objects or characters together that normally wouldn't co-exist and then give these objects or characters surprising problems or settings that are atypical for them. Perhaps a trash can and a piece of trash join forces to overcome an enemy. Or what would happen if a character such as Athena or Snow White suddenly found herself on an alien planet? Bend, twist, and retool history, fairy tales, or mythology to a new purpose to tell a good, relatable, informative story.

How do you think teachers could engage learners with humour and parody in the classroom?

In a classroom setting, discuss why humour is a powerful tool for writers and what makes something funny. Ask students to write a humorous situation for a film or book character that is not known for being funny. For instance, a character such as the stern Zeus (king of the Greek goddesses and gods) or Ares (the Greek god of war). Keep the basic structure of the myths so that they're recognizable but change or add experiences that are relevant young readers' lives. In the Pandora's Box (or more historically accurate "jar"), she opens a box and lets out various troubles and evil into the world, but hope survives. In Goddess Girls #8 *Pandora the Curious*, young Pandora opens a box that she should not open, releasing trouble bubbles that, when popped against various immortal students at Mount Olympus Academy, cause these students to act in funny or embarrassing ways that they normally would not. For instance, the brainy Athena becomes clueless and the beautiful Aphrodite becomes embarrassingly bad-mannered. This creates humour. Everyone can relate to the feeling of embarrassment, so it's empowering to read about popular Greek immortals experiencing embarrassment, too. This makes it feel less hurtful to readers who experience embarrassing moments themselves.

Zeus comes to mind as a well-known figure from myth to experiment with parody writing on. He's fascinating. He's the boss in Greek mythology. His symbols include thunder, and he has numerous opponents, siblings and friends. What would that be like as a friend or foe? As a boss of Mount Olympus, is he under a lot of pressure? What might he be afraid of? What does he enjoy doing for fun? What mistakes might he make?

What do you think about in particular when you write a picture book?
My picture book and board book creation process differs from my process for creating a chapter book or middle grade book series. I do often begin most of these books with a title. But because picture books rely on a happy marriage between both art and text, I also doodle images for picture books as part of my writing process, creating embellished stick-figures for the entire story and revising them many times, even though I don't plan to illustrate the book. I was an author-illustrator for about seven years before I segued into writing as a career. So I tend to think in images. I make hand-drawn dummies to think through the process of creating a picture book or board book. I need to see something visual in order to make sense of what art and text might appear together, and how these will best flow from page to page from the beginning to the end of a book. I envision this process as combing through long, tangled, wet hair. Another author told me that she views the process as cutting away superfluous stone to find the sculpture waiting to be discovered underneath.

When I think back to a picture book like *Zero the Hero* for the purposes of exploring your questions, I tried to recall exactly how I got the idea to make Roman Numerals the bad-guy enemies that are central to the mid-story crisis when they surround the anthropomorphic Zero and his counting number friends 1 through 9. You might think that idea just popped into my head. It did. But the reason it did is because I had already consumed copious information about my subject, mostly reading nonfiction about the concept of zero in math and about the purpose and relationships of numbers – the abilities of zero in math in particular – while trying to massage this story concept into a finished book manuscript. The idea of Roman Numerals as antagonists grew out of the fertile landscape that research about my subject (math and numbers) beforehand had created.

The story of zero is an ancient one. Its roots stretch back to the dawn of mathematics, in the time thousands of years before the first civilization, long before humans could read and write. But as natural as zero seems to us today, for ancient peoples zero was a foreign – and frightening – idea.

(From the book *Zero–The Biography of a Dangerous Idea* by Charles Seife)

How do you think art can be used in the classroom to encourage reading and writing engagement?

Art in the classroom is extremely useful. Ask students to write a story with no illustrations. Then two young authors can trade their stories and have the other student make illustrations for each other's book. This is a good way to understand what really happens in most author-illustrator collaborations, where there is often little contact between author and illustrator, an arrangement that leaves illustrators the freedom they need to create their best work. An author once told me he was surprised when he wrote a story that starred children, but the artists depicted the characters as anthropomorphic animals.

Students enjoy being read to. While a story is being read to them, have them illustrate the story in a series of boxes or just flowing around a page. These doodles might lead to something extraordinary. After making art, ask students to create written sequence statements telling what they did first, next, then, finally with regard to the steps they implemented in the art creation projects. Ask them to write an artist statement about their completed or in-progress work. This encourages communication skills, good sentence structure and word choices to describe their creative process in making an art project.

Have students create artwork that includes people, animals, and/or imaginative characters. Then ask them to write descriptions of their characters. What do they look like? Where do the subjects of their art live? What are their jobs? Their favourite things to do? Who are their friends? What problems do they need to overcome and how might they accomplish this? This can be the start of a story.

Your picture book, Little Red Writing, *focuses in its narrative on advice for aspiring young authors. Could you tell us a little more about this text in particular?*

Little Red Writing also began with the title and the idea that the main character would be an anthropomorphic red pencil with facial features and arms, who attends Pencil School with other pencils, which are each named based on the shape of the erasers atop their "heads". I also needed a "wolf-like character to pretend to be the grandmother figure to outwit the Red Riding character. What might be a scary figure to a pencil? A pencil sharpener of course! My bad-guy "wolf" character is a Wolf-3000 pencil sharpener posing as the Pencil School principal. The actual school principal is a stand-in for the true grandmother figure. I started with those plot points and the story grew from there.

Since I'm always eager to add a learning component if it can be seamlessly merged with the story plot, I had Red's teacher assign her and other pencil-students in her class to write a story. During Red's physical journey of moving through the book's pages and traveling through different parts of the school itself, Red learns about parts of speech and how to write a story. Her personal journey is proving that she is indeed brave enough to thwart the Wolf-3000's nefarious plans for the school. After all, red is traditionally the colour of bravery! One of the joys of writing children's books is weaving a deeper meaning, message, instruction, or information into an engaging story. I think of it as "faction" – the weaving of factual information into a fictional story.

Your Adventure Dolls *(aka* Dolls Hospital*) series takes a familiar childhood toy (a doll) and builds detailed and challenging stories around this childhood artefact that span centuries and wide spaces. What advice would you have for young people about taking something familiar to them and creating a story around this?*

Inanimate objects make for wonderful, unexpected star characters in a story. Assign a personality to a familiar object or animal, making it an anthropomorphic book character. Zero the Hero and Little Red Writing are anthropomorphic characters; Zero and Little Red (the pencil) each have a face, arms, and legs. They speak and walk and interact with friends and enemies.

Build your story around a shared human concern, but give this concern to a non-human main character. The great white shark in my picture book *I Am the Shark* has a shared human concern – how does he compare to others of his kind? Is he smarter? Bigger? After all, "great" is part of his name so he must be the greatest at something, right? Through the story text, it is made clear that in everyone's life there will always be someone else who is smarter or bigger or whatever. The underlying message in this book is a self-esteem-building one: "just be happy being you".

> Some childhood or teenage items such as a diary, a piece of jewellery, a hat, a favourite item of clothing, such as the pants in *The Sisterhood of the Traveling Pants* by Ann Brashares could make an intriguing main character. Or perhaps choose to feature an item that a child or teenager longs for but does not possess, and make the journey about trying to acquire the item. Pair two disparate things that are unlikely to work well together at first glance, and then find a way to make them work together to create a story. Maybe a hat befriends a shoe. Or a fork battles it out with spaghetti. The possibilities are endless.
>
> *What advice would you have for aspiring young authors who would like to follow in your footsteps?*
> Try to find your own style. Dare to do something different. Don't just write one story and then give up. Write many stories and ask others to offer you two compliments and one helpful criticism on your work. Go further than what you have learned or been taught. Do you have two book ideas? One about a monster in a time machine? And another about a superhero stuck in a bathroom toilet stall? Try combining both ideas into one book. Doing this can often lead one book that's better than either of the two original ideas were on their own. Read books that you like and some that you don't. Know that reading nonfiction can inspire and enrich your fiction writing.
>
> As you write remember that every story needs a beginning, middle, and end, plus characters, tension, and pacing. Introduce the characters and establish their problems quickly for the reader. Solve their problems, then heap on more problems that they must solve. And make sure the ending is satisfying. Two good resource books about the structure of writing are *The Writer's Journey* by Christopher Vogler and *Save the Cat* by Blake Snyder. Both are written at an adult level and contain insights into how stories and films are typically structured to meet the innate expectations of readers and film-watchers.

In her interview Joan Holub emphasises and exemplifies many of the reading and writing widely for pleasure pedagogical approaches explored in this chapter. Her focus on pleasure and personal purpose as the central aspect of her writing for young people reminds teachers why many children's and young adult literature texts are created in the first place – for pleasure, enjoyment and with the identities, worlds and experiences of young readers at heart. Her understanding of writing as world-building drawing on familiar references in ways that are relatable and current around an intriguing title or idea offers a helpful structure for the development of remixing pedagogies and practices in the classroom. The focus on personal identity throughout Joan's interview and its pedagogical power to engage and motivate learners is a central aspect of reading and writing for pleasure pedagogy.

In the classroom learners could be encouraged to consider local histories, stories and myths, alongside wider national and international stories or indeed re-imagine world experiences in their own smaller and more familiar locale. Combining objects or characters in surprising ways to tell their stories in these settings is an imaginative and identity affirming approach to creative writing in the classroom. Joan's suggestion of creating an imaginative mythology to explain the unknown of our schools or perhaps even family and community lives is an authentic and meaningful engagement of young people with learning across a variety of contexts – learning personally and socially about themselves, each other, their community, their country and their world alongside sharing and developing reading and writing skills.

Joan's parodist remixing of myth and fairy tale in her work to tell new stories connects well with personal critical literacy pedagogical approaches. Bettelheim (1989) is a seminal text for teachers who want to explore fairy tale stories with learners in their classroom and identifies the many different ways fairy tale texts offer opportunities for engaging learners in personal critical literacy practice. For Bettelheim the truth of the fairy tale is "the truth of our imagination, not that of normal causality" (Bettelheim, 1989, p. 117) as fairy tales explore "life divined from the inside" (Bettelheim, 1989, p. 24).

These cruel stories help us cope with and understand our own life experiences as Bettelheim explains how the vagueness of fairy tale (and myth) is particularly pedagogically suited to deeper and more personal critical thinking tasks because the fairy tale, at each reading, is capable of yielding new insights, questions and experiences. Teaching the fairy tale offers complex meaning and interpretive models for remixing personal experience to learners of all ages because these stories do not have single, stable origins, and exist in many different versions (Teverson, 2013).

This ambiguity and the multiple perspectives can be taken when exploring these seemingly simple tales (how would *Little Red Riding Hood* change if told from the perspective of Red's grandmother, the wolf or the woodsman, for example, or in *The Three Little Pigs* what reasons could the wolf give for destroying the houses of the pigs?). These perspectives allow learners to collaboratively question texts, authors and worlds in ways that develop personal critical literacy in shared thinking and discussion. Teverson (2013) further suggests that fairy tales appear timeless not because they have no history but because they have too many histories to count, and are plural and multi-voiced, culturally and historically layered as they carry the memory of other times. Fairy tales and myth offer powerful opportunities to explore relationships between text and context as they speak so loudly of the times in which they have been told. Investigating the many fingerprints through time on modern day fairy tales asks learners of all ages to engage personally and critically with a number of versions of the same story, considering as they read personal, social, historical and socio-political contexts that may impact on the telling of stories.

Zipes suggests that we can understand fairy tales as metaphors for how we as humans adapt to our environments and in his work on critical literacy frames fairy tales as socio-political texts. Reversals of the real world, Zipes argues that fairy tales are interesting for their modernisation as well as their timelessness and the interactions and evolutions evident in between. In his text *Creative Storytelling: Building Community Changing Lives,* Zipes (1996) outlines a three-month program of storytelling for fairy tales that introduces literary genres in a hands-on and active ways focusing on reading, writing, acting, drawing and dialogue in reading and writing widely for personal purposes in communities of practice.

Building on reading for pleasure, remix pedagogies and critical literacy, this text asks learners to innovatively use fairy tale characters, motifs and narrative strategies and aims to enable learners to tell their own stories and design their own curricular focus. Central to Zipes's approach is making close connections with personal learner experiences and what is already known collectively and socially about these stories. This aligns very closely with Joan's discussion of her approach to writing in her interview as she emphasises how her stories come from and grow out of experiences and knowledge she already has encountered in her daily life.

Developing reading for pleasure communities in the classroom and connecting with those already in existence beyond in online and virtual spaces affords learners fertile soil to nurture, grow, pollinate and transform their beginning ideas into shared stories, similar to Joan's untangling of hair or cutting away of stone to reveal the sculpture underneath. Fanfiction.net, for example, contains a number of pages dedicated to young author fan fiction based on Joan's book series *Goddess Girls* with Suzanne Williams. On this and other fan fiction sites and fandoms, individuals rewrite endings, create and remix characters, scenes and plot twists for an authentic audience of fan peers ready and willing to share feedback and comments on the work uploaded, all because, as one young writer remixing the *Goddess Girls* includes in her title, it is "just something I wanted to do".

Joan's artistic focus in text creation and read aloud pedagogies provide further inspiration for how learners might respond to personally selected texts in the classroom. Read aloud doodles or writing planning asks learners to draw and visualise their characters, or imagine what anthropomorphic characters might look like, say and do. Her conceptualisation of her writing as "faction", the weaving of factual information into a fictional story again provides a way in to remix pedagogy and activities for learners to explore in the classroom. The following table provides some ideas for classroom activities based on Joan's work and ideas. Some of the activities encourage learners to engage with online communities and affinity spaces and so further exemplify the extending of the definition of and responsibilities for supporting literacy in virtual and online spaces to include consideration of digital literacy and the online safety and well-being of children and teenagers.

FROM READERS TO WRITERS: EXPLORING FAN FICTION AND REMIX IN AFFINITY SPACES AND READING FOR PLEASURE COMMUNITIES

- **Fandoms and finding my own affinity space:** Teachers should give learners a list of fan fiction websites (e.g., fanfiction.net; wattpad.com; getunderlined.com) and ask them to find a fandom for something (book, movie, TV show, computer game) they love. Learners should research their fandom (and related spaces) and make a short presentation to the class introducing their fandom. As a part of this project learners could also be encouraged to actively engage in their chosen fan community in some way (writing, reading, commenting) and report back on this experience in their presentation as well as situating themselves within particular aspects of their affinity spaces (what they like about their chosen focus, why, how it connects to their everyday experiences out of school).

- **The classroom as affinity space for children's and young adult literature:** Teachers can use the ideas within this chapter to adapt their physical classroom space into an affinity space for children's and young adult literature, reading and writing. Some adjustments may be physical (e.g., setting the scene for reading, creating author walls or reading and writing corners, gathering sets of mentor texts for remixing activities) but many may relate to pedagogies and the planning of pleasurable, collaborative and identity affirming reading and writing activities for learners. Teacher and learner roles may also change in this new learning environment and connections could be made later to online affinity spaces and worlds as resources for classroom learning.
- **Remixing literary worlds – Alternate perspectives, universes, realities and me:** Learners can complete a wide variety of activities focused on asking them to remix their favourite and familiar stories from books, movies, TV shows and games. Some of these activities could involve learners choosing to research their favourite stories and worlds in detail and individually or collaboratively write themselves into the stories, create missing scenes, prequels and sequels, or combine two favourite worlds and characters to make something new. Joan's definition of faction as the weaving of factual information into a fictional story also provides rich stimulus and inspiration for remixing writing projects.
- **NaNoWriMo:** This website challenges writers to draft an entire novel in one month, as well as offering smaller writing challenges to engage with at any time. Learners should be introduced to this website and excellent writing resources, pep talks, blogs, events and videos and sign up for the challenge. Alternatively teachers can use this website to help plan a classroom-based (rather than online) unit of work to encourage creative writing and reading for pleasure. https://ywp.nanowrimo.org/
- **Collaborative Peer Editor Workshops:** A key aspect of fan fiction is the engagement of writers with beta readers, people who read fiction with a critical eye and the improvement of grammar, spelling, characterization and style as a central focus, in the development of their creative projects. Mirroring this approach in the classroom to develop peer editor workshops (a part of which could involve engaging with beta readers in online fandoms) encourages learners to help and support each other in the development of authentic and collaborative reading and writing for pleasure communities in the classroom.

The poems are told for you: (i)Poetry, parody and comedy in reading and writing for personal purpose and the poetry of KJ Shapiro

Written by KJ Shapiro

Parody has a long tradition across many times and cultures. Lewis Carroll famously used serious, dry poems as fodder for clever parodies like *Father William*. Many contemporary films and books for young people give a nod back to the plots and styles of Jane Austen (*Clueless*), Shakespeare (*Ten Things I Hate about You*), Blake (*A Visit to William Blake's Inn*) and Dickinson (*The Mouse of Amherst*). In my children's poetry books I similarly transform classical works by poets such as Blake, Shakespeare, Dickinson and Poe into poems with child-friendly themes like riding a bike, eating macaroni and cheese, and going to the beach. In this way, I have tried to draw on the beautiful and varied rhythms and meters of famous poems while giving children of all ages a topic that they can relate to. The benefits to children seemed obvious to me; to ignite their interest in poetry by giving them poems they would love to read over and over. I wanted them to laugh and have fun, to be touched by a thought they may not have considered, or learn something new about their world.

Each of my poems starts with an "apology" to the famous author from which the inspiration was drawn. I always intended the poems to work on two levels: to stand completely alone without any need whatsoever of the original works to appreciate the new ones, and yet also to have extra meaning for the grownups and teenagers who were familiar with the originals. Like Sesame Street's *Letter B*, *Cereal Girl* and *Monsterpiece Theater*, the humour becomes multi-determined – both the actual rhyming story is funny (for children taking it literally) and the wordplay provides a bit of amusement for those who recognize the sources.

A really good parody requires reading widely and a deep understanding of the author's style. In fact, as I wrote these poems, I began to appreciate the poets in a way that I never had before when merely a reader. It was as if I felt my way inside their way of making rhythm and rhyme, and in doing so, expanded my own skill and understanding. When authors engage with classical works in a playful and interactive way, they give permission for others to do the same. I don't believe that literature has to be static, as long as we give the proper credit; a parody can show deep respect of a poet's talents even as it sings a silly tune.

There are two ways I have found that spark the beginning of a good parody:

1. I read through poems and find one that seems fun to change around, sometimes even keeping the first line or very similar. For instance in my poem *Me* I took almost the first line from *Trees* by Joyce Kilmer – "I think that I shall never see/a poem as lovely as a tree" – and it became "I think that I will never see/another person just like me…" From there it was a matter of thinking of all the things that might make a person unique and listing them, just as Kilmer listed the things that make a tree lovely. In fact, students could use this same beginning line and take it in lots of other directions for their own parodies: "I think that I will never see…" There can also just be something about a poem itself that if I change around some of the words in the first few lines, I see how I can make a new and funny story. This method has taken me in some silly directions.
2. Sometimes it can work to have a theme or subject first I want to write on, and then go through many poems to find one that seems to have a good rhythm that would support that topic. Many types of poetry have a form, and that structure itself helps the writer to create. For instance the sonnet, the haiku and the villanelle are examples of poetic forms that have specific rules, and many writers find that the structure itself helps them to shape their ideas into poems. Writing a parody is kind of like that for me – I hang my ideas and images onto the rhyme scheme or rhythm of a classical poem. It's absolutely essential to me that the poem stand on its own, makes one laugh or think, without the reader ever having to read the original to understand it though of course, if and when learners do discover the originals I hope that will add another layer of interest.

In early years parody poems are good for building awareness of sounds and rhymes, and just plain fun. Children can read aloud and act out my poems *I Eat My Pickle, Blow, Blow, Sing Me a Song My Daddy*, and *Dressing*. The food themes in *Tiger, Tiger* and *Ketchup* also work well with this age group. After the poems are read aloud several times, children will be able to supply the rhyming word if you pause. An older age group will appreciate the themes of these poems. Many can be read and acted out, as well as talked about. *Macaroni and Cheese, Bark, Bark, Oh Mommy, My Mommy* and *A Messy Room* can stimulate talk about their own experiences. Teachers can use the poems to help them learners different rhymes and patterns, and students can begin to write their own simple rhymes.

With preteen and teen learners, it works well to introduce these poems as parodies of classic poems. Learners can try their own parodies of nursery rhymes, familiar songs, or even use my poems to make their own "take-offs". Acting out and reciting poems is fun. *The Generous Boy to His Friend* and *Her Reply* make a good dialogue or for a soliloquy *Oh Mommy, My Mommy* and *Party in Xanadu* can be acted out by the whole class. *My Birthday* has a lot of similes; encourage students to write their own poems with similes.

Other ideas would include: Write a poem from the point of view of an animal or object (like *Bark, Bark*) or as a conversation. Write a poem about a favourite food. With teenagers give students a copy of one of the original poems and its parody. (*A Red, Red Nose, Because I Could Not Stop My Bike, The Tiger*, and *To My Dawdling Daughter* are some of the poems which most closely parallel the original.) Have them note similarities (i.e., structure, rhythm, phrasing) and differences (i.e., theme) between the two. Have students pick a poet they particularly like, read some of that poet's poems and then attempt a parody or a looser "take-off". This is a great way to help them feel that they "own" classical poetry, something central to my own writing and work.

FIVE MINUTES WITH KJ SHAPIRO

How do learning, reading and enjoyment connect for you as you write your poetry?

I think of learning as an openness of the mind and spirit and sometimes the heart – depending on the lesson. I think that lessons are everywhere – in what we see, experience, hear, feel, intuit, and do; we go through something and if we are open to it and reflect on it, we can see what went well and what didn't, what we felt or thought, and what we might do differently next time. The best teachers have reflected on what they themselves have learned, whether knowledge, conceptual or experiential, have digested it and then they communicate it in a way that their audience or student can take it in.

Reading is the chance to get inside another world, whether it is someone else's perspective, a culture or time one hasn't been exposed to before, an imaginary place with magical rules, or truths about the natural environment around us. When I was a kid, reading was itself like the Magical Wardrobe that provided a portal to Narnia – one minute a child is in an ordinary closet and the next is transported to somewhere new. Or like *The Secret Garden*, words open up novel and special inner places. Reading gives us so many possibilities and visions and I think it can expand our empathy as we go inside different characters' perspectives.

Mainly I want young people to enjoy my poems – the funny images created, the way that the words sound in the rhyme patterns and the stories themselves. Poetry can often be thought of as a chore by school kids and I would never want my work to be a chore to read. I deliberately wanted these poems to be for fun and to also uplift the reader in some way. I truly hope that young people will realize that poetry can be something accessible to them for their own pleasure.

Could you tell us a little about your understanding and treatment of language and rhyme in your writing?
I have enjoyed wordplay and puns ever since I was in elementary school and have always found that humour through words is very satisfying. There is something particularly rewarding about making a good parody. To play with making parody, think of a commercial jingle or common song that you know and then try to change the words around to make a new song or rhyme, even if it is nonsense. From observations, it seems to me that human beings in general are wired in our brains to feel a certain joy with a good rhyme or rhythm. We see even very young children (sometimes especially very young children) giggling and laughing at rhyming words, even if those words don't make a story. Clapping hands and following simple rhythms is something that children as young as three find engaging.

Poems are also really meant to be read aloud! I've always treasured excellent rhythm and wonderful rhymes, which are just so engaging and enjoyable to hear. It's fun to use surprising words to rhyme, and I think that poets throughout the ages and also the songwriters and rappers of today are delighted when they can come up with some original use of rhyming words. (One of the more unusual rhymes I heard in a poem was "purple" with maple "surple", which also makes for a smile because there is of course no such word as "surple").

Classical poetry has a wide variety of beautiful rhythms (Edgar Allen Poe has some phenomenal rhyme patterns which pulls us in with the beginning). The trouble for children, though, is that these classic poems by talented poets are generally about death, loss, adult romantic love or some mixture of these themes. My idea was to transport the interesting rhythms and rhyme patterns from these poems into new poems that would speak to childhood experiences – favourite foods, daily tasks, pets, family, clothing, fun trips and so on. In the process, I worked to make them enjoyable to read even for someone who didn't know the original poem or poet in any way. Teachers can introduce their students to classical poetry by having them look behind my poems of macaroni and cheese, of ketchup and dogs, to the way that they rhyme and move across the page in rhythm. How are the poems different in style from each other?

How do you select the poets who inspire your work and ideas?
I was introduced to classical poetry in fifth grade with a teacher who had us all memorize and recite poems together as a class. So many years later, I still remember well *Beach Fever* and its first line "I must go down to the sea again" which became the basis of the second book title poem *I Must Go Down to the Beach Again*. When I first started writing the parodies for these books, I used classical poems from my memory bank of grade school and college English major, *A Red Red Rose* became *A Red Red Nose*, *Tiger, Tiger* became *The Tiger* and so on. After I exhausted my memory, I began looking through lots of poetry books for works that I could adapt to a fun poem for children. One of the great things about writing parody poems is it forces me to keep my poetry fresh in rhyme scheme and not get into a rut where all my poems sound the same.

I love Emily Dickinson's rhythms, and almost any of her poems would work well for parodies. She has a very distinct style. Edgar Allan Poe has language structures that are more complicated but they sound very satisfying to me and are fun to play with. William Blake and William Shakespeare are also writers that lend themselves well to adaptation. I also recommend Robert Frost as a great writer to imitate.

The poems in my books also serve as a springboard for students to create their own parodies. Some students have used my poems to make their own versions: i.e., "Because I could not stop my bike" became "Because I could not stop my sled". They can also take other poems they find or songs and create an adaptation of their own. In this way it also becomes easier to appreciate the original poet more – to feel a kinship even as they lean on given rhythms.

What opportunities do parody and humour afford a storyteller in telling a story (or a story within a poem) and have you any ideas for how these may be explored in the classroom?

Parody and humour are almost the same thing to me because when I think of a twist in my mind on some well-known poem, song or lyric, it almost always makes me smile. My brain enjoys the way that the original can be changed around into something new and still recognizable. I believe there are a lot of people who get the same kind of enjoyment because there are many parody songs about current events and issues online, and lots of children's books that do "take-offs" on traditional fairy tales or nursery rhymes. Making a parody can be a terrific way to reduce stress by the way – if I am in a troublesome situation and I can make a funny poem about it, my whole being relaxes and takes things less seriously.

When I make a parody, the rhyme and rhythm often come before the actual story. For instance, I did not start out thinking I would write a poem about macaroni and cheese, but as I paid attention to the rhythms of "Annabel Lee" I heard that they could be used as "macaroni and cheese" instead and then the story evolved as I followed the original poem's patterns. I like to read lots of poems out loud and see if one of them connects with me as possible to transform.

When it comes to poetry in the classroom first and most importantly, I believe that poems, and children's poetry in particular, should be read aloud. Do not just read these poems inside your head! Poetry is meant to be spoken and heard and when dramatized it is even more fun. I have loved visiting classrooms and having the students read different parts of the poems out loud and also acting them out. For instance, *Xanadu* works wonderfully as a dramatic rendition with groups of students playing the different animals. *Rotten, Lousy Flu* is also fun to act out. For ages 3 to 8, I have used puppets, hand gestures and movement to go with the poems. For example, *The Train Comes and the Train Goes* (making a toot toot sound) and *Bubbles, Bubbles* (pretending to blow bubbles) work well for the littlest ones. In fact, many young children can pretty easily learn a whole short poem by heart like *I Eat My Pickle*. This can build confidence in their language skills. I also ask the children about their own experiences with ketchup, dogs, siblings etc. to engage them with the content.

Students can use classical poems, well-known songs, and even my poems, to create their own parody versions. Making parodies will get them to pay close attention to the original source and how it sounds, and this attention could help develop their reading and writing skills.

What advice would you have for aspiring writers who want to experiment with poetry to tell their stories?

My advice to young writers would indeed be to experiment! Prose is generally more straightforward than poetry, and in poetry you can use your words in all kinds of innovative ways to tell those stories. You can put words upside down or going in a circle, you can rhyme if you like and you can also not rhyme. Find what feels true for you in your feelings and thoughts and experiences and try getting that down in words. Equally you can also make something up – a story that you create, a world that you envision. It's best to just put words down without judging or evaluating them. Try to get the words that feel right to you. There will be time later for editing and revisions. (Editing and revisions are an important part of writing, but it should come later, not as you write.)

If it feels too difficult to write a poem, start with a type that uses a structure – a haiku is a well-used example with its 5-7-5 syllable rhythm; or you could use the letters of your name or other word to make a poem about that person/thing; you can cut interesting words out of magazines. If you want to write a rhyming poem, play around with fun rhyming words. You can also listen to lots of songs and nursery rhymes and poems and perhaps draw some inspiration to create your own variations.

Read lots of different kinds of books and poems and then just play with words. Make up rhymes out loud for fun. Try not to judge yourself or criticize yourself. Write things that make you laugh if you find them humorous; chances are that others will, too. Or write things that feel true to you and your own experiences that express your feelings about something. If you want to get ideas, it can help to read lots of different other poems. It can also be useful to keep a notebook, hard copy or online, where you write for ten minutes anything that comes to mind without judgement. When I have done this regularly, I find it helps unstick the flow of words and move past "blocks". (This technique is adapted from "The Artist's Way", called *morning pages*, by Julia Cameron). Writing poetry is an excellent way to reflect and express yourself and can be enjoyed for its own sake without ever having to be in a published book. Make a habit of writing if you can, and of noticing interesting things around you. Get comfortable saying what feels true for you.

> *What for you are the essential ingredients of a good poem?*
>
> That's a hard question! For a rhyming poem, I do like good rhythms and rhymes that are not forced. The story should flow naturally and not take awkward twists just to make two words rhyme. (Dr Seuss was the master at this! He would switch around sentence structure rather than make a rhyme that wouldn't work in the story. And if he couldn't find a word that worked, he would often make one up! He was a King of Silliness.) And of course, many poems are not rhymed. For these, the way language is used is still very important and good rhythm is still important. I like a poem that feels like it has someone's true feelings, or authentic voice, or heart-felt experience in it, some kind of truth in being human or perhaps helps me to see the natural world in a new or beautiful way. A good poem can open your eyes to something new.
>
> *Can you name a well-known figure (from myth, fairy tale or wider literature) who you think would be a very interesting figure for our readers to develop a parody portrait poem of?*
>
> I think it would be fun to take any character from a fairy tale, myth, or classic work and put them in a new and silly situation. Similarly one could use famous figures like monarchs (King Henry VIII, Queen Elizabeth I), artists, scientists and inventors, presidents and so on. A parody poem can be an excellent way to let off some steam about something that is annoying you or to make a point to help society in some way. Currently I have been working on a project that is a re-telling for children of the prologue of the Canterbury Tales, updated as a silly parade of characters in a small town.

The connections KJ highlights between learning, reading and enjoyment fuse together the key concepts of reading widely for pleasure and personal purposes, reading and writing communities and critical literacy explored in this chapter. For KJ learning is everywhere and the best teachers are learners who have taken the time to critically reflect on reading and writing experiences shared with particular communities and audiences. Multiple perspectives are also important within this process as learners are encouraged to read first for pleasure and personal purpose (and read aloud) and later consider what can be learnt from such enjoyable and interactive engagements. KJ's suggestion that parody writing can also be used in the classroom to support learner well-being and personal struggles or issues learners may be experiencing offers powerful opportunities for teachers to engage learners in more complex and dark themes in reading and writing. Building confidence in learner language skills through a focus on reading and speaking aloud in dramatic and enjoyable parody focused pedagogies also allows teachers to connect with learners and the development of more personal and emotional literacies in the classroom.

In her advice to young writers KJ offers an inventive, personal and creative approach to writing poetry, suggesting we can turn words and worlds upside down in our writing, as well as reimagining grammar and sentence structure to suit the rhythm and rhyme of poetry. This reimagination of poetry and literature echoes Curwood's (2011) exploration of how students' and teachers' engagement with digital poetry, reimagining familiar poems in online and virtual contexts through technology and collaborative inquiry, can facilitate personal critical engagement, identity expression and multimodal composition.

Drawing on new literacies, and the work of Lankshear and Knobel in particular, Curwood highlights how the integration of media and technology in schools and classrooms often privileges and focuses on the digital tools themselves, rather than the new understandings of teaching, learning, participation and engagement, that occurs within and through literacy (Curwood, 2011). Referencing Lewis (2007) she concludes that:

> new technologies afford new practices, but it is the practices themselves, and the local and global contexts within which they are situated, that are central to new literacies. The logical implication… is that schools would accomplish more if, like new literacy users, they too focused on the practices rather than the tools.
> (Lewis, 2007, p. 230)

Her iPoetry project, involving exploring classic literary techniques such as mood, imagery or metaphor in nonlinear, multimodal and online spaces, understands digital poetry as a new literacy practice and empowers learners to take control of and experiment with their own learning and literacy in personally meaningful, supportive and collaborative ways and resulted in this study in the professional development of the teachers involved also. Opportunities and activities for engaging learners with iPoetry alongside other parody focused pedagogical approaches are outlined below.

WRITING WIDELY FOR PERSONAL PURPOSE: HUMOUR, PARODY AND (I)POETRY

- **From past to present – Storyboarding history:** Learners are asked to create a modern comic style storyboard reinterpretation of a poem, story or event from history. Learners should annotate their storyboard with notes explaining their creative decision making and key foci for parody and modernization. Learners should present their storyboards in groups, taking opportunities to compare and contrast features of style, parody, language and approach in both their original and modernized texts. Learners could in groups vote on their favourite texts and techniques (old and new) and host an awards ceremony to celebrate the diversity inherent in children's and young adult literature across time and space.

- **Comedy across the curriculum:** Doyne, Epstein Ojalvo and Schulten (2011) contributed an article to *The New York Times* focusing on comedy across the curriculum (https://learning.blogs.nytimes.com/2011/04/15/thats-funny-comedy-across-the-curriculum/). Classroom activities explored here begin with inviting students to focus on comedy as an acceptable and valuable genre for classroom reading and writing practices. Learners are encouraged to think about their own favourite comedians and their individual comedic styles and how learners might remix these elements in their own writing. Learners start small in their experimentation with humour and parody in the classroom. They could be asked to create or remix memes and short sketches they are familiar with from the internet and television. Later learners can reset these sketches in more local settings (home or school) and remix accordingly. Learners can research particular types of humour or parody (historical political cartons for example) and consider how techniques here can be adapted for other writing styles, genres or improvisation and speech making.

- **Our class goes viral – Viral videos, humour and parody:** Learners complete a unit of work with the central aim of creating one (or a small number) of viral videos in the classroom. Learners should begin by researching and collecting as many viral videos as they can. They should collectively analyse these videos – what makes them funny? Are they intentional or spontaneous? What multimodal elements are used in what ways – visuals, text, music, sound effects, speech? As a result of their research in groups, learners should create their own viral videos and upload these to school, local or global servers (e.g., YouTube). Views and comments should be tracked over a period of time and a viral winner video announced as the class's own viral video.

- **Musical parody:** Learners are asked to make a parody of their favourite song and share this with the class. Learners are encouraged as a part of this process to research the life and other work of the singer/band (as we might do with poets or authors in the classroom). This research should inform the creation of their musical parody. Learners could record these parodies as podcasts and share with the class to listen and respond to outside of the classroom.
- **Exploring authors, genre and style through (i)Poetry and parody:** Teachers could design an iPoetry unit similar to the work explored in Curwood (2011). Through responding to, reinterpreting and parodying poems using online technology and multimedia learners could develop their understanding of traditional poetry concepts such as simile, metaphor and image. The iPoetry produced could be shared on a school or class website and sent virtually to parents, relatives and friends, broadening the authentic audience for learner writing and engagement with literary ideas.

Conclusion

This chapter has explored pedagogical opportunities for using fan fiction, remix and parody to encourage reading and writing widely for pleasure and personal purpose in and beyond the traditional classroom setting. Understanding that literature is for life and not just for academic purposes this chapter and the previous one suggest the importance for teachers of encouraging learners to read widely and for personal purpose beyond curricular content and classroom contexts. The development of collaborative and complementary physical and virtual affinity spaces for literature appreciation, engagement and reflection plays a central role in related pedagogical approaches to literature and reading and writing for pleasure and personal purposes.

Fairy tale and poetry are identified as particularly well-suited genres for engaging with fan fiction, remix and parody in local or more global affinity groups and communities. The literature, research and children's authors discussed throughout this chapter highlight the transformative role of reading and writing widely for pleasure and personal purposes when it comes to learning and literacy in the classroom. Authentic connections, audiences and tasks in reading and writing for pleasure communities and pedagogies ensure, as Lewis suggests below, that every learner can find the magic in the tale and later the magic in the world as a result of engaging with stories in a meaningful and more critical way.

> The fairy tale land arouses a longing for he knows not what – it stirs and troubles (to his life-long enrichment) with the dim sense of something beyond his reach – and far from dulling the actual world – gives it a new dimension of depth. He does not despise real wood because he has read of enchanted woods: the reading makes all real woods a little enchanted.
>
> (Lewis, 1966, p. 58)

Bibliography

Children's and young adult literature explored in this chapter

Carroll, L. (1865). *Alice in Wonderland*. London: MacMillan.
Collins, S. (2012). *The Hunger Games Trilogy*. USA: Scholastic.
Holub, J. (2016). *Mighty Dads*. USA: Scholastic.
Holub, J. (2013). *Little Red Writing*. USA: Chronicle Books.
Holub, J. (2012). *Zero the Hero*. USA: Macmillan/Holt.
Holub, J. (2002–2004). *Doll Hospital Book Series*. OOP.
Holub, J. Williams, S. (2014–Present) *Grimmtastic Girls Book Series*. USA: Scholastic.
Holub, J. Williams, S. (2012–Present) *Heroes in Training Book Series*. USA: Simon and Schuster.
Holub, J. Williams, S. (2010–Present) *The Goddess Girls Book Series*. USA: Simon and Schuster.
Kilmer, Joyce. *Trees and Other Poems*. (New York: Doubleday Doran and Co., 1914), 18.
Shapiro, K J. (2007). *I Must Go Down to the Beach Again and Other Poems*. USA: Charlesbridge Publishing.
Shapiro, K J. (2005). *Because I Could Not Stop My Bike and Other Poems*. USA: Charlesbridge Publishing.
Spires, E. (1999). *The Mouse of Amherst*. USA: Farrar Straus Giroux.
Willard, N. (1981). *A Visit to William Blake's Inn: Poems for innocent and experienced travelers*. USA: Houghton Mifflin Harcourt.

Other possible texts for exploring literacy ideas and pedagogies highlighted in this chapter

Ahlberg, A. Ahlberg, J. (1999). *The Jolly Postman*. UK: Puffin.

This text series remix individual characters from traditional fairy tale as they live alongside each other in a new world, their stories connected and told by the postman's delivery of letters, cards, bills, presents, leaflets, annuals, newspapers, adverts.

DiRisio, C. (2017). *Brooding YA Hero: Becoming a main character (almost) as awesome as me.* USA: Sky Pony.

Born on a Twitter account, this self-help guide including activities parodies familiar tropes, themes and characters from young adult fiction.

Scieszka, J. (1992). *The Stinky Cheese Man and Other Fairly Stupid Tales.* USA: Viking Press.

This text and others by Scieszka parody traditional fairy tales, offering new perspectives on familiar stories and challenging readers to recognize a variety of multimodal storytelling techniques inserted to remodel and remix the original tales.

Chapter bibliography

Bean, T. Moni, K. (2003). Developing students' critical literacy: Exploring identity construction in young adult fiction. *Journal of Adolescent and Adult Literacy.* 46(8), 638–648.

Bettelheim, B. (1989*). The Uses of Enchantment: The meaning and importance of fairy tales.* New York: Vintage Books.

Black, R. (2008). *Adolescents and Online Fan Fiction.* New York: Peter Lang.

Chandler-Olcott, K. Mahar, D. (2003). Adolescents' anime inspired fan fictions: An exploration of multiliteracies. *Journal of Adolescent and Adult Literacy, 46*(7), 565.

Cremin, T. (2018). *Reading Communities and Books in Common.* National Association of Advisers of English. Available at www.naae.org.co.uk/reading-communities-and-books-in-common/ (accessed 24 June 2020).

Cremin, T. Mottram, M. Powell, S. Collins, R. Safford, K. (2014). *Building Communities of Engaged Readers: Reading for Pleasure.* London and New York: Routledge.

Cremin, T. Mottram, M. Powell, S. Collins, R. Safford, K. (2009). Teachers as readers: Building communities of readers. *Literacy, 43*(1), 11-19.

Curwood, J. (2013). Fan fiction, remix culture and The Potter Games. In Frankel, V. E. (Ed.), *Teaching with Harry Potter* (pp. 81–92). USA: McFarland.

Curwood, J. (2011). iPoetry: Creating space for new literacies in the English curriculum. *Journal of Adolescent and Adult Literacy*, 110–120. IRA.

Doyne, S. Epstein Ojalvo, H. Schulten, K. (2011). Comedy across the curriculum. *The New York Times. The Learning Network.* Retrieved 23 February 2021 at https://learning.blogs.nytimes.com/2011/04/15/thats-funny-comedy-across-the-curriculum/.

Eshet-Alkalai, Y. Amichai-Hamburger, Y. (2004). Experiments in digital literacy, *CyberPsychology & Behavior, 7*(4), 421–429.

Gee, J. P. (2012). Nurturing affinity spaces and game-based learning. In Constance S. Kurt, S. Sasha, B. (Eds.), *Games, Llearning*

and Society: Learning and meaning in the digital age (pp. 129–155). Cambridge: Cambridge University Press. https://doi.org/10.1017/cbo9781139031127.015.
Gottschall, J. (2012). *The Storytelling Animal: How Stories Make us Human.* New York: Houghton Mifflin Harcourt.
Janks, H. (2013). Critical literacy in teaching and research. *Education Inquiry, 4*(4), 225–242.
Jenkins, H. (1992). *Textual Poachers: Television fans and participatory culture.* New York: Routledge.
Jerrim, J. Moss, G. (2018). The link between fiction and teenagers' reading skills: International evidence from the OECD PISA study. *British Educational Research Journal, 45*(1), 161–181.
Kucirkova, N. Cremin, T. (2020) *Children Reading for Pleasure in the Digital Age: Mapping reader engagement.* London: Sage.
Lammers, J. (2012). Is the hangout… the hangout? Exploring tensions in an online gaming related fan site writing. In Hayes, E. Duncan, S. (Eds). (2012) *Learning in Video Game Affinity Spaces: New literacies and digital epistemologies.* New York: Peter Lang.
Lankshear, C. Knobel, M. (2007). Sampling 'the new' in new literacies. In Lankshear C. Knobel M. (Eds.), *A New Literacies Sampler* (pp. 1–24). New York: Peter Lang.
Lankshear, C. Knobel, M. (2006). *New Literacies: Everyday practices and classroom learning.* New York: Open University Press.
Lewis, C. (2007). New literacies. In Lankshear C. Knobel M. (Eds.), *New Literacies Sampler* (pp. 229–239). New York: Peter Lang.
Lewis, C. S. (1966). *On Stories: And other essays on literature.* Walter Hooper.
Magnifico, A. (2012). The game of Neopian writing. In Hayes, E. Duncan, S. (Eds). (2012) *Learning in Video Game Affinity Spaces: New literacies and digital epistemologes.* New York: Peter Lang.
McWilliams, J. Hickey, T. Hines, M. (2011). Using collaborative writing tools for literary analysis: Twitter, fan fiction and *The Crucible* in the secondary English classroom. *The National Association for Media Literacy Education's Journal of Media Literacy Education, 2*(3), 238–245.
Meyers, E. M. Erickson, I. Small, R. V. (2013). Digital literacy and informal learning environments: An introduction. *Learning, Media and Technology, 38*(4), 355–367.
Milovanović, A. Maksimović, J. (2020). Digital literacy: An important component of future teachers' education. In Kopas-Vukašinović, E. Stojadinović, A. (Eds.) *The Strategic Directions of the Development and Improvement of Higher Education Quality: Challenges and dilemmas. Proceedings of the International Conference Vranje – Jagodina, November 2020.* Serbia: University of Niš, Faculty of Education. University of Kragujevac, Faculty of Education.
Short, K. (2011). Reading literature in elementary classrooms. In Wolf, S. Coats, K. Enciso, P. Jenkins, C. (Eds.), *Handbook of Research on Children's and Young Adult Literature* (pp. 48–63). London: Routledge.

Su-Jeong Wee, Kyoung Jin Kim, Youngmi Lee (2019) Cinderella did not speak up: Critical literacy approach using folk/fairy tales and their parodies in an early childhood classroom, *Early Child Development and Care, 189*(11), 1874–1888, DOI: 10.1080/03004430.2017.1417856.

Teverson, A. (2013). *Fairytale – The new critical idiom.* UK: Routledge.

Thomas, A. (2007). *Youth Online: Identity and literacy in the digital age.* New York: Peter Lang.

Zipes, J. (1996). *Creative Storytelling: Building community, changing lives.* UK: Routledge.

PART

Reading and writing deeply to transform understanding

CHAPTER

5

Reading and writing through the lenses of critical literacy, social justice and historical perspective: Cultural, social and historical contexts for literacy and identity

About this chapter

This chapter begins the final part of this text with an exploration of how teachers and learners can engage with reading and writing deeply to transform understanding through a focus on critical literacy, social justice and historical perspective in the classroom. The concepts of social justice and critical literacy are defined and connected to develop a critical literacy for social justice approach to children's and young adult literature that focuses on identity, positionality and perspective. Historical literacy is also considered as a lens for interrogating history and contemporary experience, moving the focus further from knowing that to interpreting how and why, and opening up past and present as spaces for drama, dialogue and debate about social justice issues. Related pedagogies for engaging learners are developed throughout this chapter in the context of history and interrogating relationships between people, place, time and life experience. The narrative nonfiction and historical fiction children's and young adult literature discussed asks learners to consider their own lives alongside the lives of others and reflect on what can be learned about and from parallel lives and identities existing in different places and times.

About the authors

Marita Conlon-McKenna

Marita is an Irish author passionate about Irish history and storytelling. Her historical fiction novels are relatable and accessible for young readers and teenagers. She has won many awards for her work, which has been televised and translated into over 20 languages, including an International Reading Association award in the United States, The Osterreichischer Kinder und Jungendbuchpreis in Austria, the Frankfurt Book Fair Children's Choice Book Prize and a Reading Association of Ireland Award.

Marita's *Children of the Famine Trilogy* is set in Ireland at the time of the Great Irish Famine and tells the story of the O'Driscoll family. *Under the Hawthorn Tree,* the first book in the series was inspired by the discovery of a famine grave with the skeletons of three children buried under a hawthorn tree and became an instant bestseller when it was published in 1990. It tells the story of three young children, Eily, Michael and Peggy, and their journey across the barren landscape of 1840s Ireland in search of their aunt, hope and a new life together. *Wildflower Girl* follows a now 13-year-old Peggy across the Atlantic to America. *Fields of Home* returns to Ireland and the lives of Eily and Michael now struggling with responsibilities and families of their own. *Love Lucie,* set in contemporary Ireland and told entirely in letters, centres on the experiences of Lucie, a young teenager who has just lost her mother. For more information see https://maritaconlonmckenna.com.

Deborah Heiligman

Deborah is an American author whose work ranges from picture books to young adult novels. Deborah writes both fiction and nonfiction and has won numerous awards including the SCBWI Golden Kite Award, the YALSA Excellence in Nonfiction Award, the Boston Globe-Horn Book Award for nonfiction, the SCBWI Golden Kite Award for nonfiction, the Cook Prize, the Anne Izard Storytelling Award, a New York Times Notable Book and Editor's Choice Honors and an ALA Printz Honor.

In her stories Deborah draws on people as lenses for exploring familiar and more strange aspects of history as she transforms ordinary lives into celebratory works of art. *Torpedoed* chronicles the true story of the 1940 voyage of the *SS City of Benares* and its young passengers from England to Canada, a journey that ended with the sinking of the children's ship. Drawing on extensive research and primary sources to tell the tragic stories of so many of its passengers, this narrative nonfiction text offers a rich tapestry for engaging and learning about the past.

Vincent and Theo: The Van Gogh Brothers narrates the true story of the relationship between brothers Vincent and Theo and is based on almost 700 real letters exchanged between the pair. *Charles and Emma: The Darwins' Leap of Faith* explores the relationship between Charles and Emma and the impacts this had on his scientific work. Finally, *The Boy Who Loved Math: The Improbable Life of Paul Erdos* tells the true story of Paul Erdos, a young boy who loves numbers and sees them everywhere he goes. Deborah's website (www.deborahheiligman.com) is itself a rich treasure trove of history and story, and includes links to many of the primary sources she has interrogated to craft her works as well as photographs and discussion of her own research process. This incredible resource allows learners the opportunity to not only engage with history and these primary resources, but to consider also how they might respond to and write drawing on these historical documents and experiences.

Michelle Markel

Michelle Markel is an American author whose work includes both fiction and nonfiction. She has won numerous awards including the Bank Street Flora Stieglitz Straus Award, the Jane Addams Children's Book Award for Younger Children and an NCTE Orbis Pictus Honor.

Michelle's biographical work tells the story of a number of well- and lesser well-known historical figures. *The Fantastic Jungles of Henri Rousseau* shares the inspiring story of Henri, a toll collector turned self-taught artist, alongside important messages and life lessons about success, failure, determination and self-belief. *Dreamer from the Village: The Story of Marc Chagall* narrates the biography of Marc Chagall, focusing on the power of the imagination to create something new out of current experiences. *Brave Girl: Clara and the Shirtwaist Makers* engages young readers in the themes of immigration, social justice and women in history as we discover Clara Lemlich's story. Finally, *Balderdash!: John Newbery and the Boisterous Birth of Children's Books* tells the history of children's literature itself and the life of one of its founders John Newbury. For more information see www.michellemarkel.com.

Introduction

In the final part of this text the focus moves to Short's third and final purpose for children's and young adult literature in the context of literacy, reading and writing deeply to transform understanding (Short, 2011). Reading and writing deeply encourages learners to "think about and transform understanding about oneself and the world [and] involves reading to inquire into issues in children's lives and in the broader society" (Short, 2011, p. 60). It asks learners to themselves construct questions and theories about their personal understandings of the world and their own experiences in ways that open these up to collaborative dialogue in classroom practice. Reading and writing deeply to transform understanding asserts that reading and writing curriculum, content and texts should not be prescribed for learners but constructed with them "as they engage in wondering and seeking insights into their own literacy processes and literary experiences" (Short, 2011, p. 60). This chapter explores what this "wondering and seeking" might look like in classroom pedagogies and learning that focus on critical literacy, social justice and historical perspective. As a starting point for this investigation of reading and writing deeply to transform understanding it is necessary to first define and connect the related concepts of critical literacy, social justice and history.

Rizvi (1998) warns that:

> the immediate difficulty one confronts when examining the idea of social justice is the fact that it does not have a single essential

meaning – it is embedded within discourses that are historically constituted and that are sites of conflicting and divergent political endeavours.

(Rizvi, 1998, p. 47)

Moffett (1994; 1988) was one of the first educators to explicitly connect critical literacy to social justice perspectives on learning. More recently critical literacy for social justice has become an important theme in pedagogy and praxis, and for the understanding and development of identity affirming and culturally relevant pedagogies in particular (Zacher et al., 2014).

Comber (2015) exemplifies how different theories of social justice themselves underpin critical literacy and suggests a series of pedagogical moves required by teachers to engage with deeper thinking and critical literacy for social justice in the classroom. These pedagogical moves are central to the development of the critical literacy for social justice pedagogies required for reading and writing deeply explored in this chapter and include a repositioning of learners as researchers of language, a respect for student resistance, a focus on exploring minority culture constructions of literacy and an openness to problematizing classroom and public texts.

Comber further connects these pedagogical moves to the key social justice principle of engaging with the interests of the least advantaged (Connell, 1993), suggesting that teachers engaging with critical literacy for social justice should ask the following questions to themselves interrogate and reflect more deeply on their curricula, pedagogy and practice. What might constitute "curricular justice"? Whose interests are represented? What constitutes knowledge? What is open to question and negotiation? What kinds of social justice might be needed to underpin our critical literacy curriculum designs? What kinds of dilemmas are faced daily in schools serving our most disadvantaged communities?

Thinking deeply about their own practices, teachers here play a central role in leading and modelling engagement, reflection and learning in critical literacy for social justice pedagogies. In fact these pedagogies necessitate that teachers should know themselves, be culturally responsive and open to change, continually reflect on their multicultural understandings and philosophies of learning and connect personal and classroom learning to out of school worlds and experiences (Grant and Gillette, 2006). Central here also is an interrogation of the myriad and complex relationships between people, place, social class, work, wealth, poverty and education. In the field of education, critical literacy for social justice is also a lens through which teachers can read, reflect on and understand their own classroom experiences alongside curriculum, policy and education documents and reform (Cahill, 2020; 2019).

At the intersection of critical literacy and social justice teachers become "agents of history, who work towards making the world less discriminatory, more democratic, and less dehumanizing and more just" (Chomsky, 2000, p.12). History is itself a central aspect of critical literacy pedagogies for social justice as to know and understand our daily experiences, societies and worlds, and to read and write our own lives deeply to transform understanding, we need to first reflect on and explore how things came to be as they are before we can imagine how they might be changed in the future. As Comber (2015) explains without the rich context of history:

> scripted pedagogies quickly become barren landscapes for teaching and learning when stripped of significant content and concepts. Instead in such contexts, it is imperative that literacy lessons are occasions for complex and critical meaning-making, for students to assemble sophisticated analytical repertoires which they can apply to social phenomena such as poverty, youth unemployment, or workers' rights
>
> (Comber, 2015, p. 361)

Real world interventions as literacy practice: Connecting critical literacy, social justice and identity

Critical literacy understands learning to read and write deeply to transform understanding as part of the process of becoming conscious of one's experience as historically constructed within specific power relations (Anderson and Irvine, 1982). As Comber (2015) questions:

> what do the injustices associated with poverty have to do with critical literacy? Education, literacy in particular, is often purported to offer the possibility of social justice. For some "working-class" and immigrant baby boomers, completing high school and going on to higher education was indeed the ticket out of the

kinds of poverty experienced by our parents and grandparents. Nevertheless... the game has changed. Hence contemporary work in critical literacy needs to overtly question the politics of poverty: how and where is poverty produced, by what means, by whom and for whom and how are educational systems stratified to provide different kinds of education to the rich and the poor.

(Comber, 2015, p. 359)

Freire (2001) further situates this understanding of critical literacy in the relationship of learners to the world, explaining that "literacy makes sense only in these terms, as the consequence of men's beginning to reflect about their capacity for reflection, about the world, about their position in the world, about the encounter of consciousness" (Freire, 2001, p. 106). In this sense to acquire literacy:

is more than to psychologically and mechanically dominate reading and writing techniques. It is to dominate these techniques in terms of consciousness; to understand what one reads and to write what one understands; it is to communicate graphically. Acquiring literacy does not involve memorizing sentences, words, or syllables – lifeless objects unconnected to an existential universe – but rather an attitude of creation and re-creation, a self-transformation producing a stance of intervention in one's context.

(Freire, 2001, p. 86)

Here Freire lays the foundation for later emphases on identity and agency in literacy and learning (Lewis et al., 2007) in his assertion that to be critically literate involves a change or intervention in one's context or world.

Engaging learners with critical literacy in the classroom exposes the relationships between language, power, texts and worlds in ways that support learners in subsequent personal constructions and reconstructions of text. Lewison et al. (2015) highlight four dimensions of critical literacy for classroom practice as disrupting the commonplace, considering multiple viewpoints, focusing on the socio-political and taking action. Applying these dimensions to deeper explorations of multiple and often counter narratives in text supports learners in their understanding and reading of the world itself as a socially constructed text and reminds learners that there is often multiple rather than single meanings or interpretations in text and experience. An understanding of critical literacy asks learners to pay careful attention to implicit messages and real-life implications inherent in the texts they read and write, and encourages learners of all ages, abilities and experiences to reflect on and question issues beyond the text such as social justice and equity, power, race, gender alongside inherent textual and real world ideologies and practices (Janks, 2010; 2013).

Considering critical literacy in this way as a support for social justice education necessitates an understanding of what this complex concept could look like in the classroom. Bell (1997) defines social justice as:

> both a process and a goal. The goal of social justice is full and equal participation of all groups in a society that is mutually shaped to meet their needs. Social justice includes a vision of society in which the distribution of resources is equitable and all members are physically and psychologically secure... The process for attaining the goal of social justice, we believe, should also be democratic and participatory, inclusive and affirming of human agency and capacities for working collaboratively to create change.
>
> (Bell, 1997, p. 4)

Hackman (2005) further conceptualises Bell's goal of social justice to encompass student empowerment and the equitable distribution of resources and social responsibility, and process to centre on democracy, a student-centred focus, dialogue, an analysis of power and systems of power, and a prolonged emphasis on social change and student agency within and beyond the classroom and school. Her work highlights five key components, conceptualised as "tools" by Hackman, for classroom engagement with critical literacy for social justice, and these further inform the development of social justice pedagogies suggested in this chapter. These are tools for content mastery, tools for critical thinking, tools for action and social change, tools for personal reflection and tools for awareness of multicultural group dynamics.

Content mastery is the first component of effective social justice education as without factual information, historical contextualisation, a macro to micro content analysis and access to a variety of complex sources of information Hackman argues learners cannot engage in positive and proactive social change. She explains that facts explored within social justice pedagogies should represent broad and deep information and detail beyond those generally presented in mainstream media, texts and classrooms to support learners in engaging with social responsibility. Moreover, a focus on facts and historical information affords learners opportunities to reflect on the political, social and economic influences on social and cultural dynamics and human experiences. A careful understanding of historical context is an essential analytic lens for this type of social justice reflection in the classroom. As learners reflect they begin with information connected to their own lives and later and as a result develop deeper understandings of how classroom content and experiences connects with larger societal issues.

Hackman's second component of social justice education focuses on critical thinking and the analysis of oppression. Information alone is not enough to facilitate and enable societal responsibility and change and needs to be combined with a focus on critical thinking to develop effective social justice pedagogies. This component works closely with Hackman's third component's emphasis on action and social change to ensure learners are hopeful that society and experiences can change. Her fourth component of social justice education prioritises personal reflection of learners and teachers engaging in social justice pedagogies and imagining other possibilities for how the world might be. This leads to the final component of social justice education, an awareness of multicultural group dynamics, and for the teacher in particular, an understanding of the group dynamics and identities present in the classroom.

Connecting critical literacy for social justice pedagogies explicitly with identity Boylan and Woolsey (2015) understand social justice as having relational, distributive (Cochran-Smith, 2009; North, 2008) and participative (Fraser, 2008) aspects, across micro and macro ethical dimensions, and as a form of action rather than a state to be achieved (Griffiths, 2009). Examining relationships between identity and engaging with issues of social justice in the context of teacher education and preparation, their research suggests the importance of understanding the classroom itself as a site where more socially just relationships, practices and identities can be enacted. Mapping identity spaces for teacher engagement with and relationships to social justice, they suggest that pedagogical approaches focusing on deep inquiry into personal positionality and the roots of injustice, discomfort (ranging from feelings of discomfort to more emotionally challenging and provocative explorations of injustice), compassion, respect and philosophy best facilitate identity driven explorations of social justice in the classroom.

These pedagogies are informed by an understanding of learning as intimately connected to learner identities practiced in figured worlds (Holland et al., 1998; Hall, 2008). According to Holland et al. (1998), and as explored in more detail earlier in this text:

> the self is a position from which meaning is made, a position that is addressed by and answers others and the world (the physical and cultural environment). In answering (which is the stuff of existence), the self authors the world – including itself and others.
> (Holland et al., 1998, p. 173)

From this perspective participation in activities can be understood as purposeful improvisation in the service of developing an identity and authoring a self. As teachers and learners improvise and author their worlds and experiences in the classroom, figured worlds take shape around particular related practices as these worlds simultaneously recruit individuals to their practices and are reconstructed through each individual's participation.

Going deeper into history through narrative nonfiction: Learning as identity, critical literacy and social justice in the stories of Deborah Heiligman and Michelle Markel

Interrogating relationships between learning, identity and participation as suggested here aligns closely with critical literacy and social justice perspectives of learning and frames how deeper classroom engagement with these themes, reading and writing may be planned for. Understanding learning as identity makes visible issues of power and agency in our daily practice in and outside of the classroom and focuses attention on relationships between activity, agent and world (Rogoff, 2012) in learning in any given context. This emphasis on the importance of relationships and making connections in learning is a central theme of the narrative nonfiction work of Deborah Heiligman, our first children's and young adult literature author in this chapter.

FIVE MINUTES WITH DEBORAH HEILIGMAN

In your writing you work closely with primary resources. You have said that the reason for this is because you like meeting your characters on their own. Could you tell us a little more about what you mean here and your writing process for narrative nonfiction?

An editor of mine has called me a method writer and I think that's true. I use primary sources – letters, journals, diaries and for more recent people videos and interviews etc. also – to try and get inside my subject's head and heart. The longer I spend and the deeper I go, the more that happens for me as a writer. This is helpful in so many ways – not only for the story, the motivation, the detail, but also as a way to figure out what you can accept as truth and what you can't. For example, I got to know Charles Darwin so well that I felt certain that whatever he wrote in a letter or journal I could accept as truth. I did of course double check things to make sure!

Conversely, I got to know Vincent Van Gogh well enough that I could accept some things as true (what paint colours he used, what he thought about that painting or the work of other artists). I could trust him to paint a physical scene with words – he was such a great writer! But I couldn't always believe everything he said because he might have an ulterior motive. For example when he wrote to Theo about a break-up with his lover Sien and said that she was fine about it, I knew not to take that as the absolute truth. I knew that he was painting that scene in a way that put him in a decent light. He was less of a reliable narrator of his own life and certainly of other people's emotions. That said, I also knew that he had a huge heart, and over time I felt I was as good a judge as possible without going back in time as to what I could believe and what I couldn't. And that was huge. That is the kind of thing you can't do if you rely on other people's assessment of the subject's life or work.

In your writing, how the story is told seems just as important as the details and content as the tale emerges through letters, galleries, quotes, dual biographies and other documents and images... Could you talk to us a little more about this idea? Why is the form of text so important for you?

I think I find the form of my writing the same way that I find the subject's character and storyline. As I read about Charles and Emma Darwin and got to know them through their letters, I knew that what I was writing was a love story. And so I wanted it to read as a love story. Since it was during Victorian times I also wanted it to read like a Victorian novel (though all true of course). And while I was working on it I read Dickens, thought about him and Jane Austen, and tried to imbue into my narrative nonfiction the elements that those novelists used to tell their stories. I wanted the reader to come away with the same experience of reading Dickens or Austen (not that I am in any way comparing myself to them). I wanted to paint the relationship, the society, the times and the themes that were important then stylistically through the novel writing form.

With Vincent and Theo I realised a few years into the project that I wanted to reader to have a similar experience reading my book as though they were looking at a piece of Van Gogh's art. Then I thought the whole book should be like a museum show, imagining the reader walking through it like an exhibit. Because Van Gogh's style of painting and drawing varied I had the freedom to write in different styles from traditional to impressionistic, from detailed paintings to sketches of experience.

With *Torpedoed* I considered for a short time telling it as fiction, but since there was so much rich primary source material I knew it should be nonfiction. As I wrote I still wanted it to have the same suspense or pull that a novel would. I wanted it to feel like a war/adventure/personal story. I read a lot of these kinds of books and watched a lot of these kinds of movies while doing my research and as I wrote. So much so that as I worked I thought of this book as a movie for much of the time. I also tried to write scenes cinematically, picturing what the story would look like on screen, and using a lot of the techniques that a film maker would, for example, zooming in and out, including close ups and panoramas to focus on a character and then create suspense by leaving him/her out of focus for a bit. I hadn't ever written anything like that before so I read, watched and listened to models to learn how it might be done.

My stories are about connection – the connection between people and how that connection makes a huge difference in their lives. Charles Darwin wrote *The Origin of the Species* with such care and consideration because of Emma. The world wouldn't have Vincent without Theo. I spent much of the first few years of my time writing their story asking myself why did Theo put up with and support Vincent? I found Vincent so exasperating – why did Theo stick with him? The book slowly became my answer to that question. *Torpedoed* too is all about connection, community and altruism. Each book teaches me how to write that book, but I think you can probably see the same author fingerprints in each one.

Biography and history are central aspects of your storytelling. Why are these areas so important for you?

I love learning about people up close and find it fascinating to learn about people from different times. My lens into history is through people and I think biographies are a great way to learn about time periods and different values. As a teenager I read about real people because they helped me figure out who I was and I think it's the same with young people today. Who do you identify with and why? What would you have done if you were Emma or Theo or Mary Cornish? Putting yourself in other people's shoes is a great way to figure out your own values, personality and goals. I think every life is a work of art, truly. The people I choose to write about have to speak to me on a profound level, on a gut level and then on further examination on an intellectual level. And I think I have to have a strong connection to them to be able to see their life. It's the same for the reader. You connect and then you learn. You look at the world and people differently. Because you have connected. When I'm teaching writing I explore how even if you do a lot of research your job as a writer is to tell a story. So you should not use too many details that get in the way of the story – but use the details that help propel the story along.

I firmly believe when writing nonfiction that you can't make anything up. But other than that I believe in using the techniques of fiction – plot, character, setting, detail. If you want to be a writer the best thing you can do right now is read, read, read! Read especially what you love and think about why you love it. Once in a while read what you don't love or even like and think about why. Learn how to read critically but mostly read to enjoy and take note of why you enjoy it! Read texts in different forms – poetry, nonfiction, fiction – regardless of what it is you want to write. And let me just say this – one book I have not talked about yet is *The Boy Who Loved Math*. I learned so much not only about myself as the mother of a person a lot like Erdos but about my son. It opened me up to him in ways that I had not been before. So I think writing about people who are very different from you is a great way to learn about them and yourself.

Your work creates emotional portraits of experience and the human condition. What three questions would you ask aspiring authors to respond to in the development of their own emotional self-portrait?

What is your theme/motto as a person? As a writer? What makes you so angry that you want to hit a wall? What makes you smile even when you are sad?

In her interview Deborah exemplifies many key aspects of a critical literacy for social justice pedagogy. Her extensive research and use of primary sources to really get to know the people she writes about highlight how closely and actively Deborah engages with the past in the crafting of her stories. Her histories are truthful and based on fact but are also written from a position occupied by Deborah in the present. This is evident in the decisions Deborah makes about her form, writing her stories to resemble art exhibitions or films for example. Her defining of herself as a method writer emphasises the strong connections between identity, history and learning, and offers innovative opportunities for engaging with writing deeply to transform understanding in the classroom. What are the similarities and differences between imagining a character and creating a narrative characterisation of a real figure from history? What skills, literacies and activities are central to each task? How are learners, learning, writing and history positioned in each task? Aligning with Comber's (2015) suggested pedagogical move towards positioning learners as researchers of language and practice through engaging more deeply with primary sources and historical perspectives, these kinds of questions and tasks invite learners to engage with and think about the past and present in new ways.

Similarly, Deborah's explanation of how she develops her stories, working to write scenes cinematically, for example, offers further creative possibilities to teachers and learners around creating text as well as enabling critical questioning of fact, interpretation and media. Built into critical literacy for social justice pedagogies could be any of the following questions: What are the affordances and constraints of the different media in which we tell our stories? How can media impact the story, characters/figure, reader understanding and ultimately reader identity? What are the relationships between fact, interpretation, storytelling and history? How is how I see the world impacted by my position in it? How is my position in the world impacted by how I see and understand myself and others? How might a consideration of these questions develop my understandings of my own identity and positioning in the world as well as the identity and positioning of others?

Deborah's assertion of the value of using lesser known biographies and people different to ourselves as a lens into history to find out who we identify with and why speaks strongly to critical literacy for social justice pedagogies. Foregrounding deep and meaningful connection between readers, writers, characters and worlds as powerful impetus for personal and social change Deborah further exemplifies in her interview and work some of the complex relationships between learning about the world, others and ourselves. This social justice theme of critical understanding for change is also central to the work of our second children's literature author in this chapter, Michelle Markel.

FIVE MINUTES WITH MICHELLE MARKEL

Could you tell us a little about your understanding of reading?

Reading expands and enriches the tiny world young people are familiar with. It's a deeply personal experience. The books I read in my youth had a profound, lasting impact on me. My first book love was Ludwig Bemelman's *Madeline*. I didn't realize how deeply that book affected me until many years later, when I was studying abroad, as a French major. Ludwig Bemelmans is in great part responsible for my love of France, poetry and art.

I hope my books offer instruction with delight (Newbery's motto). My goal is to not only introduce young people to the subjects of my biographies, but also to give them a deeper understanding of what it means to be human, to have desires, setbacks, struggles, and joys, to have the potential for growth/transformation, no matter what culture they're born into. I hope that reading my books is an emotional, aesthetic experience for them. That's a kind of magic.

Could you tell us a little about how you plan and develop your stories? What do aspiring young authors have to consider in particular when they write narrative nonfiction stories?

After finishing my research I consider the narrative through line – the driving force of the book. For example, Rousseau's desire to be a recognized artist propels the action in *The Fantastic Jungles of Henri Rousseau*. Once I know what my subject desires, I work on the dramatic structure of the story: conflict, crisis, resolution. As themes emerge during the writing, I modify my original plan as needed. I may suppress some scenes and replace them with new ones. I may start the story later in time. I recommend that young authors ask themselves these questions about their subject: When and why did this person choose to pursue her goals? What/who influenced her? What kind of challenges did she face? How was she able to overcome obstacles? Young writers need to focus on what the subject wants and what he/she goes through in order to get it. That's the emotional heart of the story. In my books – as in all human activity – passion fuels action. Most beginning writers get lost in the forest of details.

Your stories take ordinary lives and turn them into extraordinary life lessons and celebrations of creativity, innovation and invention. How do you turn a life into a work of art?

My subjects must draw me emotionally (their work and their life stories), they must appeal to children in some way, and in most cases they need to be lesser known or celebrated figures. Allow me to use Henri Rousseau as an example. When preparing an art lesson for children I came across his *Sleeping Gypsy* and wondered, who created this mysterious, surreal, gently humorous painting? After doing some initial research, I chose to write his biography. I could empathize with Rousseau because as a writer, I've suffered multiple rejections, like he did. I believed that children would connect with Rousseau because of his charming jungle paintings, and because they can understand what it feels like to be criticized for an expressive act, how much that hurts. I knew that Rousseau was typically not included in the canon of artists (Picasso et al.) chosen for the elementary school art curriculum.

How do I bring my stories to life? Unlike encyclopaedias, which relate a string of facts, literary nonfiction includes the subject's *reactions* to events. Biographies should include moments of inspiration and responses to obstacles. That's how you humanize your subjects. One way to vividly accomplish this is through the use of setting. We each perceive our environment in different ways, depending on our sensibility and interests, our point of view. In my biography of Rousseau, I write "When Henri walks through the glass doorway, it's as though he enters into a dream. It's like he is someone else completely". If John Newbery had chosen to visit such a place, he probably would have had a different reaction. So setting provides sensory imagery, bringing the story to life, while helping with characterization.

Your work pushes the boundaries of the picture book genre in its focus on deep and powerful themes for living, identity and learning, disappointment, failure and perseverance all play a role in eventual successful endeavours. What lessons do you think your picture books have and how could they be used with older children and teenagers in the classroom?

The themes you mentioned are relevant to young people, regardless of their age. Stories about staying true to oneself, about not making

> compromises, can resonate with older children and teenagers. They're at an age when they're pressured to conform. I've heard from teachers who've used my books in high schools and even in college classrooms. Young adults are beginning to think about their careers. My biographies can provide lessons about challenging the norms of gender and class and ethnicity that can get in the way of their pursuits. Upper class women such as Leonora Carrington were not supposed to pursue careers in the arts, and neither were poor Jewish men like Chagall. Henri Rousseau lacked the resources for a basic art education. All three of these artists risked disapproval from the artistic establishment. I'd also say that because the language in all my books is fairly sophisticated, it can engage older readers, and give them models for self-expression. The literary text can be studied for sensory language, voice, setting, characterization etc.
>
> Additionally, we all have natural gifts. We need to use our individual strengths to make a change in the world. To explore this theme, teachers could do character studies of my subjects. Why did they succeed in making a change? What were their talents, assets and weaknesses? Did they do what their parents, or society, expected them to do? John Newbery refused to be a farmer; he loved books at a young age, and because of his creativity as a businessman, came up with innovative publishing ideas. Children could ask themselves about their own talents, and their concerns about the world, and how they might put them to use.
>
> Finally, literature lets us enter the consciousness of another human being. We vicariously experience what it's like to be heroic, inspired, etc. It's like a little virtual rehearsal for what we might encounter in the real world. That's empowering. One might compare the inspirations of the three artists. Leonora was inspired by fairy tales, Chagall by his memories, and Rousseau by beasts. Children might consider what subject matter engages them, that might allow them to express their emotions, either in art, in writing or some other way.

Michelle's definition of her stories as serving dual purposes of introducing her readers to history while also offering deeper understandings of what it means to be human and always have the potential for change aligns clearly with a critical literacy for social justice pedagogical approach. Her assertion that her subjects need to connect with her on an emotional level and be lesser known figures from history suggest social justice pedagogical opportunities for engaging with a plurality of personal, local, national and international stories and figures. Donelson and Nilsen (1997) suggest that when exploring histories in the classroom rather than asking all learners to read the same text, teachers should source and bring in individual copies of lots of different kinds of texts related to the particular time period or social justice issue under study and allow learners to choose for themselves the texts they want to read. This also allows for a later deeper dialoguing with history in classroom practice as different learners will have explored different but related texts, stories and perspectives.

Michelle's texts also provide rich material for engaging with Hackman's five components of social justice education previously described and her emphasis on exploring what it means to be human in her stories alongside facts and historical detail connects critical literacy and social justice approaches with an exploration of identity in the classroom. Michelle's raw and emotional portrait of artist Henri Rousseau, a toll collector who wants to be an artist despite constant and consistent negative and harsh critiques, offers stark lessons about success, failure, inspiration, rejection and determination to be seen and heard by the world. Henri knows that because of his poverty he will never travel to a real jungle but this does not matter to him because he sees one emerging from the canvas before him. John Newbury similarly has a vision for a different life for himself and a different understanding of what children's literature could be and offer children and his individual actions change the world around him and others in exciting and previously unthinkable ways. Imagining the world a little differently and being able to see possibilities for change on personal and social levels is a central tenet of critical literacy for social justice pedagogies and learning to read and write deeply and Michelle's texts offer real life examples of how individual action can make change in the world.

As we identify historical figures and explore their stories to overcome getting lost in the forest of data, as Michelle warns, learners as researchers of the past should identify and follow the through line of their narrative, the force that drives the work, and these through lines can question, respond to and address social justice issues such as gender, ethnicity and class. Michelle reminds us that we all have individual strengths for making change in the world and suggests that engaging in character or people studies could help learners better understand their own potential in this regard. The following suggests ideas for engaging learners in character study and other pedagogies focusing on reading and writing deeply to transform understanding.

> **INTERROGATING PAST AND PRESENT EXPERIENCE THROUGH NARRATIVE NONFICTION, CRITICAL LITERACY AND SOCIAL JUSTICE: CONNECTING REAL PEOPLE, PLACES AND WORLDS**
>
> - **Exploring narrative nonfiction – Viewing the present from the past:** As an introduction to the text, give each learner a different short extract from *Vincent and Theo: The Van Gogh Brothers* (the text itself is comprised of short sections). Ask learners to read their unique extracts and identify any information they can about the text (who, what, where, when, how). Learners in groups should then share their ideas and perspectives (as each will have read a different part of the story) to develop a picture of what the story is about, paying particular attention to in text cues and clues. Learners should also consider here their understanding of how the story is told. Individual groups should later present their predictions to the class. Learners should then have the opportunity to engage with the text of Vincent and Theo in full. Having read the text, learners should be directed to Deborah's website (https://deborahheiligman.com/) where they will find extensive detail on Deborah's research and writing process, as well as links to many of the primary sources used by Deborah herself. Based on exploring these resources, learners should be asked to pick a moment in the story and retell it in their own way and style, using Deborah's website, resources and primary sources as support. These retellings should then be shared with the class alongside learner reflections on what they have learned (about themselves and the world) as a result of engaging in researching and writing narrative nonfiction.
> - **Our classroom exhibition – Museums, galleries and ekphrastic poetry:** Engaging with historical and critical literacy affords teachers opportunities to engage with nontraditional spaces for learning such as museums, galleries and landmarks. Deborah's website includes fantastic resources (and teaching guides) for her texts. Activities suggested here for *Torpedoed: The True Story of the World War II Sinking of "The Children's Ship"* for example include creating maps, drama and poetry; writing a narrative from the perspective of one of the people aboard the ship; designing a memorial for the lives lost in the sinking of the ship; and exploring the website of and later writing to the Imperial War Museum. Learners could also be asked to explore particular sections of

museum or gallery websites and complete a series of tasks. They could identify a number of works of art or artefacts that interest them and try and map out the story behind them. They could use a collection of related art pieces (such as paintings) to inspire their own pieces of historical non-fiction and fiction. Learners could also be asked to write ekphrastic poetry (poetry that explores a work of art) and stage a class exhibition of these poems alongside the works that inspired them or art created by the learners themselves. Ekphrastic poetry asks learners to find a piece of art that speaks to them in some way; research and record official descriptions of the work; describe the work by free writing about everything you can see; brainstorm a list of questions about the work; make a list of personal connections to the work; and finally write a poem about the work by rereading what has been written, circling words and ideas that stand out and reassembling the words and phrases you have highlighted in different lines as a first draft of the poem.

- **Presenting the past through exploring experience and justice project:** Use probing questions (and/or provocative statements) that focus on learners' own lives and experiences to open up a discussion about social justice. Questions should focus on learner feelings and in particular their own social justice related experiences, actions and reactions. Ask learners to consider how other people (in and beyond the classroom) may have different experiences, actions and reactions of the social justice issues identified. Show learners an image of the dedication in *Brave Girl: Clara and the Shirtwaist Makers* (2016), which reads "For workers everywhere", and ask learners to think about how this dedication might connect to the class discussion on social justice. Without telling learners the story distribute different images and text excerpts for learners to explore in groups. Ask learners to use these snapshots of experience as writing prompts to reflect on social justice issues represented in any medium that they would like (prose, poetry, collage). After sharing these as a class ask learners to read and reflect on Clara's story in full. Using the selected bibliography of general and primary resources at the end of the text learners should research the themes explored in the story. The final "Table of wages" page could be used as a further writing and reflection prompt, asking learners to connect what they have researched to this visual and present day related social justice issues. Finally, learners should be encouraged to take action in some way in relation to present social justice issues identified throughout this project (Examples of these actions include writing a letter to a relevant authority, making an action plan for

how I can change my own actions, design a poster for the classroom or neighbourhood).
- **Mantle of the Expert learning communities:** Mantle of the Expert is a pedagogical approach developed by Dorothy Heathcote and involves the creation of a fictional world in the classroom where learners assume the roles of experts in a designated field. Teachers and learners become co-creators of learning and supports creativity, collaboration, communication, critical thinking and decision making. The teacher introduces a task or problem and learners roleplay and improvise as a team of experts exploring the issue, engaging in research and collaboration and producing real outputs such as letters or posters. Central here is the real context engaging with fictional worlds provides classroom practice and encouraging and supporting learners to move from inside (improvisation and role play) to outside (researching, discussing, debating and creating) these fictional worlds. Ideas underpinning this approach are reminiscent of Wenger's (1998) theorisation of communities of practice where a community engaged in a joint enterprise through mutual engagement use and co-construct shared repertoires or resources to support learning and identity development. https://www.mantleoftheexpert.com/ is an excellent resource for teachers beginning to experiment with this pedagogical approach. In her blog teacher Jenny Burrell (https://theseacompany.blogspot.com/) shares her experience with Mantle of the Expert pedagogy in a series of episodes. To start learners receive a letter from a local museum asking for help from the classroom "salvage company" to examine some objects salvaged from a shipwreck in the North Atlantic Ocean that they believe may belong to the *Titanic*. Learners have to first provide the museum with a company portfolio including training certificates, job descriptions, photographs… This example involves a visit to and collaboration with a real museum but if this is not possible teachers could resource suitable resources and alternative activities. Learners later participate in salvaging, examining, researching and restoring key artefacts and the project culminates in the organising of a Great Titanic Exhibition.
- **Engaging with popular culture through true crime podcasts and texts:** Tapping into the growing popularity of true crime podcasts and the true crime genre in young adult literature teachers could identify an age appropriate crime in history (or from more contemporary times) and develop a research and writing project around this crime for their classroom.

From knowing to interpreting the past as an extended present through historical fiction: Historical literacy and social justice in the work of Marita Conlon McKenna

Adams (2001) conceptualises historical fiction as a literacy rich, meaningful and authentic space for exploring history and developing historical literacy and critical social justice perspectives on the past. Crawford and Zygouris-Coe (2008) similarly understand the importance of:

> the use of historical fiction within the curricular context promotes a stronger engagement between the reader and the text than does use of the traditional social studies textbook. In turn, student engagement with the text promotes comprehension. Thus, instead of wading through lists of dates and isolated historical events, readers of historical fiction find themselves "walking in the shoes" of a particular character and seeing the historical world through this unique perspective. This type of viewpoint can make a tremendous difference not only in readers' understanding of historical events, but also in their understanding of the social consequences of these events.
> (Crawford and Zygouris-Coe, 2008, p. 197)

Taylor (2003) defines historical literacy as comprising of knowing and understanding events of the past; understanding narratives of the past and in particular the shape of change and continuity over time across and within multiple narratives and ambiguity; research skills; fluency in the language of history and the past; understanding historical concepts such as causation and motivation; ICT familiarity for ICT-based historical resources; making connections between the past, the self and the world today; understanding contention and contestability within historical debate; understanding how the past can be represented creatively through film, drama, music, the arts; addressing moral and ethical issues inherent in explorations of stories from the past; and being able to use historical reasoning to explain the past (Taylor, 2003). Adopting historical literacy-based approaches as a lens to interrogate past and present through historical fiction moves our focus from "fact" to interpretation, providing rich opportunities for framing literacy for social justice pedagogies and reading and writing deeply in the classroom.

Rodwell (2013) provides a wonderful resource for teachers considering engaging with historical fiction alongside historical literacy in the classroom. Drawing on Lindquist (2002) Rodwell emphasises the power of historical fiction to engage learners deeply with historical literacy, suggesting that this genre fuels learner curiosity, shares the language and everyday details of places and times inaccessible elsewhere, offers multiple perspectives on the past and supports learners in reflecting on the complexities of the past and the present. He argues that this is because historical fiction unfolds the events of the past in layers, and puts these layers in dialogue with one another in a way that encourages readers to ask why as they see and feel the world through the eyes of other people.

Bird (2009) highlights further this agentive aspect of engaging deeply with the past through historical fiction, suggesting that its readers are "in a position of privilege, [who] to a degree becomes a player in the history" (Bird, 2009, p. 20). This engagement is not necessarily straight forward and as Campbell (2008) warns us if the past is another country, historical novels are forged passports. For Campbell (2008) historical fiction tells us more about the present than the past, serving as "lectures" exploring how the present sees the past. This problematisation of knowing the past (and present), or versions of it, is central to critical literacy for social justice pedagogy. Grappling with the many issues inherent in interpreting past and present experience Campbell asks (as should we):

> How can we know the past?... After all, psychology 101 suggests that even simple events are reported inaccurately. Aren't there as many realities as witnesses? If present matters of fact are opaque, how can we possibly re-create the culture of a Manchester police station of 1973, or 19th-century naval life, let alone the world of Claudius or Spartacus?
>
> (Campbell, 2008, p. 1)

Returning to Hackman's component of content mastery, and in particular a need to explore broad and deep historical information and detail beyond those generally presented in mainstream media, texts and classrooms to support learners in engaging with social responsibility, historical fiction as a genre often serves to voice the stories of those who have been silenced or adversely affected by events in the past. This focus across a continuous and often conflicting narrative encourages learners to question issues of power, influence, privilege and voice in the past and in their own lives.

Levstik and Barton (2001) suggest that historical fiction as a genre particularises and personalises history in a way that helps learners make connections between past and present social, moral and ethical issues, concerns and dilemmas. They argue that historical fiction provides an entry point to engaging learners deeply with a wide range of other types of texts (primary sources, text books, poetry, video) in a way that helps teachers and learners co-construct semantic webs in classroom practice. They further explain how engaging with historical fiction supports learners develop more mature and social justice informed historical understandings because it encourages learners to reflect on human aspects of history and gives us a sense of history as an ongoing participatory drama (Levstik and Barton, 2001, p. 120).

Bateman and Harris (2008) also encourage teachers to explore history with learners more deeply as an extended present rather than a chronological series of events. The language used in historical fiction along with character and personal stories foci support learners in developing metacognition, abstract thinking and connecting more deeply and critically events, people and places in history to their own lives and experiences.

This way learners can begin to see their own place and agency in history and how their individual actions and positions shape their worlds in a variety of ways. The openness of narrative within historical fiction also allows space for interpretation, exploration and discussion of history in ways engaging with historical facts cannot and further enhances critical literacy for social justice pedagogies in the classroom. This understanding of the power of narrative fiction is central to the work of Marita Conlon-McKenna and is further exemplified in the words of Norton (1999) who explains that:

> through historical fiction, children can begin to visualize the sweep of history. As characters in historical fiction from many different time periods face and overcome their problems, children may discover universal truths, identify feelings and behaviours that encourage them to consider alternative ways to handle their own problems, empathize with viewpoints that are different from their own, and realize that history consists of many people who have learned to work together.
>
> (Norton, 1999, p. 523)

FIVE MINUTES WITH MARITA CONLON-MCKENNA

As a writer you have talked about the importance of keeping your own voice and identity central to your work. Could you tell us a little more about what you mean here and your writing process? How can young people develop their own voices and identities in their writing?

I am so lucky, as I learned to read very easily and it has enriched my life in every way. Reading not only helps us to learn and gain knowledge but opens our imagination to new worlds and people as we read stories and imagine ourselves within them. When I write I imagine myself in the story. This is central to my way of writing, and my hope is that through my words that somehow this same magic will pass on to my reader, no matter what age they are. It is very rewarding as so many of my readers write or tell me that they felt they were in the story. I started writing a long time ago, and I can hand on heart say that my voice has stayed the same. Perhaps it is because I started writing for my own children and wanted to be clear and simple and uncluttered in what I was writing and trying to say.

Children are a tough readership…probably the toughest a writer can have and if they don't like the story or the way you are telling it, they just simply close the book or throw it down. They are utterly honest and will not suffer bad writing or a boring story no matter what adults say. I have learned so much since those early days of writing and if you pick up *Under the Hawthorn Tree* or *Love Lucie* and put them beside any of my adult books, the voice is the same. I do not want to copy or follow the style or voice or way of writing of another writer so I usually try to avoid reading fiction or prose when I am working on the latter half of a book as I want no intrusion on the work. From writing originally for children I have learned to avoid flourishes and showing off or too much description or flowery language as my young critics would not tolerate them.

Younger writers are often so keen to write that they copy their favourite writer or their favourite book. Style, story and voice almost replicated. While it is a huge compliment to a book or writer, it is much better that they develop their own voice, their own story and a way of telling it. Writing about something unique to them makes it so much easier. For younger children handing them a prop of an animal, an object, a name on a card, or a picture, often frees them to imagine and write without any links to a book or story they read. It is so encouraging to see the different stories and voices that emerge.

I write because I want to write, but it is very important to think of your audience when you are writing for children. It is a privilege to have a child pick up your book, open it and read it and become absorbed in the world that you have created. You cannot take young readers for granted and must battle to hold their attention, fulfil their curiosity and touch their hearts with your story. Writing for children is not for the faint hearted as young expectations are high. Change and hope are two of the main elements of my writing, no matter what the age range.

Every book is a journey which makes writing exciting as it brings me to so many places. Change is everything – be it physical, emotional, or spiritual. My heroes have to move and change and grow and journey through the books so they emerge different. For without some kind of change there is no book, no story to tell. I usually find that readers each in their own way interpret and experience the character's journey and how it reflects on their own lives.

My work is often touched with some sadness, darkness and injustice for that is what helps to drive the story and its characters forward. It is difficult to read, enjoy or remember a book that does not contain some mixture of light and dark, hope and fear, good and bad. From the earliest classic fairy tales and legends to the great children's classics all contain that essential balance of shadow and sunshine. It is a part of storytelling and writing and only obvious when it is missing. It is so important to have stories that contain shadows and that inspire questions and curiosity and an interest in discovering more. Children often tell me they want to write a story but begin to tell me a story that runs along on flat lines and has little colour, shape or pace. With only a little direction and a few questions, their brains and imagination will kick in as a new more vibrant story emerges.

Irish history and giving people a voice in history are central aspects of your storytelling. Why are these areas so important for you? How do you think a focus on history in the classroom could support learning and identity development for children and teenagers?

History has always played a huge a part in my life as I am passionate about discovering more about the past. History has inspired so much of my work especially our own Irish history. I read as much historical fiction as I could when I was young and was very conscious of the lack of books about our own history. I told one of my teachers that when I grew up that I was going to write a book about the Great Irish Famine. I have never consciously set out to write so much about history but was hooked by people's stories of the past and curious to discover more about the times they lived in. I have always been drawn to stories about those that have been overlooked or almost written out of history, and find myself wanting to give them a voice.

I have learned so much from the past and the heroism of those who lived before us and encountered hardships and difficult circumstances that most of us would struggle to overcome. Yet these are our ancestors, our families, our forebears and we share so much with them, strength and courage, endurance and resilience. Pride in our past with all its complexities is important. In my writing I always hope that most of my readers experience the same empathy with my characters that I feel and relate to the challenges they face.

History has become far more exciting and accessible since I was in school with new technologies enabling teachers and students to find and discover and research even more about the past, be it on a local or global scale. It always amazes me how teachers use my books as a way for students to not only gain a better understanding of history but to inhabit it, from designing book covers and letters, to animated videos, games, puppets, and even building famine villages, famine ships and World War 11 air-raid shelters.

Your work very closely portrays people and their thoughts, feelings and experiences. How do you develop your characters in your stories? Have you any ideas for how teachers might adapt this approach in the classroom for reading and writing engagement and development?

Character is everything in my work and I initially see the main character or characters, before the story ever begins to emerge and develop. My characters are real and rounded with talents and flaws, multifaceted with a very definite opinion of the time or place or position I am putting them in. These are the heroes who will carry my book and on whom I depend, for building and creating my story. Without my characters I have nothing. When I am writing, my characters are very real to me and are flesh and blood made up of emotions, conflicts and complexities that will path their way through the book. I do believe that good characters make good books. And great characters...great books!

For teachers, getting students to understand more about the characters they are reading or writing about is paramount. What do the characters love, hate, miss, want? What makes them happy, sad, proud, nervous or scared? I find often when children are writing a story they will use the name of a friend or other boy or girl in their class.

This will automatically limit their storytelling and imagination. It is much better to say we will not use any friend or family names when we are writing. Often having a small bag or box with lots of different and varied names they can choose from is helpful if they get stuck for a name. You can also give them an idea that the story is about someone brave, sad, lonely, afraid, shy, funny. Or better still let them pick out a card or two with attributes on them. This hopefully helps to avoid them just planting a boy or girl in the story with no character development.

And remember that every book is a mixture of two vital ingredients a strong realistic character and a good story. Having just one element is not enough, you need the two. Your character or main characters will carry the story so they have to be very real and capable of standing up and filling the story you are writing. Their personality and inner self will shape how they go through the book and deal with the journey you are sending them on. Who goes in your story is a really important decision. So think about it! Are they brave or afraid, quiet or loud, clever or a bit silly, strong or weak, funny or serious? There are lots of things to think about and decide. If you have two or three characters try to make them each a little different.

The story itself needs to be set in a place or time or around an event… Be it the famine or the arrival of new baby or even moving house! Where ever or whenever you chose, remember it must not be flat and boring. The story must climb and go up and down and sometimes even zig zag a bit…with quiet bits and some exciting bits and periods, maybe sad bits or happy bits, funny bits or serious. It's up to you as you are the writer and can do what you want.

For example, *Love Lucie* was inspired by hearing about a French girl who wrote a whole load of letters to her mother after she died and posted them, only to have them returned months later by the French post office stamped with not known at this address and by the death of my best friend. It was a very difficult book to write as it started on the day of Lucie's mum's funeral and is about loss, loneliness, grief and survival. I played around with various ways to write it but kept coming back to the letters. I have always been a letter writer and kept a diary so wanted that kind of structure and I broke it down into seasons. However I think a whole book written through letters can be hard. It ties you as a writer so it is not something to take on unless you need to.

What three questions would you ask young authors to answer in a creative letter writing exercise to themselves?

> Three very important questions if you want to write a story:
>
> 1. Who is in my story?
> 2. Where are they and why?
> 3. What happens to them?

Marita's description of her writing process as something almost magical, as she imagines herself into the story, offers yet another way into history and writing that differs from researching real people and figures from the past. This experience in some ways allows Marita herself to inhabit history through the figures in her work while simultaneously learning about her own voice, identity and story and ways of telling it. Asking learners to imagine themselves as characters central to their writing connects with fan fiction and remix-based pedagogies (explored in detail in part two of this text) and also affords opportunities for making deep and meaningful learner identity connections between our selves, people and places in history and the social justice issues they have faced.

Tripp (2011) powerfully and similarly connects social justice, history and identity in her assertion that:

> what we're trying to do through historical fiction is to help our students realise they are what history is. What they do matters... What we're trying to do if to sort of trickle a moral intelligence, a mindfulness, a sense of responsibility, into being.
>
> (Tripp, 2011)

To achieve this aim she suggests that teachers should explore with learners the following questions as they read historical fiction. What's my voice? What's my view? Which side should I be on? Is there a right side? These questions would be very helpful in deeper classroom and personal explorations and reflections on Marita's *Children of the Famine Trilogy*.

Marita emphasises that change and hope are central elements of her work and without change there is, in fact, no story to tell. This is a very powerful assertion that connects deeply with critical literacy for social justice pedagogies. Marita explains that her stories bring her to so many different places and through the journey her characters, and Marita herself changes in a variety of ways. Her description of beginning pieces of writing as flat lines with little colour, shape or pace is imaginative and insightful and offers teachers and learners different ways of thinking about and planning their own writing. Later Marita develops this almost visual description of her writing process to include ups and downs, zigs and zags and a focus on different emotions at different high and low points in the story. This framework could be used by learners to visually plot the development of their own stories, with a particular emphasis at each point on the responses, reactions and emotions of the characters as they engage with each other and the world in ways that asks them to change their understandings.

Marita connects closely with critical literacy for social justice pedagogies in her discussion of her work as focusing often on giving a voice to those overlooked or written out of history. Reading historical fiction beings into focus the people who have actively shaped the histories and facts we know, reminding learners of their own agency and opportunities for activism as they engage with the making of history every day. Engaging with Marita's texts in the classroom allows for a range of exciting critical and historical literacy focused pedagogies for social justice. The following shares some ideas for developing these kinds of pedagogies for reading and writing deeply using historical fiction in the classroom.

PARTICIPATING IN HISTORY THROUGH READING AND WRITING – DEMYSTIFYING AND DRAMATISING HISTORICAL FICTION AND LITERACY

- **Inhabiting history through people study and forum theatre – History as ongoing participatory drama:** Bringing the past to life in the classroom in ways that connect with learners' experiences and identities and allows learners to inhabit past worlds, and experiences can be achieved well through the use of drama focused pedagogies. Exploring a particular time period (a 20-year time span surrounding the Great Irish Famine, for example) learners should be asked to choose a figure alive within this time span that interests them and complete a person study by researching their life. Beginning with a sharing of this person study, the class is then divided into groups with each group working to write and stage a drama involving all of the historical figures researched by the group. Supporting drama focused pedagogies as learners engage in this project include hot seating (learners engaging in question and answer sessions in character), making maps or plans of the setting of their plays, linked freeze framing (similar to hot seating but all learners freeze in motion at a particular moment in their drama and can be questioned as their characters as to what they are thinking and feeling), and writing and performing smaller conversations between two characters. Learners will then perform their plays through forum theatre. Forum theatre is a particular way of engaging with drama whereby a play or scene, usually involving some kind of oppression or social justice issue, is performed twice. In the second performance any member of the audience can shout "stop" themselves come forward and take the place of one of the characters, showing how they could change the situation in ways that might allow for a different outcome. A number of different alternatives may be explored by different audience members with the original actors improvising in character as changes to the performance are made.

- **Investigating the past – Writing history mysteries case files:** History mysteries challenge learners to approach history as detectives and think carefully about what precisely it is that historians do. History mystery activities supporting themes in classroom texts can range from asking learners to research history to find out particular details about people or events, to asking students to investigate a "history box", a box containing a variety of items collected by the teacher and related to the topic or time period to be studied, to staging a scene from history with clues and asking students to discover aspects of the past within the scene, to engaging learners in philosophical discussions in the classroom. In the context of Marita's *Children of the Famine Trilogy* learners could, for example, imagine/create/engage with the suitcase/bag packed by the young children setting out on their journey. Learners could also be asked to research and share with the class a history mystery they themselves have identified and are interested in. Learners should complete a creative writing project case file on their history mystery incorporating the following elements: background information on the selected history mystery, a plausible theory to explain it, a number of pieces of evidence from primary sources that support this theory and a short reflection on each, an alternative theory that could explain the history mystery and the reasons why this theory has not been adopted, and finally what has been learned about the mystery and myself as a result of engaging with this history mystery. Fisher, Wilkinson and Leat (2000) presents a series of historical mysteries supported by an underlying narrative and is a good starting point for engaging with history mystery pedagogies in the classroom. Using this text as a model and resource, teachers could identify and

> prepare a range of history mysteries within Marita's *Children of the Famine Trilogy* and beyond.
> - **Exploring social justice and identity through counterfactual, alternative and time slip histories:** Counterfactual histories ask and answer "what if" questions in relation to the past and serve as antidotes to determinism and feelings that there is no free will or individual agency in the sweep of history. Alternative histories re-imagine and rewrite the past while time slip histories incorporate characters travelling between times and trying to understand their experiences in a new place and time. Each of these ways of telling stories about our past brings their own affordances and constraints to reading, writing and debating history. Learners could be asked, for example, to travel back in time and write themselves, their families and friends into Marita's story of Eily, Michael and Peggy. They could also imagine an alternative or counterfactual history for the young children of Marita's story. As learners engage in these kinds of writing projects an emphasis on social justice and identity, education can be foregrounded through attention to Tripp's (2011) questions: What's my voice? What's my view? Which side should I be on? Is there a right side?

Conclusion

This chapter explores opportunities within critical and historical literacies for engaging with social justice issues through narrative nonfiction and historical fiction texts. Linking past and present experiences in ways that tell us something about ourselves and the world is a central theme throughout for reading and writing deeply to transform understanding. Narrative nonfiction and historical fiction texts are presented as complementary lenses through which our gaze comes to see past and present experience a little differently. Literature discussed in this chapter suggests that relationships between perspective, position and agency impact these personal interpretations of past and present, and result in the unique development of our own identities and critical lenses later used to make sense of and bring meaning to our lives and experiences alongside and as well as the lives and experiences of others. As Sunderland and Gibbons (2009) explain:

> historical fiction and history reflect a symbiotic rather than a parasitic relationship. Each gives to the other, from their respective strengths. Even so the common elements between literature and

history, especially through the use of narrative, the recreation of an historical era and the attempts to establish a link between the past and the present remain... Inevitably there are differences between the work of historians and writers of historical fiction, but these differences may be thought of...in terms of family resemblances. Bearing this analogy in mind historical fiction should never be thought of as the poor relation. Historical fiction can take its place at the family table in equal company with History.

(Sunderland and Gibbons, 2009, p. 27)

Bibliography

Children's and young adult literature explored in this chapter

Conlon-McKenna, M. (2013). *Under the Hawthorn Tree*. Ireland: The O'Brien Press.
Conlon-McKenna, M. (2013). *Wildflower Girl*. Ireland: The O'Brien Press.
Conlon-McKenna, M. (2013). *Fields of Home*. Ireland: The O'Brien Press.
Conlon-McKenna, M. (2012). *Love Lucie*. UK: Simon and Schuster.
Heiligman, D. (2019). *Torpedoed: The true story of the World War II sinking of "The Children's Ship"*. USA: Henry Holt & Company Inc.
Heiligman, D. (2019). *Vincent and Theo: The Van Gogh brothers*. USA: Square Fish.
Heiligman, D. (2013). *The Boy Who Loved Math: The improbable life of Paul Erdos*. USA: Macmillan.
Heiligman, D. (2011). *Charles and Emma: The Darwins' leap of faith*. USA: Macmillan.
Markel, M. (2019). *The Fantastic Jungles of Henri Rousseau (Incredible Lives for Young Readers)*. USA: Spck.
Markel, M. (2017). *Balderdash!: John Newbery and the boisterous birth of children's books*. USA: Chronicle Books LLC.
Markel, M. (2013). *Brave Girl: Clara and the shirtwaist makers*. USA: HarperCollins.
Markel, M. (2005). *Dreamer from the Village: The story of Marc Chagall*. USA: Henry Holt & Company.

Other possible texts for exploring literacy ideas and pedagogies highlighted in this chapter

Anderson, L. H. (2011). *Fever 1793*. USA: Atheneum Books for Young Readers.

This book tells the story of the 1793 yellow fever plague in Philadelphia through the eyes of fourteen-year-old Mattie Cook.

Anderson, M. T. (2017). *Symphony for the City of the Dead: Shostakovich and the Siege of Leningrad*. USA: Candlewick Press.

This text narrates the story of Russian composer Dimitri Shostakovich and his Seventh Symphony, composed during the 444 day Siege of Leningrad by Hitler in World War II.

Foreman, M. (2014). *War Game: The legendary story of the First World War football match*. USA: Pavilion Children's Books.

This book follows the story of a group of boys from playing football in the Suffolk countryside to a Christmas day in no man's land in the trenches of World War II.

Hunt, G. (2013). *1913 – Larkin's Labour War*. Ireland: The O'Brien Press.

Gerry Hunt has written a selection of historical fiction graphic novels focusing specifically on Irish history and its impacts on our present. This text focuses on a lockout without pay of workers insisting on better conditions in Dublin in 1913.

Miller, S. E. (2016). *The Borden Murders*. New York: Schwartz and Wade Books.

This true crime text examines the Borden murders and includes newspaper articles, period photos, images from the murder scene and recreations of trial events in a theorization of what may have happened in 1892.

Riordan, R. (2018). *Brooklyn House: Magician's manual*. UK: Penguin.

This book is a magician's training manual full of stories, inside information and quizzes on Ancient Egypt. Innovative and engaging in its approach, this text is an example of the style of literature that works particularly well with Mantle of the Expert pedagogies.

Chapter bibliography

Adams, H. (2001) 'Bringing History into the Classroom', *Classroom, 21*, 7, pp. 10–14.

Anderson, G., & Irvine, P. (1993). Informing critical literacy with ethnography. In Lankshear C. McLaren P. (Eds.) *Critical Literacy: Politics, praxis, and the postmodern*. Albany, NY: SUNY Press.

Bateman, D. Harris C. (2008) Time Perspectives: Examining the past, present and futures. In Marsh C. (Ed.), *Studies of Society and Environment: Exploring the teaching possibilities* (5th edn). Sydney, Pearson Education.

Bell, L. A. (1997). Theoretical foundations for social justice education. In ¹Adams, M. Bell, L. Griffin, P. (Eds.), *Teaching for Diversity and Social Justice: A sourcebook* (pp. 3–15). Routledge.

Bird, C. (2009). Past Master, *The Australian Literary Review*, 3 June.

Boylan, M. Woolsey, I. (2015). Teacher education for social justice: Mapping identity spaces. *Teaching and Teacher Education, 46*, 62–71.

Cahill, K. (2020) School markets and educational inequality in the Republic of Ireland. In *Oxford Research Encyclopedia of Education*. New York: Oxford University Press.

Cahill, K. (2019) Socio-sartorial inscriptions of social class in a study of school and identity in Ireland. *Discourse: Studies in the Cultural Politics of Education*, 40(3), 294–305.

Campbell, F. (2008). History as Fiction, Forum, *The Australian*, 1 March, http://www.theaustralian.com.au/news/history-as-fiction/story-e6frg8kf1111115651259.

Chomsky, N. (2000). *Chomsky on Miseducation*. New York: Rowman & Littlefield Publishers Inc.

Cochran-Smith, M. (2009). Toward a theory of teacher education for social justice. In Hargreaves, A. Lieberman, A. Fullan M. & Hopkins D. (Eds.), *Second International Handbook of Educational Change, Springer International Handbooks of Education*, Volume 23, Part 2, (pp. 445–467). Springer.

Comber, B. (2015). Critical literacy and social justice. *Journal of Adolescent & Adult Literacy*, 58(5).

Connell, R. W. (1993). *Schools and Social Justice*. Toronto, Canada: Our Schools/Our Selves Education Foundation.

Donelson, K. L. Nilsen A. P. (1997) *Literature in Today's Young Adults* (5th edn), New York, Addison Wesley/Longman.

Fisher, P. Wilkinson, I. Leat, D. (2000). *Think Through History*. USA: Chris Kington Publishing.

Fraser, N. (2008). *Scales of Justice: Reimagining political space in a globalizing world*. Cambridge: Polity Press.

Freire, P. (2001). *The Paulo Freire Reader* (Freire A. Macedo, D. Eds.). New York: Continuum.

Grant, C. A. Gillette, M. (2006). A candid talk to teacher educators about effectively preparing teachers who can teach everyone's children. *Journal of Teacher Education*, 57(3), 292–299.

Griffiths, M. (2009). Action research for/as/mindful of social justice. In Somekh B. Noffke S. (Eds.), *Handbook of Educational Action Research*, (pp. 85–93). London: Sage.

Hackman, H. (2005). Five essential components for social justice education. *Equity & Excellence in Education*, 38, 103–109.

Hall, K; (2008). Leaving middle childhood and moving into teenhood: small stories revealing identity and agency in: *Pedagogy and Practice: Culture and Identities*. London: Sage.

Holland, D. Lachicotte, W. Skinner, D. Cain. C. (1998). *Identity and Agency in Cultural Worlds*. Cambridge, MA: Harvard University Press.

Levstik, L. S. Barton, K. C. (2011). *Doing History: Investigating with children in elementary and middle schools* (4th edn). New York, Routledge.

Lewis, C. Enciso, P. Moje, E. B. (2007). *Reframing Sociocultural Research on Literacy: Identity, agency, and power*. Mahwah, NJ: Lawrence Erlbaum Associates.

Lewison, M. Leland, C. Harste, J. C. (2015). *Creating Critical Classrooms: Reading and writing with an edge*. London: Routledge.

Lindquist, T. (2002) Why and How I Teach with Historical Fiction, The Reading Teacher, http://teacher.scholastic.com/lessonrepro/lesson-plans/instructor/social1.htm (retrieved 4 March 2010).

Janks, H. (2010). *Literacy and Power*. New York, NY: Routledge.

Moffett, J. (1994). *The Universal Schoolhouse*. San Francisco, CA: Jossey-Bass Publishers.

Moffett, J. (1988). *Storm in the Mountains: A case study of censorship, conflict, and consciousness*. Carbondale, IL: Southern Illinois University Press.

North, C. (2008). What's all this talk about "social justice"? Mapping the terrain of education's latest catch phrase. *Teachers College Record 110*(6), 1182–1206.

Norton, D. (1999). *Through the Eyes of a Child: An introduction to children's literature* (5th edn). New Jersey, Prentice-Hall.

Pandya, J. Avila, J. (Ed.). (2014). *Moving Critical Literacies Forward: A new look at praxis across contexts*. New York, NY and London, England: Routledge.

Piketty, T. (2014). *Capital in the Twenty-First Century*. (Trans. Goldhammer A.). Cambridge, MA: The Belknap Press of Harvard University Press.

Rizvi, F. (1998). Some thoughts on contemporary theories of social justice. In Atweh, B. Kemmis, S. Weeks P. (Eds.) *Action Research in Practice: Partnerships for social justice in education* (pp. 47–56). London, UK: Routledge.

Rodwell, G. (2013). *Whose History? Engaging history students through historical fiction*. Adelaide: University of Adelaide Press.

Rogoff, B. (2012). Observing sociocultural activity on three planes: Participatory appropriation, guided participation, and apprenticeship. In Wertsch, J. (2012). *Sociocultural Studies of Mind*. UK: Cambridge University Press.

Short, K. (2011). Reading literature in elementary classrooms. In Wolf, S. Coats, K. Enciso, P. Jenkins, C. (Eds.), *Handbook of Research on Children's and Young Adult Literature* (pp. 48–63). London: Routledge

Sutherland, E. Gibbons T. (2009) Historical fiction and history: Members of the same family, *Text, 13*(2), http://www.textjournal.com.au/oct09/sutherland_gibbons.htm.

Taylor, T. (2003). *Historical Literacy. Making History: A guide for the teaching and learning of history in Australian schools*. Australia: Curriculum Corporation.

Tripp, V. (2011). *The Vitamins in the Chocolate Cake: Why use historical fiction in the classroom*, TeachingHistory.org (retrieved 31 March 2021).

Wenger, E. (1998). *Communities of Practice: Learning, meaning and identity*. UK: Cambridge University Press.

CHAPTER 6

Culturally sustaining reading and writing practice: Engaging with funds of knowledge and popular culture literacies to negotiate curriculum design with learners

About this chapter

Building on the key ideas of the previous chapter for supporting reading and writing deeply to transform understanding, this chapter outlines a funds of knowledge-based approach (Moll et al., 1992) to developing culturally sustaining pedagogies and learner-centred curriculum design approaches in the classroom. Culturally sustaining pedagogies encourage teachers to focus closely on the shifting and multiple ways that learners engage deeply with culture in a way that explicitly supports aspects of language, literacies and culture itself.

A number of key characteristics for designing culturally sustaining pedagogies are explored, namely firstly that culturally sustaining pedagogies develop through a focus on funds of knowledge, where teacher and learner roles are interchangeable and each learner as the source of their own funds of knowledge should be understood themselves as resources and assets for learning and curriculum planning. These funds of knowledge are understood in practice as flexible, adaptive, active and involving multiple persons and relationships. Reciprocity is central to developing and extending teacher and learner funds of knowledge, identities and learning in the classroom. Finally drawing on popular culture (as well as broader and more geographical understandings of culture) is central to the development of culturally sustaining pedagogies.

Negotiated Integrated Curriculum (NIC) is subsequently introduced as an approach for engaging learners in collaborative and learner led curriculum design based on these key characteristics and understandings of culturally sustaining pedagogy. Examples of what this might look in practice are shared throughout from the interviews of contributing children's and young adult literature authors and more broadly from research.

About the authors

Judi Curtin

Judi Curtin was born in London and her family relocated to Ireland when she was eight years old. A former primary school teacher she now is a novelist and children's and young adult literature author and has written a number of book series for children. Her work has been shortlisted for numerous awards and has won the Irish Book Senior Award.

Judi's stories focus on family, friendship and growing up. Her *Alice and Megan* series follows Alice and Megan's adventures and steadfast friendship as they negotiate separation, secondary school, summer holidays, camp and more. *The Eva Series* sees Eva and her friend Kate exploring old and new times, spaces and places and learning more about themselves and each other as a result. Her *Friends Forever Series* transports young Lauren to World War II London, Ancient Greece and even onboard the *Titanic*, as she forges new and old friendships along the way. Judi's most recent series, the *Lissadell* books, follows Lily, a young teenage housemaid at Lissadell House in the early part of the 20th century.

Roddy Doyle

Roddy Doyle is an Irish novelist, children's literature author, dramatist and screen writer. A former English and Geography teacher, Roddy has cofounded with Sean Love the creative writing centre Fighting Words. His work for adults and children has won numerous awards including the Irish Children's Book of the Year award, the Booker Prize and a BAFTA. He has also been shortlisted for the CILIP Carnegie Medal.

Roddy's stories for children and young adults celebrate the intimate and familial, the local and the everyday. *Brilliant* sees two young siblings try to save their uncle and their town from the Black Dog of depression. *A Greyhound of a Girl* unfolds four generations of family history as one young girl takes a journey through the past to understand her present. *Wilderness* tells dual stories of love and loss framed as family portraits in familiar and strange landscapes and experiences. Alongside Roddy's contribution to children's literature many of his adult audience aimed novels and stories can also be explored with older learners in the classroom.

Introduction

Focusing closely on Short's (2011) assertion that teachers and learners should engage in collaborative co-construction of curriculum content, learning intentions and purpose, this chapter explores how teachers can use children's and young adult literature to integrate existing learner knowledge and ways of knowing from a variety of diverse but meaningful contexts (such as home, community, popular culture) into classroom literacy practice. As Wearmouth and Berrymann (2009) assert:

> [learners should] have access to materials and experiences with which to build an image of the world and themselves, where they can locate themselves in the world, distance themselves and interpret their lives in multiple ways, to see themselves anew, look for different experiences and try out different selves with the possibility of different future trajectories. For many students

school creates a conflict between their social and personal lives outside and their intellectual engagement inside. Schools therefore need to engage students' identities on a trajectory that is meaningful to them.

(Wearmouth and Berryman, 2009, p. 200)

Culturally responsive pedagogies that reflect and support these existing deep and authentic learner literacy trajectories, alongside explicit investigation of language and culture itself in out of school contexts are developed through a particular focus on funds of knowledge (Moll et al., 1992) and popular culture literacies.

Culturally responsive pedagogy understands literacy and learning experiences as situated in and impacted by the personal, cultural, social and historical contexts in which they are encountered in ways similar to those explored throughout this text. Additionally, and as this text also asserts, culture itself is identified as a context in which learning takes place. As a result, learning is itself a transaction occurring within the culturally structured social and natural environments of which learners are a part (Wearmouth, 2017). The particular characteristics of these contexts then, whether they refer to classrooms, bedrooms or community spaces, impact what is defined as valued learning and literacy practice. As Wearmouth (2017) explains, "a classroom context has a cultural history through which are established particular literacy related outcomes that direct much of the activities related to literacy learning within it" (Wearmouth, 2017, p. 10).

Culturally responsive approaches understand the power of these cultural histories of practice and encourage teachers to prioritise the diversity, experiences, identities and cultures of learners in their classroom planning for and practice of curriculum, assessment and learning. They posit literacy as a value laden practice and question what contexts, aspects and experiences of literacy are undervalued in classroom (as opposed to home for example) contexts, asserting that in any given context or situation that we can only ever learn what is around us to be learnt (McDermott, 1993). The research and literature explored in this chapter offer opportunities for teachers to engage deeply with learners through the development of culturally responsive and sustaining pedagogies, culturally relevant research and team led activities, and active and learner-centred curriculum planning and design (through experimentation with Negotiated Integrated Curriculum and beyond) in the classroom.

The value of literacy in funds of knowledge-based culturally sustaining pedagogies

Understanding what (valued) literacy looks, sounds and feels like in our classrooms, as well as being aware that this experience of literacy may be very different from how literacy is valued, understood and experienced in the homes of our learners, is a first step in the development of culturally sustaining pedagogical approaches for reading and writing deeply. Talking about and problematising literacy, and indeed learning itself, should be a feature of culturally sustaining classroom practices as learners engage in a wide variety of different tasks and experiences, and should work to continually negotiate with and make visible for learners the evolution of what counts as literacy in this setting. Volk and de Acosta (2001) highlight the inherent values within these kinds of conversations about literacy in their suggestion that:

> as teachers learn what counts as literacy at home, it would be equally important for them to make explicit what counts as literacy in their own classrooms to themselves as well as to the children and to their families. Once that is clear, they can experiment with techniques and materials used at home in ways that complement their own approaches. [...] By interweaving different approaches, teachers will make it possible for children to draw on what they learn in both settings when interacting with print.
>
> Volk and de Acosta, 2001, p. 221

Ladson-Billings (1995) in her problematisation of the links between schooling and culture in research, policy and practice introduces the concept of culturally responsive pedagogy as a pedagogy of opposition not unlike critical pedagogy but specifically committed to the collective empowerment of learners through the achievement of academic success, cultural competence and critical consciousness (Ladson-Billings, 1995). Building on this definition, Gay (2010) asserts the importance of understanding learners themselves as resources and explains that teachers should focus on using the deep cultural knowledge, prior experiences, frames of reference and performance styles of learners to make learning encounters more relevant to and effective for them. She suggests that teachers need to "teach to and through the strengths" (Gay, 2010, p. 31) of learners, understanding each learner as a unique asset for literacy and learning.

Paris and Alim (2017) further extend our understanding of culturally focused pedagogical approaches by suggesting that teachers not only draw on but also work to sustain learner experiences and understandings of their own past and presently evolving culture in daily classroom practice. In this way culturally sustaining pedagogy aims to support linguistic, literate and cultural pluralism as a means for positive learner transformations through the development of relevant and meaningful learning experiences. As Paris (2016) explains, culturally sustaining pedagogy

> takes dynamic cultural and linguistic dexterity as a necessary good, and sees the outcome of learning as additive, rather than subtractive, as remaining whole rather than framed as broken, as critically enriching strengths rather than replacing deficits.
> (Paris, 2016, p. 6)

This definition asks teachers to focus more closely on the shifting and multiple ways that learners engage with culture in a way that explicitly supports aspects of language, literacies and culture. In practice teachers and learners should work together to co-construct classroom, curricular and assessment spaces that foster collaboration, discussion, reconstruction and the sustaining of individual and shared identities and cultures.

Central to this culturally sustaining pedagogical approach are the repertoires of practice (Gutierrez and Rogoff, 2003) acquired by learners in their histories of involvement in a range of different cultural practices. Understanding culture as "history in the present" (Cole, 1996, p. 110), Moll et al.'s (1992) funds of knowledge approach explicitly employs learner participation in home and community practices to redesign classroom literacy and learning activities as relevant and meaningful learner experiences. They argue that while their conceptualisation of funds of knowledge does not replace the anthropological concept of culture it is more precise for the purposes of pedagogical development because of its emphasis on strategic knowledge and related activities in home and community social, economic and productive practices for example.

Funds of knowledge are bodies of everyday knowledge learned through participation in home and community practices (Moll et al., 1992). Examples of home funds of knowledge include agricultural knowledge, material and scientific knowledge such as carpentry or construction, religious knowledge, household management knowledge and so on. As individuals engage in these home practices knowledge in one area impacts and connects with learning in another because, as Moll et al. argue:

> the teacher in these home based contexts of learning will know the child as a whole person, not merely as a student, taking into account or having knowledge about the multiple spheres of activity within which the child is enmeshed. In comparison, the typical teacher student relationship seems thin and single stranded, as the teacher knows the students only from their performance within rather limited classroom contexts.
> (Moll et al., 1992, p. 134)

In home settings where home funds of knowledge of particular areas are absent or need to be supplemented with community funds of knowledge, Moll et al. further explain how relationships with individuals outside the households are activated to meet either household or individual needs, a stark contrast with the sense of isolation and encapsulation from personal, social and community worlds and resources felt in traditional classroom settings (Moll et al., 1992). A key characteristic of these dynamic and evolving networks of practice for home and community knowledge is that they are "flexible, adaptive, and active, and may involve multiple persons from outside the homes; in our terms, they are thick and multi-stranded, meaning that one may have multiple relationships with the same person or with various persons" (Moll et al., 1992, p. 133).

Additionally in these home and community settings, teacher and learner roles are fluid and flexible, allowing for many opportunities for different individuals to connect and interact through shared but varied interests and understandings. In this way no one individual or act embodies the culture of a particular community of practice as funds of knowledge themselves are shared non-fixed, social, cultural and historical practices that evolve within changing sociocultural contexts (Gonzalez, 2005). This means that funds of knowledge are understood not as knowledge to be attained so that a particular person or group can be understood, but as resources for engagement and interactional possibilities around meaningful and authentic contexts and experiences.

Adapting this approach to classroom practice repositions teachers and learners as collaborators in shared experiences, which themselves lead to dialogue. In turn, learning as identities of and relationships between teachers and learners develop across multiple possible trajectories alongside exploration of new ideas, knowledge and deep learning. There are many paths to learning and many different ways to know and to share that knowledge. As a community (of practice), the class group draws on its own varied and rich resources, learning assets and funds of knowledge available as each individual collaborates in mutual engagement around a joint enterprise through a shared and evolving repertoire of dialogue and resources (Wenger, 1998).

Another key characteristic of funds of knowledge is reciprocity, "an attempt to establish a social relationship on an enduring basis. Whether symmetrical or asymmetrical, the exchange expresses and symbolizes human social interdependence" (Velez-Ibanez, 1988, p. 29). As Moll et al. (1992) explain, each interaction in home and community contexts, which itself leads to the developments of long-term relationships, entails a variety of diverse and practical activities and contexts for learning. Also significant is that through these exchanges surrounding home and community learning knowledge is obtained by the learner through personal interest and questioning rather than being imposed by the expert or teacher.

Moll et al. (1992) assert that this reciprocity at the heart of a funds of knowledge approach embodies and supports a multitude of cultural and cognitive resources with rich possibilities for participatory pedagogies and broader classroom use. Their research positions teachers and learners as active participants and researchers in the collaborative and deep investigation and reconstruction of home, community and school-based practices, settings and cultures. The roles of teacher and learner are also interchangeable as knowledge is exchanged and meaningful research of authentic material remains a central activity.

Moll et al. (1992) further highlight how, in their research, engaging with funds of knowledge in the classroom acted as a catalyst for developing research teams of learners to investigate topics of interest to them. As a part of this process a focus on methods for research and reflection on experiences is central to culturally sustaining pedagogies incorporating a funds of knowledge approach to teaching and learning. In this way engaging funds of knowledge in classroom settings supports the "transforming [of] students' diversities into pedagogical assets" (Moll and Gonzalez, 1997, p. 89).

Exploring funds of knowledge and literacy values: Collaborative explorations of authentic language, culture and personal experience in the work of Roddy Doyle

The explicit focus within culturally sustaining pedagogies on the shifting and multiple ways that learners engage with culture in a way that explicitly supports collaborative explorations of language, literacy and culture itself aligns very closely with the writing of Roddy Doyle and its explicit focus on authentic language, dialogue and communication within familial and community traditions and culture. Additionally his foundation Fighting Words (https://www.fightingwords.ie/), co-founded with Sean Love in 2009, emphasises authentic engagement with real and meaningful personal, community and cultural learning as central to the creative writing process. His interview further explores this work and his writing, building on these understandings and considering possibilities for teaching, learning and classroom practice.

FIVE MINUTES WITH RODDY DOYLE

How do you define and understand learning through engaging with children's and young adult literature in the classroom?

I don't think I'd define learning; it seems too restrictive. When I feel I know – or have been given a glimpse of – something new, or I'm being invited to look at something known (a word, a phrase, a situation) from a new angle, which adds meaning to the word or phrase or situation, I feel I'm learning. The most important thing for the learner and the teacher: they are the same person. The teacher learns; the pupil teaches.

I also think, though, that it's important that the teacher be seen to enjoy the book as much as the students. 'Reading for pleasure' is key. It must be a pleasure, 'pleasure' in its broadest sense. Children love to see the familiar in what they read, and the unfamiliar. It's the same with adults. I became a writer because I became addicted to the pleasure of reading, the joy of following a line of print across a page, and down the page, turning the page, swallowing the words as I went. I became that addict when I was 7. I started writing in a disciplined way when I was 22. It's all about words, really – taking in the words of others, making them our own, then reassembling them into our own stories.

Authentic language, dialogue and communication are central to your writing. Why are these areas so important to your storytelling?

If you're writing fiction, a made-up story, it's important to make it seem real, so that the reader, and the writer, will become involved in the story and the lives of the characters. So, choosing a character name that could be real makes the character seem more real. It also helps if the characters seem to be speaking real language, words we'd hear if we were witnessing a real situation. 'Like' is great for capturing the rhythm of young people speaking: 'It isn't my fault, like.' It's all about small, but important decisions and individual words that will make the story seem authentic, whether it's about working class Dubliners or talking animals or singing bananas.

Voices (of children, adults, animals and ghosts) in dialogue fill your stories. How can we tell stories and bring characters to life in this way?

Say, you have two characters – an adult and a child. Get the adult to say something, write it down, something short. Look at what you've written. Does it look like something an adult would say? Woman or man, is there a difference? Do you adjust it slightly to make it something a man, a father, would say? What about a grandfather? Is there a word you can include in the sentence to make it seem like it's an elderly man, maybe even an elderly Irishman? Try to hear what the characters – the adult and the child – are saying, in the same way that you hear real people.

I wrote about a talking dog called Rover. I decided to make him a Dublin dog, and the job became easier. I gave the dog a Dublin accent. Ghosts were once living people, so why wouldn't they speak like the people they used to be? I wrote about a ghost in my book, *A Greyhound of a Girl*. I gave her a slightly old-fashioned way of talking, a few words that my mother used to say, to make it seem like she learnt her English a long time ago. The best thing to do is to write a piece of dialogue first, then examine it and make little alterations, so that the words seem like the words of a real person, someone you might hear any day, in your home, in school, on TV, in a film.

Your stories depict physical, emotional and symbolic journeys through rural and urban places, experiences and childhoods across generations while emphasising familial and community continuity and tradition in a changing world. What kinds of activities would you plan for to explore these themes with young people in the classroom?

It might be a good idea to ask about family stories and myths, to get the students to go home and ask, to gather names and places and dates and then fashion a piece of fiction out of it. It doesn't have to be a big event, or something from far history. It could be something that's talked about or laughed about at family get-togethers – a stolen bike, a great-grandparent in the War of Independence, a granny cocooned in the lockdown. *A Greyhound of a Girl* is quite close to my mother's story; I just added the ghost. It stopped being family history and became a piece of fiction.

Could you tell us a little about your work with Fighting Words? Are there any particular approaches to creative writing and learning used that could be adapted in the classroom?

Fighting Words was founded in Dublin, by myself and Sean Love, in 2009. What we wanted to do was create an environment that made creative writing as inviting and as doable as possible for children and young people. The writing starts as a collective exercise. A class sits in front of a screen and writes a story, together. They don't plan it first, and no one tells them what they can't do. They plan as they go, by changing their minds, or adding to a sentence.

Secondary students start with a short piece of dialogue – two students play two characters; they're given a situation and talk for a minute while someone types their words onto the screen. It's great fun and powerful – the students are watching their words appear on the screen. They then assemble the story around the dialogue – they give the characters names, they choose the location, they decide whether to write in the past or present tense. Quite soon, they individually begin to own the story, which is when the group breaks up and they all start to write their own versions. There is no planning, no description of characters before the story starts – they get to know the characters as they write. Spelling the punctuation do not matter until the first draft is finished; there is no right and wrong. We are now working with the DCU Institute of Education and are supported by the Department of Education. We are also running writing courses for teachers, and an anthology of work by Junior Cert teachers, called *Visions and Revisions*, has just been published by Fighting Words. We have centres throughout the country and our website is www.fightingwords.ie.

Your books explore lighter and darker aspects of contemporary childhood. What ideas would you have for teachers about broaching these darker aspects of experience in the classroom?

At Fighting Words, when we work with teenagers, we let them write what they want. We try to give them the freedom to write what they want, as well as possible. If there are issues (foul language, racism, sexism) we let them appear in the first draft but then discuss them with the student, in the context of making it a better story. It's a good idea to forewarn them, individually, as they write: 'There might be a problem with that line', 'I don't think a publisher will let you include that word.' Students, when writing something that they want to write, become very proprietorial about what they write. They want it to be the best it can be, and they want to it to be read. It's a negotiation. Trust the writer. This is where writing two, three or four drafts becomes vital. 'Issues' can be dealt with in the re-writing and editing. If, for example, a young woman is writing about a bad experience, it's importance that she be given the space to choose the words, to experiment with them, to feel that she and the work won't be judged until it's officially finished and she's had a chance to delete words or alter phrases, or change her mind and write something different. Trust the writer. Let them plan the story as they write. Write yourself.

What was your favourite childhood book growing up? Why?

Just William, by Richmal Crompton, was my favourite book because it describes the world of boys so brilliantly and so funnily. What I particularly liked was that the adults are almost all idiots and William and his friends always get away with things. I remember being surprised when I discovered that Richmal Crompton was a woman. She was a teacher. She must have loved being in the company of children.

What advice would you have for aspiring young authors who would like to follow in your footsteps?

The best piece of advice I can offer is: don't try to follow in my footsteps. Trust your own footsteps. I made up my own work rules, my own habits, my do's and don't's, as I got into the discipline of writing. I wrote at a time that suited me. I gradually began to know what I wanted to write about. But it took time. There were a lot of false starts and a lot of very bad writing before I began to feel that I was doing something that I really wanted to do. So, my second piece of advice is: don't be in a hurry. My third piece of advice is: just write, start filling pages. Gradually, you'll begin to know what you're doing, and why. Think of

> something to start with, and get going. Don't worry if you don't have a big plan. The plan will emerge as you write.
>
> *As both an author and teacher what do you think are the essential ingredients of a good story?*
> Characters that we like or dislike. or both. Characters are the most important thing, then what they do (the plot) and what they say (the dialogue) and where it happens and everything else about the story becomes important. We get to know the characters as we write about them. It's very like getting to know a new friend, a gradual thing. All of this – the creation of the characters and the story they bring us through – is done with words. We, the writers, you and me, choose the words.
>
> *Could you challenge our aspiring authors by offering a sentence or two as an opening to a story that they could complete?*
> 'I held the cold, metal handle – but I hesitated. I knew: when I opened the door my life was going to change forever.'

Roddy's affirmation that the learner and the teacher are the same person is the foundation of the culturally sustaining pedagogical approaches developed in this chapter. His understanding of the deep processes, anchored in real world communication and dialogue, through which the words of others become our own to be used in new ways in the stories we tell the world about ourselves echo Gutierrez and Rogoff's (2003) and Wenger's (1998) shared repertoires of practice and exemplifies Cole's (1996) conceptualisation of culture as history in the making and every day.

His suggestion that as we write we should try to hear what the characters are saying and how (a young child, a woman, a grandfather), altering our dialogue as a result, connects our creative writing with real people, places and voices we hear around us every day, and offers many rich creative approaches and activities for writing in the classroom. Building on the funds of knowledge already available to us, writing a story or dialogue becomes not such an abstract task but one that evolves from the dialogues and communities of practice of which we are already a part and mark our identities not only as teachers and learners, but also as readers, footballers, sisters, artists. Thinking about context and subject matter for our stories, Roddy's own writing experiences and ideas about starting with a family story or myth talked and laughed about at family get-togethers offers further rich possibilities for culturally sustaining classroom activities and writing projects.

The pedagogical approach Roddy describes as central to creative writing at Fighting Words exemplifies many of the characteristics of culturally sustaining pedagogies explored in this chapter. The collective and collaborative initial writing activity, focusing on a dialogue with older learners, involves little or no teacher intervention as learners are themselves understood as resources and draw on their own words and worlds in the production of their text. The story then assembles around the dialogue, as characters and locations emerge in an order of events somewhat different to traditional approaches to planning and writing stories in the classroom. Finally each learner works individually to develop their own version of the story in ways that they want to and connect with their own previous learning and experiences.

As a part of the negotiation at the heart of this process, learners have the opportunity to draft and redraft their work, something central to the work of authors yet something that learners working as authors do not often have opportunities to experiment with in traditional classroom approaches to creative writing. Traditional classroom approaches to writing focus heavily on the importance of planning before writing our stories, yet the authors' experiences in this chapter and book suggest in reality a more fluid and evolving approach to writing in professional practice. The alternative approach offered by Roddy and Fighting Words of trusting the writer and letting them plan as they write, again opens up new and innovative opportunities for engaging learners in creative writing in the classroom. Knowing what we want to write about is gradual and in his final comments Roddy again returns to the centrality and power of the words themselves for telling our stories.

FUNDS OF KNOWLEDGE AND CULTURALLY SUSTAINING PEDAGOGIES: EXPLORING OUR WORDS AND WORLDS THROUGH AUTHENTIC LANGUAGE AND LITERACY PRACTICE

- **Rewriting our words and worlds team project:** A focus on the everyday words and worlds we are familiar with facilitates opportunities to sustain and extend learner funds of knowledge. Learners are asked to engage in a team project around sharing experiences focusing on their words and worlds in creative ways. Learners should be given agency to choose their own activities here but activities suggested by the teacher could include watching a new episode of a favourite national soap opera (or a scene from a movie known or unknown in class) without sound and writing the dialogue; watching a (familiar popular culture) soap opera or movie clip from outside of the learner's own country without sound and rewriting the dialogue as though it is set in the learner's own country, city or town; walking around your house or community to find a sight, sound, smell or overheard conversation that can form the basis of a story; bringing familiar and personal items, tastes, sounds or smells into the classroom and sharing these as inspiration for collaborative story writing; writing a dialogue with or a story told from the perspective of your pet or an animal in the community (What would they think and how would they understand a normal experience for us? What would they sound like? What would they say?); researching a phrase often heard at home or in the community (perhaps a saying a parent or grandparent uses often) and writing a story about the first time it was ever said.

- **The limits of my language are the limits of my world (Wittgenstein, 1921):** In *Brilliant* (Doyle, 2015) he tells us that "*Brilliant* was a brilliant word. It lit everything around it. It was hard to see the gloom when the word was constantly bustling all over the city, like a firework display that never ended". Taking this quote as a starting point, learners are asked to think about their own use of language and the language used in their communities. Building on the themes explored in *Brilliant*, learners are asked to think about what language and words are used specifically when they or their family and friends talk about their feelings. What kind of feelings are talked about and what language is used? Why? Reflecting more broadly, what kinds of words do we hear and use every day in our homes and communities? Where might these words come from and how do they mediate our experiences? How powerful are the words we use every day? What do they do? How? Why? Could changing our words help change our worlds or understandings of our experiences in different ways?
- **Connecting with culture and cultural difference:** Learners are asked to write a story about someone who has just started to question something they have always believed. Adapting the pedagogical approach at Fighting Words learners will initially focus on collaboratively writing a dialogue, where their main character's feelings come to a head. Using the dialogue as a springboard into the story, learners collaboratively discuss and explore opportunities for other story elements (including plot,

> character, setting, writing style) before individually writing a first draft of their own version of the story. Learners share their stories with the class, and the teacher prompts some deeper reflection on the experiences of the characters shared in the group. Questions such as what kinds of beliefs do people take for granted and why; why might we question our beliefs and how would we feel doing this; and how can we come to better understand ourselves and our world through thinking about familiar experiences and understandings in new ways could be useful as discussion points. Following this discussion learners are asked to complete a second draft of their individual story, using what they have discussed to now write themselves as a new character into the story. In this they should consider how they will position themselves in dialogue with the main character and his/her evolving understandings and beliefs.

Sharing words and worlds of experience in the work of Judi Curtin: Popular culture and Negotiated Integrated Curriculum (NIC)

The explicit focus on language (as both a repository and a creator of culture and experience) evidenced in these sample classroom activities and more broadly in the work of Roddy Doyle is also a central concern of our second children's and young adult literature author contributing to this chapter, Judi Curtin. Her interview explores further opportunities for engaging with culturally sustaining pedagogies for reading and writing deeply to transform understanding.

> ### FIVE MINUTES WITH JUDI CURTIN
>
> *Could you tell us a little about your understanding of reading and how you use language in your writing?*
>
> For me, the enjoyment of reading is central. No matter how worthy a book may seem in its language and story, if young people are not engaged, then the book is a failure. My ideal reader enjoys the reading experience, and the language used, and then perhaps (hopefully) reflects on the characters and the events about which they have read.
>
> Almost all of my books are written in the first person, narrated by a young person living in Ireland today. This puts some limitations on

the language I can use. I am not afraid of putting challenging words in my books, but if they do not fit the character's voice, then the book will not read well. As I have been writing children's books since 2003, the fluidity of language means that children in the older books sound a little different to the more recent ones. Getting the language right is a balancing act; following trends too closely can mean that the books date faster.

Your work very closely portrays the thoughts, feelings and experiences of your young characters. Why is this such an important focus for you?

For me, characters, and how they develop, are more interesting than plot. The first-person narrative allows me to inhabit my character, and present the world as it appears to them. I get to know my character very well – what drives them, what they are afraid of, what their biggest problem is etc. For a story to work, all of this has to be clear before the first word is written, so character questionnaires and profiles can be very helpful in the classroom. In workshops, I sometimes ask a child to "be" their character, and other children interview them, asking about their lives, hopes and dreams etc – a fun and valuable exercise.

Your books explore lighter and darker aspects of contemporary childhood. Do you think it is important to explore lighter and darker pedagogies in the classroom?

Life is rarely simple, and we do children no favours if we pretend that it is. Children will experience difficulties in their lives, and reading about similar struggles can help them to put things into perspective. Publishers and libraries can be most helpful if teachers wish to find texts that explore issues that might arise in the classroom, or individual children's lives.

What was your favourite childhood book growing up? Why?

My favourite childhood book is *The Voyage of The Dawn Treader* by C. S. Lewis. When young, I did not have access to the rest of the Narnia series, so I re-read this one many times. (I read the others in adulthood, but I don't think it is an accident that *Dawn Treader* remains my favourite.) I loved the idea of the ordinary characters taking a most-extra-ordinary journey. The mixture of fantasy and more realistic elements appealed to me, and the language was beautiful. I can still remember phrases that I have not read for many years.

> *In your work you engage readers in humorous but heartfelt perspectives of the real world. What advice would you have for aspiring young authors who would like to follow in your footsteps?*
>
> Aspiring young authors need to read all kinds of texts and genres, until they find one that appeals to them. Writing improves with practice, so writing a little every day is a good idea – diaries, poems, short stories and longer works. Enter competitions, not necessarily to win, but to get used to crafting your work until it is as good as it can possibly be. Unless you have come up with an exceptional, one-of-a-kind plot, character development is key. Most books map a character's journey through an hour, a day or a life. Characters don't have to be loveable, but (usually) the reader has to care what happens to them – and this can only happen if the writer cares too.
>
> *In* Time After Time *Molly and Beth travel back in time and learn a lot about the world, their families and themselves. Could you suggest a journey (for example the daily walk home from school, car ride to visit grandparents, driving with friends to a concert) that could form the basis of an interesting creative writing activity for our aspiring authors?*
>
> Doorways are always exciting, and a few steps through the opening can take you anywhere. Look at the door nearest to you, and imagine where it can take you.

Judi's interview further emphasises the power of funds of knowledge already in existence for engagement, connection and learning, as she explains that all her books are written in the first person and narrated by a young person living in Ireland today. Her assertion that as a result of the fluidity of language the children in her older books sound a little different than those in more recent ones is a very interesting one and opens opportunities for learners and teachers to study childhood itself in children's and young adult literature, as represented in a variety of different kinds of texts from a number of different time periods, places and cultures.

Her understanding that to write well we need to know and share the worlds of our characters has particular resonance with culturally sustaining pedagogical approaches and, like Roddy, Judi suggests that this experiencing and knowing of character is more interesting and may come before consideration of other story elements such as plot. This multifaceted and connective focus on people and deeper reflection on understanding our characters themselves aligns closely with funds of knowledge-based approaches and encourages creative and imaginative explorations of character in classroom practice. An example of these kinds of agentic and personally resonant explorations is alluded to by Melrose (2012) when he states:

> in what can only be described as an authorial intervention, Milan Kundera's narrator in *The Unbearable Lightness of Being* (Kundera, 1984) found himself staring back at his characters, back to when he first saw them as a shadow or a silhouette in the window, back to the point before they were taught how to speak, and I always liked this idea of stumbling across a ghosted idea of a character in story. It is characters that interest us most when we read fiction. The what happens next is almost always about the person in the story: the girl abducted by pirates; the boy who lived…
>
> (Melrose, 2012, p. 167)

Judi's perspective on the importance of knowing as fully as possible our characters and their worlds aligns very well with Melrose's assertion and the research of Hicks (2001), in particular her emphasis on understanding a reader (or a learner) as a person with a history. For Hicks this history is both local and cultural and is built on meaningful texts, resources and activities encountered by young people in their homes and communities. Following the learning experiences of one young boy, Jake, at home, kindergarten and school, Hicks concludes that in school, where Jake felt no connection with things that interested or engaged him, he "lived his life in a kind of a cultural borderland, one that entailed increasing resistance on his part" (Hicks, 2001, p. 222). Taking opportunities in the classroom to know our learners and their worlds, including also making a space for these worlds and home and community characters in the classroom, is an essential aspect of culturally sustaining pedagogies and will allow learners to build on and better know familiar and new characters, settings and stories.

Judi's own favourite childhood book and her resulting love of ordinary characters going on extra ordinary journeys in a mix of reality and fantasy settings and language across an hour, a day, a year or a life, encourages pedagogical opportunities for the sharing and extending of existing community funds of knowledge through writing in bursts or short compositions, revisiting our understanding of the ordinary and the extra ordinary at each draft. Her focus on the learner/writer and their own concerns, interests and motivations throughout her interview alludes to the final key characteristic of culturally sustaining pedagogies we would like to discuss in the chapter, namely the importance of drawing on popular culture (as well as broader and more geographical understandings of culture), with specific reference to employing Negotiated Integrated Curriculum (NIC) pedagogical approaches in classroom practice. As Dyson (2000) very creatively explains:

> The state curriculum framework for the new millennium seems to have shut its textual door to keep out the noise of society at work and at play. I am standing outside that door, a tote bag slipping off my shoulder as lively children peek over its top. Those children are not blank tapes, waiting patiently for someone to select the voices they should record. Out of my bag come strands of love songs, sports reports, Godzilla adventures and orchestrated hybrids of varied voices. Wanting admission, feeling wary, I whisper loudly into the bag: 'SH!' But it's a bit late for shushing the children. No way I – we – are getting in that door.
>
> (Dyson, 2000, p. 363)

In our negotiation of culture in the classroom an important aspect is the inclusion of popular culture as a means through which learners can communicate and extend their shared funds of knowledge. This is central to the development of culturally sustaining pedagogies as these familiar popular culture texts, stories and experiences form a part of the basis for many learner daily interactions and understandings outside of the classroom, as well as mediating, reframing and recontextualising through story wider cultural home and community understandings and beliefs. As such popular culture texts provide context for classroom learning, it is important we remember that:

> Adults, whether parents or teachers, cannot simply provide children with meaningful contexts for learning. Contexts are not prefabricated; they are interactional accomplishments. Children must participate in their construction. To do so children have no choice but to draw on their history of past experiences. In school literacy learning, then, children reframe aspects of new practices (new concepts, new symbolic tools, new social demands) within old familiar ones. This reframing allows them a sense of competence and agency – indeed, this allows them sense.
>
> (Dyson, 2000, p. 353)

In her research Dyson (2000) evidences how one learner, Dexter:

> made school literacy sensible by attending to letters that he could situate within the familiar frames of valued practices... At the same time the school practice of analytic talk about letters seemed to make salient certain aspects of those old practices (like that D on Lester's record cover).
>
> (Dyson, 2000, p. 354)

Dyson argues that this dialectic process of frame shifting across practices, media, social activities, ideologies and cultures learners, such as Dexter, gain insight into and expand their knowledge. Understanding the rich possibilities for learning inherent in this process, she asserts the need for pedagogical practices that not only assume but depend on variations in any child, class or community bank of known resources and learning assets, and require rethinking of our preconceived understandings of childhood, culture, popular culture and even literacy itself.

Marsh and Millard's (2000) comprehensive text *Literacy and Popular Culture: Using Children's Culture in the Classroom* highlights the hybrid nature of text making outside of the classroom as a character from a computer game can be sketched, talked about or to and even played with (in imaginary play). The recontextualization of text and knowledge children engage in outside of the classroom allow texts from home to be multimodal and have longer and different time scales attached to them than classroom texts. This positions popular culture itself as a context in which teachers and learners can share, talk about and explore old and new knowledge. Developing this context as an opportunity for learning in the classroom, teachers and learners could work together to co-construct a curriculum through engaging with a Negotiated Integrated Curriculum (NIC) approach.

NIC suggests that all learning should be negotiated with learners and focus on issues of concern to them and originates in the work of Boomer (1992) and Beane (1997). It is a

> curriculum design that is concerned with enhancing the possibilities for personal and social integration through the organisation of curriculum around the concerns of students, collaboratively identified by educators and young people, without regard for subject area boundaries (Beane, 1997, p.19)...a community

> approach to learning where the participation of young people in central decision making processes and meaningful work in a social setting is guided and supported by their teachers.
>
> (Fitzpatrick, 2016, p. ii)

Negotiating the curriculum "means deliberately planning to invite students to contribute to, and to modify the educational program, so that they will have a real investment both in the learning journey and the outcomes" (Boomer, 1992, p. 140). This approach prioritises learner voice, agency and the social construction of knowledge between education stakeholders and places these concepts central to classroom curriculum development. Subjects and curricular topics within subjects should be drawn upon to address these issues of concern or questions to promote cultural congruence as learners are supported in the development of personal and sociocultural identities through collaborative engagement in shared practice (Oyserman et al., 2011) and this should be guided by the shared intent of the community of practice (teacher and learners) to integrate or make connections across subject disciplines and real lives. In this way teacher and learner previous experiences, understandings and present intentions develop through discussion into shared intent for further research and reflection (Boomer, 1992).

Planning for an NIC is a bottom up approach to curricular planning focused on the lived experiences and concerns of learners. It involves ten stages: 1) listing personal concerns; 2) grouping personal concerns; 3) listing world concerns; 4) grouping world concerns; 5) finding themes for investigation through the connecting of personal and world concerns; 6) sharing and rationalising themes to prevent overlap; 7) learners vote on themes for curricular development to engage with on this unit; 8) learners connect questions to themes and focus on what makes a good question; 9) learners suggest initial learning activities to address the questions previously developed; and 10) learner questions and activities are used as the basis for curriculum planning by the teacher separate to the learners to also allow for teacher agency and pedagogical decision making. These ten stages encompass exploration of personal knowledge (self-concerns and ways of knowing about the self), social knowledge (social and world issues), explanatory knowledge (content that names, describes and interprets) and technical knowledge (ways of investigating, communicating and analysing topics) (Beane, 1997, p. 49).

As the unit progresses it is very important that the teacher invites learners often to continually co-construct and enact the shared learning journey. At different points of the journey, different groups of learners and teachers will take the lead on different tasks, and this negotiation of roles and content knowledge (building on individual funds of knowledge and understanding learners themselves as learning assets) supports individual and whole class learning. Learners will often need a physical (classroom notice board) or virtual (class blog) space to keep track of the progress of their investigation as well as new learning paths and trajectories. The first activity in the table of sample classroom activities following outlines precisely how teachers and learners can engage with a Negotiated Integrated Curriculum pedagogical approach in their classroom.

As a final example of engaging learners in collaborative co-construction of curriculum Schwartz (2015) adapts a funds of knowledge approach to the use of new media and popular culture in a collaborative redesign of an adolescent writing classroom through formative and design experiments. Formative and design experiments are an approach to research that involves interventions, guided by theory, in authentic academic contexts that aim to positively transform practice. Engaging on this project the teacher and learners collaboratively redesigned three essays: an identity essay that focuses on learner understanding of their own positionality, experiences and identity; a community essay that asks learners to collaboratively research and write about their communities and culture; and a multimodal visual response essay that asks learners to engage with new media and popular culture in detail in the development of two pieces of work using media of their own choosing. Her findings suggest that this kind of pedagogical approach situates teachers and learners as ethnographers of youth experiences and cultures, supports teachers and learners as co-designers of curriculum and expands the semiotic resources, tools and genres available for meaning making in classrooms.

POPULAR CULTURE AND NEGOTIATED INTEGRATED CURRICULUM: RESEARCHING OURSELVES, OUR WORLDS AND THE MEANINGS OF CHILDHOOD

- **Negotiated Integrated Curriculum class research project:** Learners are asked to share what they each are most concerned about (to include personal and global issues) and would like to learn more about this term. They should reflect and/or complete some small research on their concerns which they will then present to the class. With the help of their teacher, learners should work to identify themes across the range of class presentations and vote on a theme that the class will research and learn about. Learners should then refine and focus their selected theme by connecting and listing related key issues under their theme. This forms the core curriculum of the unit. Teachers and learners together should then generate questions that learners can research based on their selected theme and related issues. The teacher may first have to talk with learners around what makes a good question. Once questions are generated, learners will again, in groups, generate activities that could answer these questions. The teacher and learners then together plan a time frame and structure for their collaborative research project, assigning roles and responsibilities as necessary. In this example learners are asked to reflect on their own personal and global concerns but this approach could be adapted also to ask learners to develop their own curriculum and practice in relation to their concerns or interest in a specific theme within a subject or key text, for example. For an example of this approach in action, visit https://ncca.ie/media/4283/negotiated-integrated-curriculum-and-well-being-10-step-process.pdf (O'Reilly, 2020). The design as outlined here focuses on learner understandings of themselves and their world but this could be adapted to a narrower focus (asking students to complete this activity in relation to a novel or poet under study).

- **Research project – Childhood in popular culture:** Learners are asked to share with the class a character from a story (text, video, game) from popular culture that they like or dislike. The character should be around the same age as the learner. Learners should share as much information as is possible about their character including in particular drawings or images of their character and their world as well as dialogue excerpts from the character. As a team the class should then explore collectively the characters shared, moving to consider also the worlds in which these characters live. Learners should be encouraged to question what it means to be a child or adolescent for these characters in these worlds and further reflect on the concept of childhood itself. What does it mean to be a child or adolescent? Is it fixed or context and culture dependent? What does it mean for me?
- **Research project – Childhood in children's and young adult literature:** Learners are introduced to some extracts selected

> by the teacher from Judi's *Friends Forever* series. These extracts should focus on characters living in other times (for example Violet on her evacuation journey from World War II London; Mary, a third-class passenger on the *Titanic*). Learners should discuss these extracts in groups, exploring what life is like for these children, as well as how Lauren and Tilly make sense of and understand their experiences in different time periods. Using these extracts as a model, learners individually select and research a historic event or time period that interests them. As a part of this research they have to develop a short presentation on the time period or event and also create a character profile of a child/teenager living at this time. In small groups learners then present their time periods/events to each other. In following activities learners collaboratively burst write a short story extract in which all of their characters meet each other having, like Lauren and Tilly, time travelled in turn to each of the time periods chosen by the learners. What would an Irish child or teenager from 1845 famine Ireland have to say to a young person from the United States or the Soviet Union in 1957 interested in the space race having both found themselves in 79CE Pompeii? This research project could extend to a wider and deeper exploration, with older learners in particular, of the way childhood is represented and portrayed in children's and young adult literature, connecting to questions of motive, political and social contexts and so on. How do history, geography, society and culture impact on our understanding and representation of children and childhood?

Conclusion

This chapter has outlined a funds of knowledge-based approach to developing culturally sustaining pedagogies for reading and writing deeply to transform understanding in the classroom. From this perspective learners are understood as resources and learning assets and promoting an authentic context for engagement is a central concern when planning for or designing curriculum. A number of key characteristics for designing opportunities for learning in these contexts are developed, beginning with the understanding that culturally sustaining pedagogies develop through a focus on funds of knowledge (Moll et al., 1992) and popular culture literacies, where teacher and learner roles are interchangeable. Each learner is the source of their own funds of knowledge and should be understood themselves as resources and assets for learning and curriculum planning. These funds of knowledge are understood as flexible, adaptive, active and involving multiple persons and relationships. Reciprocity is central to developing and extending funds of knowledge. Drawing on popular culture (as well as broader and more geographical understandings of culture) is central to the development of culturally sustaining pedagogies. Negotiated Integrated Curriculum (NIC) is explored as an approach for engaging learners in collaborative and learner led curriculum design based on these key characteristics and examples of what this might look like in practice are shared from the research. As we engage with stories in the classroom we are reminded in this chapter of Blishen (1986) who tells us that:

> stories admit children to a world infinitely larger than that lived by the most travelled child. They extend the sense of time and place… Stories are also rehearsals for the managing of human relationships, and assessing of human character… They learn through fiction to make themselves at home in situations which courage, cowardice, fear, love, jealousy, hate, loom large.
>
> (Blishen, 1986)

Bibliography

Children's and young adult literature explored in this chapter

Curtin, J. (2014). *Alice Next Door*. Ireland: The O'Brien Press.
Curtin, J. (2011). *Friends Forever*. Ireland: Penguin.
Curtin, J. (2010). *Eva's Journey*. Ireland: The O' Brien Press.
Doyle, R. (2018). *Wilderness*. Ireland: Scholastic.
Doyle, R. (2017). *A Greyhound of a Girl*. Ireland: Scholastic.
Doyle, R. (2015). *Brilliant*. Ireland: Amulet Books.
Doyle, R. (2014). *The Rover Adventures*. Ireland: Scholastic.

Other possible texts for exploring literacy ideas and pedagogies highlighted in this chapter

Baker, J. (2010). *Mirror*. Australia: Walker Books.

This picture book presents two stories to be read simultaneously, one from the left and the other from the right, about two young boys, one growing up in Sydney, Australia, and the other from Morocco. As the story develops it becomes clear how our lives reflect each other's and that we are all connected in different ways.

Lowell, P. (2009). *Returnable Girl*. USA: Skyscape.

This text tells the story of Ronnie, a 13-year-old girl in foster care who longs to belong somewhere and with a family. Written in the form of journals and in the voice of teenager Ronnie, this book deals with many sensitive issues for teenagers.

Neri, G. (2010). *Yummy: The Last Days of a Southside Shorty*. USA: Lee and Low Books.

This graphic dramatization is based on real life events that occurred in Chicago in 1994 when a 14-year-old girl was killed by a stray bullet in a gang shooting. The book tells the story of her killer's, 11-year-old Yummy, three days on the run from the police and his own gang through the eyes of a fictional classmate, Roger.

Shakur, T. (2006). *The Rose That Grew from Concrete*. UK: Simon and Schuster.

This is a collection of poems written by Tupac Shakur when he was a teenager. The poems are reproduced from his own original journals and include additional edits that offer further insight into his writing and experiences.

Chapter bibliography

Beane, J. (1997). *Curriculum Integration: Designing the core of democratic education*. New York: Teachers College Press.

Blishen, E. (1986) *The Power of Story: The good book guide to children's books* (pp. 9–10). Middlesex, England: Penguin Books.

Boomer, G. Onore, C. Lester, N. Cook, J. (1992). *Negotiating the Curriculum: Educating for the 21st century*. US: Routledge.

Cole, M. (1996). *Cultural Psychology: A once and future discipline*. Cambridge, MA: Harvard University Press.

Dyson, A. H. (2000). On Reframing Children's Words: The perils, promises and pleasures of writing children, *Research in the Teaching of English, 34*, 352–67.

Fitzpatrick, L. (2016). *Negotiating the Curriculum: An integrated approach supporting meaningful learning through learner and professional agency*. PhD Thesis. Ireland: University of Limerick.

Gay, G. (2010). *Culturally Responsive Teaching: Theory, research and practice*. New York: Teachers College Press.

González, N. (2005). Beyond culture: The hybridity of funds of knowledge. In González, N. Moll, L. Amanti C. (Eds.), *Funds of Knowledge: Theorizing practices in households, communities, and classrooms* (pp. 29–46). Mahwah, NJ: Lawrence Erlbaum Associates.

Gutiérrez, K. Rogoff, B. (2003). Cultural ways of learning: Individual traits or repertoires of practice. *Educational Researcher, 32*(5), 19–25. doi:10.3102/0013189X032005019.

Hicks, D. (2001). Literacies and masculinities in the life of a young working-class boy, *Language Arts, 78*(3), 217–226.

Ladson-Billings, G. (1995). Toward a theory of culturally relevant pedagogy. *American Educational Research Journal, 32*(3), 465–491.

Ladson-Billings, G. (1995). But that's just good teaching! The case for culturally relevant pedagogy. *Theory into Practice*, Vol. 34, No. 3 (pp. 159–165), Culturally Relevant Teaching (Summer, 1995). USA: Lawrence Erlbaum Associates.

Marsh, J. Millard, E. (2000). *Literacy and Popular Culture: Using children's culture in the classroom*. UK: Routledge.

McDermott, R. P. (1993) The acquisition of a child by a learning disability. In Chaiklin S. Lave J. (Eds). *Understanding Practice: Perspectives on activity and context*. Cambridge: Cambridge University Press.

Melrose, A. (2012). *Here Comes the Bogeyman: Exploring contemporary issues in writing for children*. UK: Routledge.

Moll, L. Amanti, C. Neff, D. Gonzalez, N. (1992). Funds of knowledge for teaching: Using a qualitative approach to connect homes and classrooms. *Theory into Practice*, *31*, 132–141.

Moll, L. Gonzalez, N. (1997). Teachers as social scientists: Learning about culture from household research. In Hall P. M. (Ed.), *Race, Ethnicity and Multiculturalism: Missouri symposium on research and educational policy, Vol. 1* (89–144). New York: Garland.

O'Reilly, J. (2020). *Negotiated Integrated Curriculum: A way to realise student wellbeing*. Ireland: University of Limerick. Assessed at https://ncca.ie/media/4283/negotiated-integrated-curriculum-and-wellbeing-10-step-process.pdf.

Oyserrman, D. Johnson, E. James, L. (2011). Seeing the destination but not the path: Effects of socioeconomic disadvantages on school focused possible self-content and linked behavioral strategies. *Self and Identity*, *10*(4), 474–492.

Paris, D. (2016). *On Educating Culturally Sustaining Teachers: Teaching works*. USA: University of Michigan.

Paris, D. Alim, S. H. (2017). *Culturally Sustaining Pedagogies: Teaching and learning for justice in a changing world*. Columbia: Teachers College Press.

Schwartz, L. (2015) A funds of knowledge approach to the appropriation of new media in a high school writing classroom. *Interactive Learning Environments*, *23*(5), 595–612.

Velez-Ibanez, C. G. (1988). Networks of exchange among Mexicans in the U.S. and Mexico: Local level mediating responses to national and international transformations. *Urban Anthropology*, *17*(1), 27–51.

Volk, D. de Acosta, M. (2001). Many differing ladders, many ways to climb: Literacy events in the bilingual classroom, homes, and community of three Puerto Rican kindergartners. *Journal of Early Childhood Literacy*, *1*, 193–224.

Wearmouth, J. (2017). Employing culturally responsive pedagogy to foster literacy learning in schools, *Cogent Education*, *4*(1), 1295824, doi: 10.1080/2331186X.2017.1295824.

Wearmouth, J. Berryman, M. (2009). *Inclusion through Participation in Communities of Practice in Schools*. Wellington: Dunmore Publishing.

Wenger, E. (1998). *Communities of Practice: Learning, meaning and identity*. Cambridge: Cambridge University Press.

Wittgenstein, L. (1921). *Tractatus*. New York: Harcourt, Brace and Company Inc.

CHAPTER

7

Reading and writing about dark knowledge: Exploring alternative ways of knowing through philosophy, psychology and mental health literacy

About this chapter

This chapter recontextualises and advances the funds of knowledge-based approach outlined in the previous chapter by considering in more detail issues of power and value in relation to knowledge and learning that may emerge in the development of funds of knowledge-based pedagogies. Building on the work of Zipin (2009), a dual focus on recontextualising not only knowledge (what we know) but the perspectives that lead to that knowledge from lifeworlds to schools (how we know) is central to this chapter. The children's and young adult literature texts explored here are texts that engage with dark, difficult and challenging themes and life experiences for young people and adolescents, knowledge that is often not explored in depth in classroom settings. Related pedagogies combine explorations of this dark knowledge with philosophical oriented classroom approaches and are designed in ways that connect with real and meaningful learner ways of knowing outside of school. While the focus remains on darker funds of knowledge this chapter suggests that the pedagogies to engage with these challenging themes should remain positive. Finally, in the context of engaging with dark funds of knowledge through authentic ways of knowing, this chapter considers opportunities for developing positive oriented pedagogies and activities around Mental Health Literacy in the classroom.

About the authors

Kevin Brooks

Kevin Brooks is an English writer, poet and musician whose work explores the darker sides of adolescence through the eyes of a variety of different teenage narrators. The powerful, emotional and realistic portraits of young people and their lives developed in his stories are told from a position of marginality and isolation as these teenagers share a sense of being different and other from the crowd. As human as they are controversial, Kevin's novels spotlight difficult adolescent questions, perspectives, feelings and experiences more often overlooked in children's and young adult literature.

Kevin's work has won numerous awards including a CILIP Carnegie Medal, a Deutscher Jugendliteraturpreis, a Kingston Youth Book Award, a Buxtehude Bulle Award, a North East Book Award, a White Raven Award, a Branford Boase Award and an Angus Book Award. *The Bunker Diary* is the fragmented journal of Linus, a 16-year-old runaway, who wakes up alone in a dark bunker, abducted by Him, a nihilistic tormentor watching and waiting from above. *Killing God* (UK title)/*Dawn* (USA title) tells the story of two Dawns, one retreated to the furthest reaches of her mind while the other struggles to come to terms with her life, addict mother, missing father and dark secrets by vowing to kill God even if she doesn't believe he can exist. *iBoy*, adapted to film in 2017, explores themes of violence, sexual abuse, revenge and power as Tom turns vigilante to protect his friend Lucy.

Cethan Leahy

Cethan Leahy is an Irish writer, filmmaker, dramatist, illustrator and magazine editor. His work sympathetically balances the stigma, experience and associated feelings of mental illness with a humour in storytelling and a depth of understanding of the reality of young people's experience of mental illness.

Cethan's debut novel *Tuesdays Are Just as Bad* was published in 2018 and has won the Mercier Press Fiction Competition and the Senior Category Great Reads Award, as well as being shortlisted for the CBI Book of the Year Award. This novel follows young teenager Adam, haunted by a ghost of himself after a failed suicide attempt, as he faces depression, suicidal thoughts and teenage life head on, in the company of his ghostly self and narrator of his story, both a friend and a foe.

Neal Shusterman

American novelist and screenwriter, Neal Shusterman is the *New York Times* best-selling author of more than 30 award-winning novels. His work explores dystology (a term Neal coined to describe his dystopian book series), utopian and fantasy worlds, asking difficult questions about real world experiences. Many of Neal's books and series have been adapted for television and film, including film adaptations of his novels *Challenger Deep* with 20th Century Fox, *Scythe* with Universal and *Dry* with Paramount Pictures, as well as television series adaptations of *Unwind* with Constantin Films and *Game Changer* with Netflix.

Neal's books and films have won numerous awards including the National Book Award for Young People's Literature, the Boston Globe Horn Book Award, the California Young Reader Medal, the Michael L. Printz Award Honour Book, the American Library Association Best Books for Young Adults Award, the Golden Kite Award for Fiction and the CINE Golden Eagle Award. Affirming "the power of narrative to describe the indescribable" (Judges Citation, National Book Awards 2015 for Young People's Literature), *Challenger Deep* tells the story of Caden Bosch, a young teenager struggling with schizophrenia simultaneously inhabiting parallel real and fantasy worlds. *The Skinjacker Trilogy* explores questions of life, death and what might exist in between for the afterlights, young people who on death reach Everlost after a nine-month sleep, a place filled with all the things and places that no longer exist.

Introduction

Zipin's (2009) Australian Redesigning Pedagogies in the North (RPiN) project aims to recontextualise what he terms as lifeworld-based funds of knowledge into school-based curriculum based on the funds of knowledge approach (Gonzalez et al., 2005) outlined in detail in the previous chapter. His experiences on this project highlight clearly two problematic tendencies in the enactment of this approach in classroom settings. These are "problematic tendencies to build curriculum around light (positive) but not dark learner funds of knowledge; and knowledge content(s) but not ways of knowing and transacting knowledge (funds of pedagogy)" (Zipin, 2009, p. 317). For Zipin it is essential that teachers reflect on and come to understand the many different kinds knowledge and how they may be known and experienced by learners in and out of school contexts. Knowledge, just like literacy itself, is never neutral and carries inherent meaning and differential value dependent on how it is understood by those engaging with it. Foreshadowing Caden's struggle in Neal's text explored in detail later in this chapter knowledge is conceptualised here as a process rather than a product, requiring problematising, problem solving and creative thinking to revisit experience from multiple perspectives. As Caden himself writes:

> Don Quixote – the famous literary madman – fought windmills. People think he saw giants when he looked at them, but those of us who've been there know the truth. He saw windmills, just like everyone else – but he *believed* they were giants. The scariest thing of all is never knowing what you're suddenly going to believe.
> (Caden, in Shusterman, 2020, eBook)

Recontextualizing the funds of knowledge-based pedagogical approaches explored in detail in the previous chapter to focus more explicitly on these darker funds of knowledge this chapter calls into question what kinds of knowledge are traditionally privileged in curriculum planning and practice, why and how. This questioning refers to what knowledge is learnt as well as how knowledge is known and shared in home and school communities of practice. As a result, this chapter highlights Mental Health Literacy as an important and central focus for teacher planning and practice, connecting this highly relevant literacy learning to our focus on dark funds of knowledge, authentic experiences, alternative ways of knowing and philosophically and positively oriented pedagogy development.

Building on Short's assertion that children's and young adult literature affords learners opportunities for intensive engagement and critical inquiry into personal, societal, scientific and philosophical issues through texts that "have multiple layers of meaning, and challenge readers to linger longer over ideas, words, characterisations, setting descriptions and relationships among literary forms and themes" (Short, 2011, p. 61) this chapter focuses explicitly on dark knowledge and alternative ways of knowing. These kinds of knowledge and experience have always held a particular fascination for individuals, often beginning in childhood, but are not often widely explored in classroom practice. As Davis (2005) highlights:

> What do children dream about? All sorts of things, but one odd thing. They have a tendency to dream, and play, about monsters. Wild animals. Fear of darkness. Falling from trees. Jungles. Fighting. Being eaten. And traditional children's stories reflect these dreams. Why? My children were brought up in Mosely, Birmingham (UK). No monsters, no jungles, no serious danger of being eaten by wild animals.
>
> (Tom Davis, 2005)

Exposing dark funds of knowledge as threshold concepts for literacy and learning: Exploring school and lifeworld knowledge and ways of knowing

The term dark funds of knowledge is used to define knowledge about difficult aspects of life that some learners experience or are aware of, such as poverty, violence, mental illness or abuse. According to Zipin (2009) these dark funds of knowledge accumulated by learners as a result of living in or having experience of difficult circumstance mediate how learners and their families understand and participate in school worlds, cultures, practices and meaning making in relation to defining and sharing knowledge. These difficult aspects of experience can also be understood in an educative context as threshold concepts incorporating the following two key characteristics, "it is transformative, leading to a significant shift in perception or a new world view; and it is irreversible, unlikely to be forgotten and more or less impossible to unlearn" (Bradbeer, 2005, p. 3).

Zipin reflects on the differences that may exist between school and lifeworld knowledge (what we know) and knowledge sharing (how we know) for some learners in terms of exchange value and use value. He suggests that cultural artefacts, knowledge and learning prioritised in traditional classrooms and curriculum become imbued with high exchange value and hold power as "elite models of literacy that 'win' in school 'markets'" (Zipin, 2009, p. 319). As a result these literacies are abstracted out of their lifeworld use value, a value that connects closely to the communicative and performative uses of literacy in local and community practices. Redesigning curriculum on a use value rather than an exchange value basis will, Zipin suggests, foster transformative dark funds of knowledge-based pedagogies that encourage reflection and pro-action towards social, community and personal change through a focus on understanding rather than avoiding these dark funds of knowledge or the consequences for learners of living in difficult circumstance.

Zipin's (2009) RpiN project reimagines classroom curriculum in this way as based on use value in learner lifeworlds and in so doing recontextualises learners as ethnographers and researchers of their own lifeworlds. On this project learners teach each other through the use of authentic cultural artefacts from homes and communities that carry rich identity resources. As an example of this kind of engagement one historical unit of work explored on the study focused on asking learners to teach about the practices, uses and meaning they themselves make of local historical sites.

Remarkable for all involved were the vastly different perspectives emerging of community, home and school practices and settings when a focus on darker funds of knowledge is encouraged in the classroom. Interesting also was the teacher participant insight that learners who taught about "light" aspects did not perceive the "darker" aspects and vice versa. Teacher participants were also overwhelmed by the dark aspects explored by some learners that had not previously been perceived by teachers, explaining:

> when you reflect on the problems of violence and abuse, and mental health…that my kids actually talked very eloquently about, and disturbingly about, you realise that, and they were saying, they don't know what the answers are, and I'm thinking "Neither do I".
>
> (Zipin, 2009, p. 321)

Zipin highlights here a key insight for teachers wishing to engage with darker funds of knowledge in the classroom. Within his project the activity and discussion of dark knowledge and experiences itself interrupted institutional cultures and mechanisms that sustain boundaries between dark knowledge and the curriculum and enabled learners to reflect more deeply on the diversity that exists across collective human experience. Further he suggests that "in letting dark sides of students' lives into articulate classroom consciousness, 'normal' themes of instituted curricula now seem like 'going through the motions' and avoiding 'big questions' that could vitalise curriculum" (Zipin, 2009, p. 321).

Zipin's belief in the potential of learner exposure to life's big and more difficult questions to vitalise curriculum and practice challenges teachers to redefine the classroom as a space for thinking and talking about our own lives and experiences in ways that connect meaningfully with local and wider knowledge, ways of knowing and practice. Biesta (2011) similarly identifies exposure as the quality of human interaction that "makes the event of the incoming of uniqueness possible" (Biesta, 2011, p. 317) and allows us to think about, understand and act in new ways.

The kinds of exposures to philosophical or existential questions in the context of personal and identity centred inquiry that drive unique learning and action are often a natural aspect of learner experience and lifeworlds. Adapting these real world ways of knowing to the classroom, Murris (2016) explores a pedagogy of exposure as a means of supporting learners in their investigation of the big ideas and difficult questions central to their experience. Pedagogies of exposure aim to support authentic, deep and critical reflection and incorporate philosophical or inquiry oriented approaches such as, for example, P4C (Philosophy for Children), first introduced by Lipman et al. (1980).

Communities of inquiry for reading deeply to transform understanding: Philosophically oriented real encounters with our world in the work of Kevin Brooks

P4C (Philosophy for Children) emphasises the intertwined, complex and mutually constituting relationships that exists between text, philosophy and pedagogy. Lipman compares traditional academic philosophy to memorising inscriptions in a graveyard and instead suggests that pedagogies for philosophy in the classroom should design for active encounters and experiences that make philosophy a way of life rather than curriculum content. As he explains we cannot "educate for enquiry unless we have education as enquiry – unless, that is, the qualitative character we desire to have in the end is loaded into the means" (Lipman, 1991, p. 245).

Lipman suggests that a community of inquiry be developed as a pedagogical approach for exploring these kinds of universal philosophical themes and questions. Features of these communities of inquiry to be developed in classroom practice and activities include an understanding of problematic situations; doubt; questioning; a search for meaning; inclusiveness; participation; distributed thinking; relationships; deliberation; modelling; thinking for oneself and challenging as a procedure (Lipman, 2011). From this perspective learners become questioners and the teachers their facilitators. Scholl et al. (2009) suggest that community of inquiry pedagogies move through the following five stages – the offering and exploration of a text; the construction of an agenda for investigation based on student's questions; solidifying the community; using exercises and discussion plans; and encouraging further responses.

Through engagement in communities of inquiry in the classroom Lipman believes that learners develop similar individual personal reflective habits and are better equipped to ponder other big questions not yet explored in the classroom. Further Cavell (1979) suggests that such communal and shared explorations of big ideas forces learners and teachers alike to confront through action their own culture and experiences from new and different perspectives. As he explains:

> If the child, little or big, asks me: Why do we eat animals? Or Why are some people poor and others rich? Or What is God? Or Why do I have to go to school? Or... Why is there anything at all? Or How did God get here?, I may find my answers thin, I may feel run out of reasons without being willing to say "This is what I do" (what I say, what I sense, what I know), and honour that.
>
> (Cavell, 1979, p. 125)

A number of national and international organisations explicitly promote exposure to philosophy in schools, offering a variety of resources to support philosophically oriented pedagogical development (for example, SAPERE in the UK, SOPHIA in the EU and the Federation of Australian Philosophy in Schools Association in Australia). A focus on understanding dark knowledge and experience as assets for discussion, literacy development and learning has also been explored in other classroom-based research (see for example, Comber, Thomson and Wells, 2001, and Jones, 2004). Summarising his own experiences with dark knowledge and ways of knowing on his research project Zipin (2009) asserts that the "shades of grey complexities of students' lives, if made curricular, pose stronger threats to institutional 'normalities' than do clear cut 'positives', and are thus more likely to incite barriers and sanctions" (Zipes, 2009, p. 323). This perspective on learning and particular focus on darker knowledge and experience is further exemplified in the work of and interview with our first children's and young adult literature author in this chapter, Kevin Brooks.

FIVE MINUTES WITH KEVIN BROOKS

Could you tell us a little about your understanding of learning?

I was fortunate enough to get a pretty "good" education (and at a time when exams weren't quite the be-all and end-all they seem to be now), and one of things I'm always grateful for is that I wasn't just taught *about* things, and how to pass exams, I was also taught how to think and learn for myself, which has proved far more useful throughout my life than most of the other things I learned.

I also had a very good English teacher who encouraged me to read books that weren't on the curriculum, just stuff that he thought I might like (e.g., Salinger, Kerouac, Richard Brautigan). And if I didn't like it, I didn't have to read it. I was already an avid reader anyway, so it wasn't as if I wouldn't have loved books without his help, but the point is that if kids who aren't natural readers aren't given the chance to at least try reading stuff that they might actually enjoy, then it can be the case that their only experience of books/literature is the academic study of set texts, and if they don't like doing that – which is perfectly possible (and completely understandable) – there's a fair chance they'll grow up with the belief that they don't like reading. No one *has* to like reading, of course, but no one should have to dislike it for the wrong reason either.

And lastly – and I realise I'm beginning to sound like an old man harking back to the rose-tinted good old days, but that's honestly *not* the case (*really* honestly!) – but I think it's fair to say that young people today are generally more sheltered than they used to be (and in my experience this is more prevalent in the UK than in other countries), and I think this can lead to a certain naivety about some of life's realties. I'm not saying it was better or worse when I was young, just that it was different. On weekends and school holidays, for example (aged 10, 11, 12ish), spending long days out and about with friends, getting up to God-knows-what, with no one knowing where we were; or walking/taking the bus to and from school, usually on my own, with only a book for company; then as a teenager, hitchhiking home in the middle of the night; and leaving home at 18, moving to London on my own. I'd hate to have to do any of that again, and I think I probably hated most of it at the time, but there's no question that I learned a massive amount about the world and myself from those kinds of experiences, and I think I would have been a different person without them. Whether that's a good thing or not, I'll never know. But it's definitely *some*thing.

Could you tell us a little about your understanding of reading?
I've always believed that when you read a story, that story becomes yours. It's in your head, part of you, it belongs to you. And it means whatever it means to you. For me, that's how a book becomes a story, i.e., by being read, by becoming not just one story but countless different stories, all of them both unique and shared.

Your texts engage with dark themes and experiences. Do you think it is important that young people are exposed to both lighter and darker aspects of life experience in and outside of the classroom?
Young people are just as aware of these dark themes as anyone else – in fact, if anything, they're generally more aware of them, and more capable of dealing with them, than a lot of "adults". Books are about life, and life is about all kinds of stuff – good, bad, light, dark – and the idea of *not* engaging with certain themes has never made sense to me.

The Bunker Diary *is a deeply challenging and affective read on many levels. Its diary form allows readers to connect intimately with Linus and his experiences. Why did you decide to write this story in diary form?*
Writing in the form of a diary creates a very close relationship between narrator and reader, and for me – as both a writer and reader – that relationship is crucial. If it works, if the reader feels the narrator is talking directly to them, allowing them to experience their innermost thoughts and experiences, the story can become something quite special, something that becomes part of you. A lot of the books that have

stayed with me all my life are stories told in diary/journal form: *My Side of the Mountain* (Jean George), *The Collector* (John Fowles) [a huge influence on *The Bunker Diary*] and pretty much anything by JD Salinger, but especially his long short stories (which aren't written in diary form as such, but they read as if they are).

From a writing point of view, there are some drawbacks to using the diary form, and the one that I'm always very aware of is striking the right balance between authenticity and storytelling. The writing has to read like a real diary, but at the same time it can't have too much of the uninteresting/boring/mundane stuff that a lot of real diaries contain. And it has to read like a story without being too obvious that it *is* a story.

Lastly, and for me, very importantly, one of the key advantages the diary form has over straightforward first-person narration is that it allows you to kill off your narrator at the end.

Time plays a central role in The Bunker Diary. *Could you tell us a little more about the role of time in your writing?*

The concept of time is a theme that I keep coming back to in almost all of my books, sometimes only in passing, and other times in a bit more depth – but not *too* much. For me, it's just one of those (metaphysical/existential) things that I've always found both fascinating and troubling (e.g., death, existence, consciousness, the self, the human condition) the big stuff, if you like, the kind of stuff that we naturally think about when we're young, but because there aren't any answers, and/or it's just too hard to think about, we tend to give up on and forget about as we get older.

Your central characters share a sense of being different, isolated and other from the crowd. Why does this position interests you and why do you tell your stories from this perspective?

It's probably not so much a position that interests me as a position I've always been in – different, isolated, other, no real sense of belonging. It can be a really tough way to be when you're young, and it means a lot to me that my books seem to resonate with kids in that position, but I'm very happy being like that now. I like being on my own, it's my favourite thing! And I like being on the outside looking in, and they're both perfect perspectives for me as a writer *and* for my characters.

What was your favourite childhood text growing up? Why?

One of my all-time favourites was *My Side of the Mountain* by Jean George. It's the diary of a boy who runs away from home and spends a year living on his own in the woods. I loved it simply for letting me be that boy in the woods, which I could never have been in reality no matter how much I wanted to. And I also loved it, and still do, for a deceptively simple sentence that's never left me. In the story the boy raises a peregrine falcon and teaches it to hunt, and there's a scene in the book where he's sheltering from a snow storm with the falcon, and he thinks to himself – *What makes a bird a bird and a boy a boy?* It's still as wonderful to me now as it was 50-odd years ago when I first read it. I also adored and devoured *Peanuts* cartoon books.

What for you are the essential ingredients of a good story?
It has to have a story – of whatever kind – that takes you in, and it has to have characters who can come to life in your head. Ideally it should be thoughtful and thought-provoking to at least some degree, and although it doesn't *have* to be superbly "well-written" – though it's wonderful if it is – it can't be badly written. I know this is a purely personal judgement. I've read and enjoyed plenty of books that aren't generally considered to be well written, and I've always believed that you should read whatever you like, no matter what anyone else might think of it. It's just that, for me purely as a reader, I can't become part of the story, or it can't become part of me, if there's something about the writing that keeps reminding me that it *is* a story.

But I think the most essential ingredient of a story is the indefinable something that makes it stay in your mind/heart/soul when you've finished reading it. That, for me, is when it truly becomes a story.

Your books deal with some very dark themes. What advice would you have for young writers who wish to explore similar themes in their own writing?
I never consciously set out to write about the darker side of things, it just happens that way because writing comes from within you, and to a certain extent it's always going to reflect who and what you are, and I'm a fairly dark-hearted person.

Another attraction of the darker side is that I like writing about powerful emotions, and for me the most powerful emotions, the feelings that affect us the most, are the darker ones (hatred, despair, fear, grief, misery) – they stay with us, they shape us, they make for strong writing.

Norman Mailer once described writing as "the spooky art", by which he meant that a lot of it comes from the unconscious or subconscious self, and it's true that writers don't always know what they're doing, or why.

> The trick is to accept this, and don't try to understand it too much, but just have faith in it. Trust your feelings, they probably know what they're doing.
>
> *Could you suggest a short creative writing activity for our readers based on the characters and experiences in* The Bunker Diary?
> Time plays a central role in *The Bunker Diary*, and Linus struggles to understand what it actually is. In one sentence only, how would *you* answer the question: What is time?

Kevin's assertion of the importance of not only learning about things but also how to think and learn for ourselves is central to the literature and pedagogies explored in this chapter. Asking different and difficult questions for and about ourselves and our worlds to learn in new ways is a recurring theme in each author's interview in this chapter as they together suggest that when we challenge ourselves to think or see the world differently we learn. Kevin's discussion of his own experiences growing up and his understanding that he would have been a different person without these experiences further emphasises the powerful impact all of our life experiences (and certainly not just the positive ones) have on our identity development and learning. This understanding also translates to our reading preferences as Kevin reminds us that "books are about life, and life is about all kinds of stuff".

Looking to his own writing and books Kevin describes his interest in time as both fascinating and troubling. He identifies this recurring theme for him alongside others such as death and existence as "the big stuff", reflecting that these are themes more naturally thought about in and by youth as because there are no easy answers we tend to forget them in later life. These existential themes, or "the big stuff" of life, explore the problem of human existence and dark knowledge from experiential perspectives. Allowing learners more opportunities to engage with, develop and share their own questions and ideas related to these big experiences central to our lives but not yet fully understood would support learner beginning exploration of dark knowledge, as the focus remains on dark knowledge that is a part of our collective experience.

This philosophically oriented approach affords opportunities for learners and teachers to engage together in philosophical discussions about their understandings and experiences in new ways that meaningfully connect classroom content (knowledge) with real life experiences, feelings and identities. Kizel and Lee (2016) suggest that a first step in the development of philosophically oriented pedagogical approaches for teachers and learners is a series of shifts in perspective. These shifts include a shift from understandings of learning as providing a corpus of answers to a place for questions; a shift in focus from preparedness for the future to understanding the present; a shift from classroom activities with predetermined content to a focus on improvisation and individualisation in content and practice; and a shift in classroom interactions from teacher as expert to a community of inquiry.

Philosophically oriented pedagogical approaches redefine classroom interaction as a living, breathing, vigorous space with the central aim of fostering creativity, caring and concern (Wartenberg, 2009). Makaiau and Miller's (2012) paper *The Philosopher's Pedagogy* offers a workable framework for teachers who want to develop philosophically oriented pedagogies in the classroom. They suggest six key interconnected principles for the philosophical reimagining of pedagogies, activities and learning. Firstly, classroom practice and dialogue should centre on the importance of examining one's own life and personal experience, incorporating a sense of curiosity and critical reflection of the meaning of these into curriculum content and developing teacher and learner relationships. Secondly, learning must be understood as a shared activity between teachers and learners working together as a community of inquiry.

Thirdly, the understanding of classroom content shifts from a static focus on content within specific subject areas and related texts to an interactive exploration of the thoughts, ideas and beliefs of the learners in relation to discipline content and texts. Fourthly, teachers should commit to understanding philosophy as central to education and encourage learning about ourselves in ways that foster positive learner identities. Fifthly, philosophy must be an active and living classroom practice with many opportunities for learners to voice and investigate collaboratively personal questions and experiences. Finally in this reimagining of pedagogy, teachers have to define and plan for assessment in ways that complement philosophically oriented inquiry and reflective practice.

Considering what this might look like in classroom practice, Makaiau and Miller further distinguish between investigations of "Big P" and "little p" philosophy. Big P philosophy concerns itself with the investigation of the "big" and more existential questions of life from the perspective of related established collective understandings and knowledge. Little p philosophy by contrast focuses on investigating present problematic personal experiences in ways that ask us to rethink our positions. It is:

> a way of approaching and dealing with content in order to come to a deeper understanding of it. This shift in perspective moves philosophy from canonical texts and the problems of philosophy to the activity of inquiry...[so that] the center of gravity of philosophy moves from the published and/or established ideas of others, to our own thoughts, questions, experiences, and reflections. The focal point of the activity resides in us and in our dealings with the world and the problems that life throws our way.
> (Makaiau and Miller, 2012, p. 10)

Engaging with Big P and little P philosophy in the classroom, learners could be encouraged to first read and share ideas on their own personally selected big questions and themes. The power of this authentic and meaningful engagement and learning through the asking of difficult (or even impossible) philosophical questions is evidenced in Kevin's interview as he remembers his favourite childhood text, the gift it afforded him (to be that boy in the woods), and the impossible question left to him by the text: What makes a bird a bird and a boy a boy?

Following on from this more philosophical investigation of dark and difficult knowledge teachers could, as outlined by Kevin, focus on the powerful emotions that affect us all, connecting here more closely with local and personal contexts and the little p philosophy that we use every day to make sense of our world and experiences. Classroom activities might here shift from reading to offer more opportunities for writing, asking learners to engage with "the spooky art" from within their unconscious or subconscious self. The following provides some ideas for developing classroom pedagogies and activities in this way.

ENCOUNTERING DIFFICULT KNOWLEDGE AND EXPERIENCE THROUGH PHILOSOPHY AND INQUIRY: WHAT IS TIME – THE MOST UNRELIABLE NARRATOR OF ALL TO EXPERIENCE? (PHILOSOPHY WITH A BIG AND LITTLE P)

Aristotle tells us that time is the most unknown of all unknown things. Building on Kevin's suggested activity, following the articulation of their own one sentence definitions of time, learners engage in a variety of activities that support their exploration of this concept and related big and more personal questions in more detail. Teachers could begin by sharing Linus's own reflection on time where he states:

> the clock on the wall is nothing. It's just a machine that makes three bits of metal go round in a circle. The Man Upstairs isn't messing with time, He's just messing with a machine... Monday, Tuesday, Wednesday... they're only words, they don't have any real meaning. Down here is down here. A day is a day. The time is now. That's all there is to it.
> (Linus in *The Bunker Diary*, 2013, p. 120)

The following website provides a wealth of information for teachers and learners to begin their own guided investigations of time http://www.exactlywhatistime.com/definition-of-time/.

Learners first choose to participate in small communities of inquiry based on alignments in their shared definitions of time, and then further investigate these and other definitions and understandings of time evident in popular culture, literature, online websites and so on. Each community of inquiry has as a central goal the outlining of their collective understanding of time based on these investigations, highlighting and explaining essential specific aspects of time. To support these investigations the teacher should share some conceptualisations of time from literature such as Linus's reflection above as well as real world perspectives on time such as, for example, Einstein's assertion that space and time are modes by which we think, not conditions under which we live.

The exploration of time within these smaller inquiry groups should be supported by activities that ask the full class to come together as one community of inquiry also to encourage the sharing and debating of different emerging and evolving perceptions of time. In these whole class engagements teachers could focus on ideas to support learner thinking and breaking down of this big concept (time) such as asking learners to consider and engage in activities around understanding some of the following:

- how time is measured (in daily life, maths, science, history, different literature genres such as science fiction) and the implications this has for our understanding of time;
- personifications of time in literature, story (such as Father Time in *The Chronicles of Narnia*) and film (such as Sacha Baron Cohen's portrayal of Time in *Alice Through the Looking Glass*);

- what would happen if time stopped or did not exist (perhaps making reference to *Alice in Wonderland*'s Mad Hatter's endless Tea Party that cannot stop);
- daily activities as subtle time markers;
- time in contexts that do not relate to everyday contexts and so on.

Learners should also be encouraged to explicitly reflect on the differences between the understanding of time inherent in these conceptualisations and our perception of time as we engage in daily life. Why does time seem to move faster at some points than others? Is time a reality or a perception of reality relative to experience. When we talk about time (sometimes, all the time, never, today) what are we actually talking about? Is time a mix of things? But what is most important? What does time mean to me? Can we imagine any alternative concepts to the concept of time that we may be able to use to make sense of experience?

Having shared and debated their understandings of time developed as a result of engaging in this project learners could be asked individually to write a short story that features "Time" as a central character. What does Time look like? Say? Do? Where does Time exist? What is Time's purpose and what is Time's story?

Authentic ways of knowing and deep funds of pedagogy: Connecting education, emotion and lived experience in the work of Neal Shusterman

Extending our understanding of funds of knowledge, Zipin (2009) suggests that in tandem with a focus on dark knowledge and experiences (what is known), teachers should also consider carefully how curriculum and classroom practice reflects lifeworld-based ways of teaching and learning (how we know), how teaching and learning processes transact in learners' lives outside of school, and what makes pedagogic relations themselves educative. He suggests:

> as cultural learning resources ways of knowing and transacting knowledge cut deeper than knowledge contents, in that they are not only embedded in locales but embodied in people, as deep, more or less subconscious dispositions… that structure perceptions and actions among agents who cohabit given social spaces and networks. School use of lifeworld funds of pedagogy would thus elicit far deeper resonances of familiarity than knowledge

> contents alone. Indeed, pedagogic interaction with learners is an art at the very heart of teachers' work. As professional practitioners of this art, teachers who appreciate the worth of researching and using lifeworld funds of knowledge have incentive also to research and use funds of pedagogy from lifeworld sites.
>
> (Zipin, 2009, p. 325)

On his RPiN project, this understanding led to a need to look for pedagogies in learner lifeworlds outside of the classroom, intersubjective ways of knowing and transacting knowledge that Zipin terms funds of pedagogy. This focus emerged in teacher roundtable discussions as a result of many teacher comments such as the following:

> I think I'm being forward thinking and using a lot of methodologies, like multiple intelligences and Bloom's taxonomy – that's just layering something on top of students; it's not necessarily picking up what students feel, and how it reflects their worlds.
>
> (Teacher participant, Zipin, 2009, p. 323)

An understanding of the power of funds of pedagogy for school and life world teaching and learning suggests that knowledge (as) content is not the same as ways of knowing and transacting knowledge (how we know and can share our knowledge). As a result both funds of knowledge and funds of pedagogy need to be considered to recontextualise pedagogical practice for exploring dark knowledge and experiences. From this perspective rather than reflecting on what makes particular knowledge in life or in literature dark or difficult (Britzman, 2000), teachers should focus more intently on what can be done with dark funds of knowledge in classroom practice (Marshall and Toohey, 2010).

Teachers and learners together need to pay attention, not only to dark knowledge but also to the ways in which this dark knowledge is experienced, talked about and transacted outside of the classroom. In this way there is potential for transformation as perceptions and aspects of dark knowledge and experience can change through dialogue as it moves through modes, generations, cultures and contexts (Marshall and Toohey, 2010). Becker's (2014) study of one man's engagement with the emotionally difficult aspects of his cultural heritage evidences how:

> being able to access his funds of (difficult) knowledge multimodally, through a documentary which contains visual, gestural,

auditory, and linguistic designs, seemed to have affordances that allowed Victor to go beyond merely learning about "that time," and to enter into a kind of experience of it.

(Becker, 2014, p. 25)

This insight for pedagogy development resonates greatly with the work of Neal Shusterman, the second children's and young adult literature author contributing to this chapter, whose novels centre on the lifeworlds of young people experiencing difficult, dark or troubling circumstance and emotion. In particular his book *Challenger Deep* connects very closely with the themes explored in this section as within this text Neal and his son Brendan together have

> mined personal experience of mental illness with his son Brendan, whose line drawings mirror Caden's fragmentation in swirling lines eerily reminiscent of Van Gogh. It's a powerful collaboration, and crucial to the novel's credibility. As Caden says, "There is no such thing as a 'correct' diagnosis," and though his story doesn't necessarily represent a "typical" experience of mental illness, it turns symptoms into lived reality in ways readers won't easily forget.
>
> (Publisher's Weekly Starred Review, 2015)

FIVE MINUTES WITH NEAL SHUSTERMAN

Could you tell us a little about your understanding of reading?

I've always believed that reading is a proactive, rather than passive endeavour. The greatest joy of reading is engaging, making choices with the main characters, working to figure things out, and feeling triumphant when you do. When you're challenged as a reader, the story means so much more, and you take so much more with you when you're done. I've had adults tell me that they read one of my books when they were in their teens, and they remember it more than a lot of other books they read at the time. That's one of the greatest compliments an author can get.

You have written a number of highly engaging and imaginative book series set in familiar and less familiar teenage worlds. Could you tell us a little about your process as a writer?

I usually begin with a concept that I feel has not been explored enough. Most of the time it's a question that makes me uncomfortable, because I can't figure out the answer. The book is then an exercise in looking at the question/problem from as many different angles as I can. For instance, in *Scythe*, I wanted to pose the opposite question than is covered in dystopian stories. Not what happens when the world goes wrong, but what happens when the world goes right. What happens to us when we achieve everything we want as a society, the way in which we want it. There are consequences when things go "right." I wanted to explore those consequences.

Has your experience as a script writer influenced your approach?
I think every kind of writing you do exercises your skills as a writer. Writing for a visual medium, and writing prose build complementary skill sets.

The fictional futures and worlds of your texts engage with darker themes. What kinds of opportunities do your texts afford young people to engage with these themes?
"Dark" is relative, and I think misleading. I don't see my stories as dark, I see them as being layered, and having depth. They are always stories of light, stories of hope, but to get to a place of greater light, characters need to face troubling challenges. The most troubling of challenges is never anything in the outside world, it's overcoming one's own demons and fears.

Do you think it is important that young people are exposed to more challenging aspects of life experience in the classroom?
Yes. One of the greatest disservices we can do to young people is to shelter them from reality, and prevent them from developing the life skills needed to face the world. Stories that address difficult issues in a nonthreatening, safe way help them to develop the perspective they'll need to face the world they will be inheriting.

What ideas would you have for teachers about broaching these more difficult aspects of experience with students?
It's all about discussion, and from I've seen, it's always driven by the students, and moderated by the teacher. When given the opportunity, kids will rise to the occasion and surprise you. A parent once came up to me and said, "My daughter read *Unwind*, then made me read it so we could talk about it. I never knew my kid thought that deeply."

Challenger Deep *invites readers to experience what is perhaps the darkest place in all of your writing, but this world and experience is a very real (and personal) one. Could you talk to us a little about this text in particular? Why did you want to write about this theme in particular and share some of your and your family's personal experiences in this story?*

In any creative field, it's hard to separate your creative life from your personal life. Sometimes they come together in powerful ways. *Challenger Deep* was inspired by one of my own kid's experiences with mental illness during his teenage years. Some of the things that happened in the book actually did happen in real life. The book is also part surreal fantasy, and the fantasy elements were all inspired by artwork he did when he was in the depths of his illness. The book was therapy for us; trying to make meaning out of a very difficult time, and rather than linger in the depths, use it to shine a light to help guide others through those treacherous canyons. More than any other book I've written, *Challenger Deep* was a labour of love.

Challenger Deep *is a deeply challenging and affective read on many levels. Your unusual narrative structure sets your story in a world that feels like it is on the verge of implosion, as themes, experiences and characters appear and fragment in one reality and then another. Readers are brought as close as may be possible to the experience of mental illness and the struggle of a teenage boy trying to understand himself and his place in the world. Could you talk to us a little about your ideas here?*

There are four different things going on in *Challenger Deep*, and from the beginning, I knew that I wanted to structure it this way: 1) The real world, and what's happening to Caden leading up to his hospitalization. 2) The "fantasy" of the journey across the sea, which is later revealed to be the delusional version of things that really happened. 3) The melding of those worlds into a hybrid fantasy/reality. 4) Caden's observations on life that are set apart from the narrative.

I wrote the book in nonlinear vignettes, broken down into those four categories, then when I felt I had enough, I began to put them together like a puzzle. Literally – color-coded pages printed out and spread out on the living room floor. I juggled them, then juggled them again, figuring out where there were holes, and where I needed more material, and kept working until every piece fit into place. I'd never written a book like that before. I learned a lot in the process!

What do you hope your readers will take from Caden's story?

I've seen stories about mental illness before. "About" is the key word there. I didn't want to write a story "about" mental illness. I wanted to take the reader through a psychotic episode. Mental illness is confusing, terrifying; you don't know what or who to believe. You can't trust your own judgment, but you're wary of trusting others. But in that chaos you begin to see patterns, and you begin to pull the truth together. That's what I tried to do with the book. I wanted readers to come as close as I could bring them to experiencing a schizophrenic episode, then coming out the other end with a fresh grasp of reality. My hope is that *Challenger Deep* will give readers new understanding and empathy for those suffering from mental illness, and for readers who are grappling with it themselves, to realize that they are not alone.

Challenger Deep includes a number of your son's drawings at key points in the text which themselves tell some of the story of Caden's experience. Why did you include these powerful images in your story?

He did hundreds of those drawings while he was struggling, and they are like a window into the heart and mind of mental illness. The drawings were the inspiration for just about everything that happened on the "journey" part of the story. When I submitted the book, I told my editor that the drawings MUST be a part of the book, and she agreed wholeheartedly.

Set within Caden's story we meet other young people struggling with mental illness. Caden's interpretation of their experience through powerful imagery in real and imagined worlds affords mental illness a physical shape and story uncommon in literature. Callie and Calliope are both physically trapped in their respective realities, until Callie can leave her window for the other side of the glass and Calliope is freed to dance across the waves. Hal's story will stay with me for a long time as the boy navigator who becomes ultimately, a physical representation of his own illness, as he succumbs barely recognisable as himself, in the painful and poetic image of one thousand pages lost at sea. Why did you take such an approach to the description of mental illness in your story? What can we learn from Hal and Callie's stories?

Hal's story is the tragedy that often accompanies mental illness. I didn't want to pretend that there's always a happy ending, or that there's even an ending, because life goes on until it doesn't. We don't know at the end of the story if Hal lived or died, because no one would tell Caden. Not knowing can be as terrible as knowing. Callie's story is one of tentative hope. She's free, but is she? She's been hospitalized before, there's no way to know for sure if this is the last time. Again, the uncertainty of not knowing. Caden faces that, too, at the end, and makes peace with the idea that "The Captain" is still out there (representing his illness), and he may journey with the Captain again. But he's at peace with the fact that it's not happening today.

What was your favourite childhood text growing up?
Charlie and the Chocolate Factory. I was enthralled by Roald Dahl's imagination, and remember thinking to myself "I want to be able to do that!"

In your work you take a number of very innovative approaches to writing in terms of form, style, narration, theme and so on. What advice would you have for aspiring young authors who would like to follow in your footsteps?
It's all about writing and rewriting. The more you do the better you get. Also read and write out of your comfort zone – challenge yourself to read and write other genres. That's how you become a well-rounded writer.

What for you are the essential ingredients of a good story?
Characters you care about, who feel real, and stories that don't take the obvious, predictable path. I've read lots of stories where the characters don't behave authentically, and the things that happen are exactly what you expect will happen. When you're writing, you should always try to blaze new paths, rather than following the well-worn ones. That's a challenge, but it's a worthwhile one!

What advice would you have for young people who want to use writing or drawing as a way of creatively engaging with their own challenging personal life experiences?
Writing is a powerful way of exorcising your own demons, because in a story, you are in control. You are empowered to fix everything that's broken and to choose what doesn't get fixed. The best kind of wish-fulfilment isn't wild fantasy, it's solving the problems of the life you're living, or at least gaining a better understanding of them.

One of the unique features of your work is the way you see and share your real and fictive worlds with readers. Could you offer readers inspiration for a short creative writing activity by sharing a brief description

> *of a world you have not yet explored in your writing but you think would make an interesting setting for a great story?*
>
> Okay, here's an idea that I've been toying with, but I don't know what to do with, so I'll throw it out there. What if the problem of feeding an overpopulated world isn't about feeding people, but re-designing people to generate their own food. Like plants. If we could use CRISPR (gene editing) to give human beings skin capable of photosynthesis, people wouldn't need food anymore. But would that create a new class system? Those who don't get to eat, because they don't have to, and those who can still indulge in sumptuous meals? It's one of the ongoing themes in my books, that whenever we naively think we're solving a problem, we rarely are. We're just shifting the problem somewhere else. So there you go, some *food* for thought (ouch!).

Neal's understanding of the importance of challenging the reader to engage with and think about worlds and experiences within texts in meaningful ways asks readers to be active and become a part of the story in ways that encourage learning and identity development. His assertion that his stories are born from concepts not fully explored or questions that make Neal himself uncomfortable connect closely with the focus on dark funds of knowledge throughout this chapter. Describing his books as exercises in looking at questions or problems from as many different angles as possible offers teachers a new way to engage learners in their own writing projects, one that focuses on the learners themselves and their feelings about their own lifeworld experiences. Similarly, his suggestion that the most troubling challenges come from within rather outside the individual connects dark knowledge with personal experience in powerful ways. The value of stories in relation to this understanding, for Neal, is that they allow young people opportunities to discuss and develop perspectives and identities they will later need to face the world. His suggestion that his stories are not themselves dark but layered experiences reiterates key messages from literature previously discussed in relation to the importance of questioning what can be done with dark funds of knowledge rather than focusing on categorizing or defining particular knowledge as dark or difficult.

Challenger Deep is a powerful example of writing not to be understood but to understand and make meaning out of a difficult time or experience. In his interview Neal shares how writing the book was therapeutic and the story fantasy elements were inspired by his son Brendan's artwork. Looking to the experiences, feelings and actions of his son at a time of extreme difficulty and challenge, Neal and Brendan together craft a deeply complex and multi-layered story from authentic artefacts and real events from this time. The following excerpt exemplifies their approach here, as this meaning making is always shadowed by the ominous figure of the caption himself, a perpetuating symbol of mental illness throughout the text.

> There are two things you know. One: You were there. Two: You couldn't have been there. Holding these two incompatible truths together takes skill at juggling. Of course juggling requires a third ball to keep the rhythm smooth. That third ball is time – which bounces much more wildly than any of us would like to believe… there are nights where you can't sleep, because these things you juggle take all of your concentration. You fear that one ball might drop, and then what? You don't dare imagine beyond that moment. Because waiting in that moment is the Captain. He's patient. And he waits. Always.
>
> (Caden, in Shusterman, 2020, eBook)

Neal asserts strongly that he did not want to write a story about mental illness in this text. Instead he aims to take his reader through a psychotic episode so that they can come out the other end with new experience and understanding. Writing his story in nonlinear vignettes that later become the puzzle that he himself must solve to tell Caden's story embodies in many ways the experience of both mental illness and recovery as pages moved across the floor until every piece fit into place. In writing this text authenticity and personal experiences are foregrounded in a way that will later tell another story, the story of Caden, but first Neal and Brendan's own stories must be shared, journeyed through and reconciled. Adapting this powerful process to developing pedagogies for writing invites teachers and learners to define writing in new ways and with new purpose, shape and form.

Caden's story does not end in tragedy but uncertainty and, as Neal warns, sometimes not knowing can be as terrible as knowing. Sometimes there is no (happy) ending and writing that engages with dark funds of knowledge cannot always "end" because there is still further to travel. Designing pedagogies for writing about dark knowledge in the classroom teachers (and learners) may first have to redefine their own understandings of purpose, shape and form as writing becomes a tool for deeply powerful and personal learning rather than a measure of learning itself. Within this perspective learners are supported to create and recreate based on their own experiences in ways that ensures that they remain in control, while, as Neal asserts, "exorcising your own demons…empowered to fix everything that's broken – and to choose what doesn't get fixed".

AUTHENTIC LEARNING CONTEXTS FOR DEEP FUNDS OF PEDAGOGY: REIMAGINING EDUCATION THROUGH THE LENSES OF EMOTION AND LIVED EXPERIENCE

Adventuring through our own lives – Making and taking the choices that matter: This collaborative interactive story writing project asks learners to write a Choose Your Own Adventure (CYOA) or hypermedia story based on their exploration of the genre. In CYOA novels or hyperlinked story presentations (told through digital and software tools such as Netstory https://netstory.io, Google docs, Google presentations, Google Forms or Microsoft PowerPoint) readers make decisions for one or more of the main characters in ways that significantly impact plot, character development and story ending. As a result these stories develop in a nonlinear fashion based on a reader's active and personally chosen investigation of the different narrative paths within. Learners should be first introduced to this style of storytelling through web-based examples and sites for reading, adding to and creating CYOA stories, such as for example https://editthis.info/create_your_own_story/Main_Page.

Learners are divided into groups of four and brainstorm ideas for the story they would like to write considering in particular story elements such as character, plot, setting and style. As a part of the plot development, learners also have to agree on a central dilemma their main character will face. Connecting with Neal's own suggestion and the focus on dark knowledge and lived experience throughout this chapter learners should be encouraged to choose a theme, question or dilemma that challenges or unsettles them personally around which to base their story. This collaborative and shared approach to writing also works well to encourage learners who do not necessarily enjoy writing in classroom practice. Once learners have agreed on the key story elements for their project, they will together write the introduction (or beginning scene(s)). The conclusion of this introduction should leave the main character facing two possible choices for progressing the story.

The group of four learners should then divide into two pairs with two learners in each pair collaboratively creating the middle section of the story, which may offer the reader further choices to make on behalf of the main character. Each pair should take responsibility for following one of the story arcs or paths facing the main character at the end of the introduction. Again, this middle section should end with two possible actions for the main character. Finally, within the groups of four, each individual learner selects one of the four choices now facing the main character and writes the ending of the story should this be the path chosen by the reader. Learners should be encouraged to stop writing and discuss options and story development together as a full group at all stages of the creative process.

Learners may need support in the development of their writing projects. Encouraging the use of cultural artefacts and local and real knowledge of theme related experiences facilitates learner interrogation of dark knowledge based on real emotions and lived experiences. To focus learner writing on personally resonant and difficult themes, teachers could use tools such as https://www.squibler.io/plot-generator. This website asks writers to write continuously based on a random or otherwise generated prompt for a set amount of time (between five minutes and one hour). Writers need to continue to type because if they stop, the game is lost and they can either save what they were able to produce, start over, or, in hardcore mode, should they stop before the timer, their work is lost forever. Mirroring Neal's nonlinear approach to writing taken in *Challenger Deep*, learners could then connect these shorter writing extracts to tell the story within their relevant sections in particular ways.

As a final step the learners will have to decide how they will present their story to readers within the class. Their story should now comprise one introduction, two middles and four possible endings. Should learners decide on a multimedia approach (rather than the more traditional text-based approach), they should search for interesting images, music and sound effects that could support their storytelling. Websites such as http://www.pics4learning.com/ could help learners here. Later whole class and individual readings of these stories afford teachers opportunities to further explore lived experiences and support emerging perspectives on these important and learner chosen dark themes and knowledge.

Living with dark knowledge within: Positive pedagogies for Mental Health Literacy and well-being and the work of Cethan Leahy

Neal's powerful portrayal of the lived experience of mental illness in *Challenger Deep* shares intimately and immediately with readers the reality of mental health, illness and care experiences for many young people and adolescents. Caden's expression of mourning for all that he has lost is beyond powerful as he tells us:

> I mourn for the songs that will never reach my ears again. For the words and stories that lie on eternally unopened pages. And I mourn my fifteenth year. And how I will never, from now until the end of time, be able to complete it the way it should have been. Rewinding, and living it again, this time without the captain and the parrot and the pills and the shoe lace free bowels of the White Plastic Kitchen. The stars will go dark and the universe will end before I get this year back.
> (Caden, in Shusterman, 2020, eBook)

The World Health Organisation tells us that 50% of mental health disorders begin before the age of 14, with 70% beginning before the age of 18 (WHO, 2019). Developing pedagogies around dark funds of knowledge affords teachers opportunities to explore with learners aspects of Mental Health Literacy (MHL) in ways that can normalise mental health and disorders as a part of everyday experience. Understanding the deeply complex, difficult and sensitive nature of this kind of pedagogical development the final part of this chapter explores some beginning considerations for teachers and learners in developing classroom pedagogies and activities that focus explicitly on MHL. Teachers engaging with these kinds of pedagogies are strongly encouraged to explore in more detail the literature and research summarised here before they begin designing related pedagogies or activities.

MHL is defined as the knowledge and beliefs about obtaining and maintaining positive mental health, reducing stigma related to mental illness, increasing help-seeking efficacy, and understanding mental health concerns and how to address them (Jorm, 2012; Kutcher et al., 2016). Understanding MHL may lead to better outcomes for learners who themselves experience mental health disorders or support family members or friends with a mental health disorder. Stigma associated with mental health disorders includes self stigma (negative thoughts about oneself) and public stigma (negative thoughts about other people), and can have a significant impact of the development of learner identity, self-esteem and self-worth (Barney et al., 2006).

Gillman et al. (2014) suggest that positive psychology can be adapted to classroom practice as a tool for the development of positive pedagogies and related resources that focus on learner mental health, well-being and identity. The fundamental goal of positive education is to promote flourishing or positive mental health within the school community (Norrish, Williams, O'Connor and Robinson, 2013). Flourishing is defined in the literature as meaning both feeling good and doing good (Huppert and So, 2013).

Norrish et al. (2013) highlight six key aspects of experience as central foci for positive education – these are positive emotions, engagement, accomplishment, purpose, relationships and health. Positively oriented pedagogical approaches support learner positive sense of self; capacity and willingness to engage positively and productively in life and learning; overall sense of well-being; and resiliency and coping skills when faced with challenges.

O'Brien (2017) further defines positive learning identity for well-being as "those positively framed self-perceptions, personal values, psychological dispositions, and affective orientations, as well as the personal knowledge and academic capabilities, that the learner brings to bear in order to participate in, and make meaning from, a specific learning setting" (O'Brien, 2017, p. 256).

This focus on positive mental health perspectives in pedagogical development shifts the impetus of teachers "from a preoccupation with repairing weakness to enhancement of positive quantities" (Clonan et al., 2004, p. 101). This move from deficit to strength and asset-based understandings of learning and learner experiences offers many opportunities to teachers for developing positively oriented approaches and pedagogies to exploring dark knowledge and more challenging aspects of MHL in the classroom.

The Pan-Canadian Joint Consortium for School Health (JCSH) (2010) presents a comprehensive review of literature exploring a number of positive mental health concepts relevant for MHL pedagogical development. These include social-emotional learning, positive (strength-focused) youth development, resiliency, protective factors, diversity, acceptance and understanding of student mental health needs, connectedness, strength-based perspectives, mental fitness, and self-efficacy. They also explore the concept of mental fitness, central to which are learner feelings about and understandings of relatedness (our need for belonging and connection to and closeness with family, peers and other significant individuals); competence (our need for recognizing and using our personal strengths and gifts in achieving personal goals); and autonomy (our need for personal freedom to make choices or decisions that affect our lives). Additionally, in partnership with the Canadian Mental Health Association and freely available online, *The Mental Health and High School Curriculum Guide* is a comprehensive resource for learning about and engaging with MHL in the classroom.

O'Brien and Blue's (2017) Australian action research study exploring how teachers can promote the development of learners' positive learning identities and well-being focus on a number of these key positive mental health concepts and highlight a number of pedagogical practices that support positivity and relatedly MHL in the classroom. They refer to these practices as positive pedagogies that target the development of positive learner cognitions, emotions and experiences, and suggest that personal, psychological and social resources required to engage with these kinds of pedagogies may need to be built as a first step within the classroom space and community of practice. These positive pedagogical practices include planning around sayings and thinkings (thinking positively to learn and using positive language when learning); doings (acting positively and productively when learning and doing learning activities to develop a positive sense of self as a capable learner); and relatings (relating to other learners in a positive way that assists others to learn).

O'Brien and Blue (2017) also highlight a range of spaces that each need to be considered in positive pedagogy development. These include the semantic space (creating particular forms of language and meaning that are shared positive dispositions using mutual understandings); the temporal space (timing, length and pacing of activities and interactions); the physical space (affordances and constraints of locations available, resources and actions); the social space (where shared encounters occur and are explored in further dialogue and interpretation); and the mental space (how do learners feel as they engage in activities across all previously mentioned spaces). Per-Åke Rosvall's (2020) study on the perspectives of students with mental health problems on improving school environments and practices further illustrates the complexity of these spaces for learners with mental health issues or concerns in the following learner interview comment.

> So, I think you can't disconnect yourself from the world, but rather continue to fight and look forward, not stand still or look back. To move forward all the time. It doesn't need to be fast. You can move really slow but still progress and not stand still. At your own pace, move forward a bit, rest and then move forward, so you don't cut off completely.
> (Per-Åke Rosvall, 2020, Interview, Student 2, p. 169)

This learner comment evidences the messy and complex nature of managing mental health on an ongoing basis. The struggle does not end and progress is hard won. Implications for teachers include the importance of understanding the often very difficult relationships that exist between the learner, their experiences, their emotions and the many different spaces in which they might be asked to reflect on or engage with these lived experiences or their own emerging identities or worlds.

Sustersic Gawlik et al. (2018) offer an interesting model for promoting mental health awareness and well-being across a range of physical and semantic spaces. Their *I Will Help You* initiative aims to spread awareness and spark discussions around mental health and illness. HELP is an acronym that captures the key goals of the initiative – Heighten awareness of mental illness, Encourage others to speak about their experiences, Listen and be open minded and Provoke a chain reaction. Activities completed on this initiative include the making of short videos to explore key themes and issues in mental health and spread awareness of Mental Health First Aid (MHFA) (O'Neill et al., 2014). Mental Health First Aid is a process of recognizing the signs and symptoms of mental illness in the self and others and seeking or providing help for the person in need (O'Neill et al., 2014). The work and interview of our final children's and young adult literature author contributing to this chapter, Cethan Leahy, further explore the myriad personal and public spaces and faces of mental health care, stigma and disorder for young people and adolescents.

FIVE MINUTES WITH CETHAN LEAHY

Could you tell us a little about your understanding of learning and reading?

I take learning to mean discovering something new and taking the time and effort to incorporate this into your worldview or your practice. It's important for the teacher and the learner that it seems useful in some way (both for work or personal achievement)

I understand reading novels as a desire to explore a subject or story fully. In my work, I would like readers to find themselves in the work and wonder what the book would look like with them in it. The exciting part of this book is that it is an answer to a universal question "If you were to meet yourself, would you like what you saw?" I think the best books ask a question and expect the reader to give an answer.

Could you tell us a little about your process as a writer? Has your experience as a film maker and editor influenced your approach? What do you think about as you plan and write a story?

Rather than writing reams of words and editing them down afterwards, I instead write the bare outline of a scene and build up the prose over successive drafts. Every word matters because I never put down anything that felt unnecessary just to get to the word count (That's not saying I don't edit or change things after the fact. Just that I tend not to have much excess prose to be deleted.)

The influence of film work may be strongest seen here as it's important for me to have a clear vision of a scene before I start, how it will start, how it will finish. Some writers find this approach creatively restricting – that you are turning your work in progress into a semantic process – but I personally can't get far if I don't know where my destination is.

I like to plan a story as much as possible in advance. A writer Sinead Moriarty once gave the advice in a workshop of setting out your chapters in advance. This had the advantage of giving a road map but also it meant that if you were feeling stuck or unmotivated for a chapter, you could skip to a chapter you want to write. Often you end up with all the chapters you wanted to write written and then you realise that you don't need to write the in-between chapters or you find better, more interesting ways of linking your existing chapters together.

Your unusual narration that makes the familiar strange gives voice to depression and darker aspects of experience long before we ever hear

Adam speak. This is one of the many unique aspects of your text that makes visible the complex workings of a depressed adolescent mind and a boy trying to understand his place in the world. Could you talk to us a little about your ideas here? Why did you decide to narrate your story in this way?

One of the difficulties of depicting depression is that if you tell the story through the person with it, it can easily get oppressive to read or risk suicidal ideation. However, I've read other work that depicts it from the perspective of a by-standing character, which reduced the suicidal character to a cipher and in turn accidentally romanticised suicide. With the ghost, I'm splitting the difference. It's told from the depressed boy's perspective (or at least close to it) without revelling in such a mindset.

In the first draft, the ghost was specifically pushing Adam towards suicide when he gets jealous, but it didn't work. For one, it was too bleak. Also it could only go two ways, it either would lose the reader since the ghost was your entry character or if they related to the ghost too much, it would have felt irresponsible. The final version of the ghost who wants only to nudge him toward depression to order to have him to himself I believe softened the plot choice and in reality is closer to how people experience depression.

The voice that narrates your story can be understood as a metaphor for depression and your novel itself as an emotional journey to a point of no return for one ordinary teenage boy. Why did you decide to tackle such difficult themes in your novel?

Funnily enough I didn't set out to tackle such a big subject at the start. My original idea was a boy who was knocked down and when he revived, his ghost was there. I knew it was a good idea for something but the problem was that there was no conflict between them and so I started to explore the idea of what would be the worst thing about essentially being stuck with yourself the entire time. Depression came then as a natural theme to discuss and I followed the idea to its natural conclusion.

What I wanted for readers to take from the book is that depression was an ongoing condition that is managed, rather than defeated and provide a nonjudgemental view of the people who struggle with it and have on some level to make peace with it. I made a very deliberate choice to set the book after Adam's initial attempt to kill himself to demonstrate this.

Do you think it is important that young people are exposed to both lighter and darker aspects of life experience? What ideas would you have for teachers about broaching these darker aspects of experience in the classroom?

It was important for me that the book avoid being oppressively dark all the time, since it's closer to real life that you have ups and downs, and while things are bad now, it can get better and vice versa. As a writer for teenagers, I partly feel that I'm responsible for preparing my readers for a richer inner life. The film critic Roger Ebert referred to film as the "Great Empathy Machine" and it's something I think about often. I'm not saying that books should be morality tales or even traditional narratives but if a reader doesn't learn or recognise some humanity from a text, I think it's functionally useless.

One thing that got added later in the book was the insertion of Leonard Cohen song titles as section headings. The reason for this was as a teenager, my parents were big fans of him while I thought he was just depressing. As an adult, I came around to him and realised that his lyrics were often very funny, so this was a little clue to me and the reader that it was possible to tackle tougher material with a sense of humour.

For teachers broaching this text, I would focus on the idea that every character is going through something, and perhaps encourage the reader to imagine what each problem looks like from another perspective within the book. I like to think of each friend living in their own YA novel and we are seeing segments of it on the way.

Your book includes a number of texts within a text (text messages, homework assignments, stories) which themselves tell some of the story of Adam's experience. How does this add to the telling of your story?

I have a pretty insufferable love of meta text, so I get a kick out of a ghost telling the story of a boy telling stories that obliquely refer to his ghost (I at one point considered a twist revealing that the ghost section was written by Adam as a way to deal with his depression. I dismissed it fairly quickly though as a little glib). I felt the stories and different texts were important to convey the lives of the characters outside the fairly biased view of the ghost.

Your book affirms writing as a possible coping mechanism for young people, a way of giving voice to their worries and insecurities and addressing the world. Could you talk a little more about the theme of writing as supporting well-being and affirming identity in your story?

I would very much discourage autobiographical readings of the book, but I did revisit some of my teenage writing to a reference. (The story of the underage sex worker is lifted almost verbatim from a larger short story I wrote as a 16-year-old. It only got bleaker from there!) I look back on work from that time as a bit overkill, but from this perspective I can see how important they were for me to work out what I felt about the world. I think anything creative does allow you to sort through the anxieties of your life, whether it's optimistic or pessimistic. It's also a little corner of the universe that you have total dominion over and I think everyone needs that place to explore their identity.

Your book depicts aspects of an emotional journey through childhood and adolescence that is real for many young people. Your close up on Adam and his experience develops as a study in identity. What opportunities do you think your story offers for supporting positive identity development inside and outside of the classroom with young people?

I wanted to do a few things differently from what is expected just because even the most well-meaning books can offer pressures. For example, Aoife and Adam's make-out scene is written to be as romantic and positive as possible but also they don't actually have sex. This wasn't out of prudishness but a desire to demonstrate that sex isn't everything and you don't need to do it if you aren't ready. I also depicted the bully character as sympathetically as possible without softening his edges. My hope is that empathy is possible (also I find scenes in books where our protagonist handily beats their school bully a little cringe and wishful thinking on the author's part).

What was your favourite childhood text growing up? Why?

Always a hard question! For the purposes of this, I would say *His Dark Materials* by Philip Pullman. It was a whole big world just a bit askew from ours, and being raised Catholic, the big theological questions asked in a very direct manner appealed to me. Interestingly I wasn't much of a fantasy reader as a kid (this and *Earthsea* were pretty much it) but I think the moral greyness made it a more relatable text than a battle between Good and Evil. That and I like polar bears.

In your work you take a number of very innovative approaches to writing in terms of form, style, narration, theme and so on. What advice would you have for aspiring young authors who would like to follow in your footsteps?

My biggest piece of advice is to read books and read outside your favourite genres. I've meet people who want to be writers but don't read for fear of being too influenced by other writers. This is silly, since you can't escape your influences anyway and also you are depriving yourself of new ideas and perspectives. When you go back to your writing, your base of knowledge will be richer and you find way to use them.

What for you are the essential ingredients of a good story?
I'm hesitant to say once I say the essential ingredients, I will immediately think of something that goes against that. So with that in mind, I would say all I need are a good ending, compelling characters and no time wasting (this doesn't mean a story can't go on tangents or move slowly. Just sometimes you can tell when a writer is just getting their word count up).

What advice would you have for young writers who wish to explore darker themes in their own writing? What advice would you have also for young people who want to use writing and self-expression as a way of creatively engaging with their own personal life experiences?
I would say when tackling dark themes, don't be afraid to use a little humour. Try not to fall for the glamourous aspects of dark subject matter and at the start, it's good to be clear to yourself why you are tackling this subject matter.

My advice for self-expression is not to wait for the perfect circumstances and to use the tools you have at hand. If you have a good idea on the go, don't wait till you find a notebook, use the notes app on your phone or message yourself. Also don't be afraid to follow an idea down strange paths. Your final work may seem far away from where you started and that's okay.

Your book includes in text a number of shorter stories by Adam and some of his friends in a variety of styles and themes. Could you suggest a title for a short creative writing exercise for the aspiring authors who will read this book that might allow them to explore and apply some of the ideas explored here in these questions?
The title of Tuesdays comes from a misremembered song lyric, so I will suggest another lyric, this time by a singer Nicole Reynolds "Side by Side like Invisible Ghosts" (a long title so feel free to chop it up)!

Cethan, connecting closely with the other author perspectives in this chapter, begins his interview by explaining that his novel *Tuesdays Are Just as Bad* sets out to answer what he terms a universal question: If you were to meet yourself, would you like what you saw? The character of the ghost, who also becomes a symbol and voice for the depression Adam suffers, hints at deeper and darker aspects of ourselves and identities that challenge our well-being and mental health in daily experience. His voice echoes the small voices, doubts and problematic feelings many young people cope with every day. In this story his voice looms large but Cethan's sensitive portrayal of Adam's experience reminds us that quieter voices can make life just as difficult.

Cethan's discussion of his writing process and treatment of the ghost figure in his interview emphasises key and insightful considerations for teachers and learners engaging with similar and challenging themes. Engaging with these deeply personal and affective themes in the classroom cannot just happen, each step must be very carefully reflected on and planned for in ways that support positive pedagogies and identity development for learners. In his interview, for example, Cethan stresses the importance of his decision to set his story after Adam's initial suicide attempt so as too present depression as an ongoing condition with ups and downs that is managed rather than defeated and normalise related thoughts and feelings as part of daily experience. In the classroom normalising these deeper, darker feelings about ourselves and our worlds means that collectively we can talk about them in ways that bring worrying thoughts to light and invite new and positive actions in response to this sharing and dialogue. Using Cethan's own text as a model here would remind us of the power of friendship, understanding and a sense of humour to help us through difficult circumstance.

Within Adam's story are woven many other stories, voices and texts in ways that invite teachers to plan related writing activities in more innovative ways. Cethan explains how, in his book, he imagines each character living in their own young adult novel, and this idea is certainly very interesting from a creative writing perspective. Each text in this chapter presents a number of characters who, alongside the central figures of Linus, Caden and Adam, live through difficult circumstance as a result of dark and challenging knowledge and experience.

Choosing to tell one of their stories in more detail would allow learners freedom and scope to explore issues and particular experiences they themselves want to, whatever their reason may be. Going a step further here learners might be asked to consider their own lives and experiences – if they were to write themselves into a young adult novel what kind of novel would this be? Why? Who would be the supporting characters? How would the novel end? What paths become available to you and which ones will you take? And perhaps most importantly here, echoing Neal's final words also, Cethan reminds us the power and importance of having opportunities to reflect on life experiences through writing/creating/self-expression with the reflection rather than the writing being the goal and purpose.

As emphasised throughout this chapter engaging with these dark themes is not writing for writing's sake. It is something altogether different, and in Cethan's own words, unfolds in "a little corner of the universe that you have total dominion over and I think everyone needs that space to explore their identity". The following shares some ideas for positively oriented pedagogies that focus on MHL in the classroom.

POSITIVE PEDAGOGIES FOR MENTAL HEALTH LITERACY: REPURPOSING CLASSROOM LITERACY TO NORMALISE PERSONAL STRUGGLES AND FOSTER POSITIVE IDENTITY DEVELOPMENT

- **Restorative justice pedagogy to reconcile difficult and dark knowledge – Feeling good and doing good:** Restorative justice pedagogy has its foundation in philosophical understandings of experience that emphasize the inherent worth and well-being of all people, the belief that humans are profoundly relational, and the goal to replace punitive, managerial structures of schooling with those that emphasize the building and repairing of relationships (Vaandering, 2014) and complements well the central ideas around dark knowledge and experiences explored in this chapter.

  Redefining classroom space as a place for positive social and emotional learning, learners join together in a circle to explore their feelings and emotions in relation to difficult and dark knowledge. To begin circle time each learner is asked to share one word that describes their mood and/or day. Learners could also be asked to keep and share a mood diary (a log where learners write down short descriptions of their mood at various nominated times during a 24-hour period). In smaller groups within the circle learners should explore their diaries, identifying and discussing their overall balance between positive and negative moods and feelings. Based on this discussion and/or their current mood learners are asked to individually write affective statements that describe how they are feeling. Affective statements are personal expressions of feeling in response to the positive or negative behaviour of others. These "I" based statements challenge traditional classroom dynamics and teach empathy based on exploration of real life experiences. Following on from their affective statements, learners are asked to consider how they can use or adapt the content within these statements to feel good and do good over the next 24 hours. Learners must identify three actions for each they will now focus on.

- **Writing to understand my Stranger Song:** In Cethan's opening chapter of *Tuesdays Are Just as Bad*, the ghost narrates a difficult day in Adam's life, his first day back at school after a suicide attempt. Having read and discussed this chapter, learners are asked to think about a difficult day or period in their own lives. As a creative writing project learners are asked to write an account of this difficult experience narrated in the same way, by their own strange ghost of themselves. Learners should be encouraged to think about how their ghost might see or understand this more distanced experience in similar and dissimilar ways. What other voices impact our understandings, feelings and choices in this story? What different viewpoints could be taken on the experience? What other choices could have been made?

- **Managing mental health fitness – Building strength and resiliency:**

In large print in blue biro it said: SORRY.

Sorry. Sorry with a full stop…

I looked at him. He looked sorry. I couldn't understand. Why was he sorry? Phillip drove him to it with his bullying and blame, Aoife drove him to it with her selfishness, his parents drove him to it with their lack of understanding.

He was sitting there.

'Why are you saying sorry?'

'It's my fault.'

'How is it your fault?'

'I dunno. My general existence.'

(Adam, in Leahy, 2018, eBook)

Learners complete a character study of Adam with a particular emphasis on the strengths he possesses or has access to to help him through difficult experiences. What positive emotions, engagement, accomplishments, purposes, relationships and mental health experiences

> can be found in the story? How could Adam develop and use these strengths to shield against particular experiences? What opportunities are taken and missed in this regard and why? Moving from the story to our own experiences, why is it important to have shields identified and ready to deploy against challenging circumstances? Can anyone survive without these kinds of shields and supports? What shields do learners each individually need? What shields do learners already possess and/or have drawn on in the past and how? What shields might learners need for the future? How can we get ready for future possible difficult experiences?

Conclusion

This chapter explores difficult and dark knowledge and ways of knowing from funds of knowledge, funds of pedagogy, philosophical and mental health literacy perspectives in ways that encourage intensive and critical deep reading and writing practices to transform understandings of ourselves and our worlds. The foreboding figure of the Captain, a symbol for mental illness and embodiment of this difficult and dark knowledge and experience, waits on the wings from beginning to end, the only constant as forever an experiential and interactional possibility. The children's and young adult literature texts explored throughout this chapter all emphasise the importance of connecting deeply with and questioning authentically and critically real and personal lived experiences to further learning and positive identity development in darker spaces. Each text and author also carefully acknowledge that dark and difficult knowledge and experience do not just go away and designing any classroom-based activities or pedagogies that engage with dark knowledge requires an understanding of the exploration of these kinds of experiences as an ongoing and necessary part of daily classroom practice. As Caden warns us:

> even before there was a ship, there was the Captain. The story began with him, you suspect it will end with him and everything between is the powdery meal of windmills that might be giants grinding bones to make their bread. Tread lightly, or you'll wake them.
>
> (Caden, in Shusterman, 2020, eBook)

Bibliography

Children's and young adult literature explored in this chapter

Brooks, K. (2013). *The Bunker Diary*. UK: Penguin.
Brooks, K. (2010). *iBoy*. UK: Penguin.
Brooks, K. (2009). *Killing God*. UK: Penguin.
Carroll, L. (1898). *Alice in Wonderland*. UK: Macmillan.
Leahy, C. (2018). *Tuesdays Are Just as Bad*. Ireland: Mercier.
Lewis, C. S. (1950–1956). *The Chronicles of Narnia Series*. New York: Harper Collins.
Shusterman, S. (2021). *Game Changer*. USA: Walker Books.
Shusterman, S. (2020). *Challenger Deep*. USA: Walker Books.
Shusterman, S. (2018). *Scythe*. USA: Walker Books.
Shusterman, S. (2018). *Dry*. USA: Walker Books.
Shusterman, S. (2011). *The Skinjacker Trilogy*. USA: Simon and Shuster Books for Young Readers.
Shusterman, S. (2009). *Unwind*. UK: Simon and Shuster Children's UK.

Other possible texts for exploring literacy ideas and pedagogies highlighted in this chapter

Chbosky, S. (2013). *The Perks of Being a Wallflower*. UK: Simon and Schuster.

Written as letters this text explores adolescence from a unique teenage perspective as Charlie himself narrates "So, this is my life. And I want you to know that I am both happy and sad and I'm still trying to figure out how that could be" (Charlie in Chbosky, 2013, eBook).

Lobel, A. (2016). *Frog and Toad: The complete collection*. UK: Harper Collins.
Lobel, A. (1982). *Owl at Home*. UK: Harper Collins.

Frog and Toad tells the story of the unlikely friendship between two very different characters, Frog and Toad, whom Lobel has identified as different aspects of himself. These stories ask readers to reflect deeply within and teach empathy, philosophy and the complexities of the human condition. In the nihilist *Owl at Home*, Owl brews a special tea from his tears by thinking about all the sad things in the world.

Rapp, A. (2012). *The Children and the Wolves*. USA: Candlewick.

This book tells the story of three young teenagers who kidnap a four-year-old girl and keep her in a basement.

Chapter bibliography

Barney L. J. Griffiths K. M. Jorm A. F. Christensen H. (2006). Stigma about depression and its impact on help-seeking intentions. *Australian & New Zealand Journal of Psychiatry*, 40(1), 51–54.

Becker, A. (2014). Funds of (difficult) knowledge and the affordances of multimodality: The case of Victor, *Journal of Language and Literacy Education, 10*(2), 17–33.

Biesta, G. J. J. (2011). Philosophy, exposure, and children: How to resist the instrumentalisation of philosophy in education, Vansieleghem N. Kennedy D. (Eds.), Special issue: Philosophy for children in transition: Problems and prospects. *Journal of Philosophy of Education, 45*(2), 305–321.

Bradbeer, J. (2005), Threshold concepts and troublesome knowledge in the GEES disciplines, *Planet, 15*(3).

Britzman, D. P. (2000). If the story cannot end: Deferred action, ambivalence, and difficult knowledge. In Simon, R. I. Rosenberg, S. Eppert C. (Eds.), *Between Hope and Despair: Pedagogy and the remembrance of historical trauma* (pp. 27–57). Lanham, MD: Rowman & Littlefield Publishers.

Cavell, S. (1979). *The Claim of Reason*. Oxford: Oxford University Press.

Clonan, S. M., Chafouleas, S. M., McDougal, J. L., & Riley-Tillman, T. C. (2004). Positive psychology goes to school: Are we there yet? *Psychology in the Schools, 41*(1), 101–109.

Comber, B. Thomson, P. Wells, M. (2001). Critical literacy finds a 'place': Writing and social action in a neighbourhood school. *Elementary School Journal, 101*, 451–464.

Davis, T. (2005). *Lecture on Jung*. University of Birmingham, UK.

Gilman, R. Huebner, E. S. Furlong M. J. (2014). Toward a science and practice of positive psychology in schools: A Conceptual framework. In Furlong, M. J. Gilman, R. Huebner E. S. (Eds.), *Handbook of Positive Psychology in Schools* (2nd edn) (pp. 3–11). New York, NY: Routledge.

Gonzalez, N. Moll, L. C. Amanti, C. (Eds.) (2005). *Funds of Knowledge: Theorizing practices in households, communities and classrooms*. Mahwah, NJ: Lawrence Erlbaum Associates.

Huppert, F. A. So, T. T. C. (2013). Flourishing across Europe: Application of a new conceptual framework for defining well-being. *Social Indicators Research, 110*(3), 837–861. https://doi.org/10.1007/s11205-011-9966-7.

Joint Consortium for School Health. (2010). *Schools as a Setting for Promoting Positive Mental Health: Better practices and perspectives*. JCSH. Retrieved at https://www.jcsh-cces.ca/upload/JCSH%20Positive%20Mental%20Health%20Lit%20Review%20Mar%202010.pdf.

Jones, S. (2004). Living poverty and literacy learning: Sanctioning topics of students' lives. *Language Arts, 81*, 461–469.

Jorm, A. (2012). Mental health literacy. *American Psychologist, 67*(3), 231–243. doi:10.1037/a0025957.

Judges citation. (2015). https://www.nationalbook.org/books/challenger-deep/.

Kizel, A. Lee, J. (reviewing editor). (2016). Philosophy with children as an educational platform for self-determined learning. *Cogent Education, 3*(1), doi:10.1080/2331186X.2016.1244026.

Kutcher, S. Wei, Y. (2018). *Mental Health and High School Curriculum Guide*. Available at http://teenmentalhealth.org/curriculum/.

Kutcher, S. Wei, Y. Coniglio, C. (2016). Mental health literacy: Past, present, and future. *Canadian Journal of Psychiatry, 61*(3), 154–158. doi:10.1177/0706743715616609.

Lipman, M. (2011). Philosophy for children: Some assumptions and implications. *Ethics in Progress, 2*(1), 3–16.

Lipman, M. (1991). *Thinking in Education*. Cambridge, MA: Cambridge University Press.

Lipman, M. Sharp, A. M. Oscanyan, F. S. (1980). *Philosophy in the Classroom* (2nd edn). Philadelphia: Temple University Press.

Makaiau, A. S. Miller, C. (2012). The Philosopher's Pedagogy. *Educational Perspectives, 44*(1–2), 8–19.

Marshall, E. Toohey, K. (2010). Representing family: Community funds of knowledge, bilingualism, and multimodality. *Harvard Educational Review, 80*(2), 221–242.

Murris, K. (2016). Philosophy with picturebooks. In Peters, M. A. (Ed), *Encyclopedia of Educational Philosophy and Theory*. doi:10.1007/978-981-287-532-7_164-1.

Norrish, J. M. Williams, P. O'Connor, M. Robinson, J. (2013). An applied framework for positive education. *International Journal of Wellbeing, 3*(2), 147–161.

O'Brien, M. (2017). Positive behaviour management: Building positive learning identities and engagement in learning. In Pendergast, D. Bahr, N. Main K. (Eds.) *Teaching Middle Years: Rethinking curriculum, pedagogy and assessment* (pp. 243–264). Sydney, NSW: Allen and Unwin.

O'Brien, M. Blue, L. (2017). Towards a positive pedagogy: designing pedagogical practices that facilitate positivity within the classroom, *Educational Action Research*, doi:10.1080/09650792.2017.1339620.

O'Neill, A. M. Leyva, V. L. Humble, M. N. Lewis, M. L. Garcia, J. A. (2014). Mental health first aid USA: The implementation of a mental health first aid training program in a rural healthcare setting. *Contemporary Rural Social Work, 6*, 117–125.

Per-Åke R. (2020). Perspectives of students with mental health problems on improving the school environment and practice. *Education Inquiry, 11*(3), 159–174, doi:10.1080/20004508.2019.1687394.

Publishers Weekly. (2015, 13 February). Shusterman, N. *Challenger Deep, starred review. Publishers Weekly*, Retrieved from https://www.storyman.com/books/challenger-deep/.

Scholl, R. Nichols, K. Burgh, G. (2009). *Philosophy for children: Towards pedagogical transformation*. Refereed paper presented at 'Teacher education crossing borders: Cultures, contexts, communities and curriculum' the annual conference of the Australian Teacher Education Association (ATEA), Albury, 28 June – 1 July.

Sustersic Gawlik, K. Jeu, G. Reisinger, V. (2018). The 'I Will Help You' mental health initiative: A pedagogy for nursing leadership and a call to action for nurses. *Journal of Professional Nursing, 34*(5), 364–368, https://doi.org/10.1016/j.profnurs.2017.12.010.

Vaandering, D. (2014). Implementing restorative justice practice in schools: What pedagogy reveals. *Journal of Peace Education*, 11(1). http://www.tandfonline.com.

Wartenberg, T. E. (2009). *Big Ideas for Little Kids: Teaching philosophy through children's literature*. Lanham, MD: Rowman & Littlefield.

World Health Organization. (2019). *Child and adolescent mental health*. Available at https://www.who.int/mental_health/ maternal-child/ child_adolescent/en/.

Zipin, L. (2013). Engaging middle years learners by making their communities curricular: A Funds of Knowledge approach. *Curriculum Perspectives*, *33*(3), 1–12.

Zipin, L. Sellar, S. Brennan, M. Gale, T. (2013). Educating for futures in marginalized regions: A sociological framework for rethinking and researching aspirations. *Educational Philosophy and Theory*. doi: 10.1080/00131857.2013.839376.

Zipin, L. (2009) Dark funds of knowledge, deep funds of pedagogy: exploring boundaries between lifeworlds and schools, *Discourse: Studies in the Cultural Politics of Education*, *30*(3), 317–331.

Index

absurdism 29
activism 74, 100, 116–17, 120, 202
adolescence 27, 110, 115, 238, 271
aesthetic literacy 62
affect 61, 73, 76–88, 103, 122, 246, 257, 265, 273–5
affinity spaces 6, 133, 138–54, 165
agency 36, 61, 71, 84, 179–82. 196, 202–4, 222, 228–30
alphabet books 22
alternate realities 128–9
annotated spreads 39
anthropomorphic 147–53
artefacts 35, 41, 100–4, 117–23, 192–3, 242, 261–3
arts based literacies 17, 60, 72–6, 88, 90
attitude 5, 71, 179
audience 15, 22, 81, 106, 123–36, 140–2, 153, 165, 203,
authenticity 36, 98, 247, 261
author study 29, 40, 123
autobiography 98–9, 110, 117, 123–4

Bazerman, C 105–7, 123
Bettelheim, B 151
biography 117–19, 123, 128, 185, 188
book talk 50, 137
bottom up 70, 230
boundaries 2, 83–4, 91, 229, 243

Cahill, K 178
challenging and controversial texts 42, 238, 246, 257
character 45–6, 65–77, 79–87, 103, 109–12, 141–62, 183–6, 195–204, 218–29, 255–63, 269–76

childhood 18, 32–3, 57, 72–5, 149, 218–33, 271
choice 1–5, 18–20, 62, 137–43, 255, 262–3, 266,
choose Your Own Adventure story 262
co-construction 211
cognition 59, 196, 266
collaboration 62, 78, 82, 100, 193
collage 40, 49–50, 75, 99, 192
Comber, B 22, 177, 179, 245
comics 28, 36, 39, 136
communication 4, 15–18, 24, 118
communities of practice 71, 121, 136, 193, 221, 240
comprehension 4, 17, 122, 137, 194
conflict 26, 187, 212, 269
Conlon McKenna, M 194–204
connection 32, 72, 103–4, 120, 128, 184–6
consciousness 32, 109, 179, 189, 213, 243
content mastery 180, 195
context 3–6, 27, 71, 76, 106, 179–82, 212, 229
counterfactual and time slip stories 204
creativity 69, 78, 82–7, 188–93, 136
Cremin, T 103, 105, 121, 136–8
critical inquiry 6, 83, 241
critical thinking 50, 60, 140, 151, 180–1, 193
crossover picture books 42, 47
Curwood, J 141–3, 163–4
culturally sustaining 6, 209–17, 221–8, 233
curiosity 26, 32, 60–2, 66, 77, 82, 195, 198
curriculum design 6, 209, 229, 234
Curtin, J 210, 224–31

Index

dance 5, 18, 56–61, 74, 88
dark funds of knowledge 33, 238–42, 254, 260–1, 264
day dream 80, 87
defamiliarisation 111, 116
dialogue 50, 83–4, 102, 138–9, 216–24
diary 68, 115, 120, 125, 140, 150, 200, 246–7, 274
discussion 62, 69, 137, 152, 192, 214, 230
Doyle, R 211–24
Drama 5, 56, 60, 65, 74, 122, 191, 202–3
drawing 17, 28–32, 38

editing 39, 120, 161, 220, 260, 268
Eisner, E 48, 59–61, 77
ekphrastic poetry 191–2
emotion 2, 37, 46–7, 90, 253
emotional literacies 4, 13, 33, 37, 52, 101, 163
empathy 43, 65, 129, 158, 199, 258, 271, 275
environmentalism 48, 72, 74

faction 149, 153–4
fairy tale 35, 134, 145, 151–2, 162
fan fiction 6, 23, 134, 139, 141–3, 153–4, 165, 201
feeling 2, 25–8, 36, 41, 88, 274
fiction effect 136, 138
film 14, 19, 27–8, 34–9, 45, 61, 74, 109, 146, 150, 184, 268–70
flash fiction 40
flash forward writing 99, 122
Fleischman, P 98, 118, 124–9
folklore 66
Forde, P. 57–76
formative and design experiments 231
forum theatre 202–3
framing 20, 22, 31–2, 37–9, 42
free indirect speech 100, 112, 115, 118
funds of knowledge 33, 209–34, 237–60
funds of pedagogy 240, 253–4

Gee, J.P. 2, 138
gender 63, 138, 180, 189–90,
genre 97–107, 118–27, 141–42, 154–5, 262
Gonzalez, N 33, 215–16, 240
graphic life writing 23
graphic novel 14, 36
Greene, M 60–2, 73–6

Hall, K 3, 8, 70, 182
Hasak-Lowy, T 5, 99, 107–17
Heiligman, D 6, 175, 182–91
Hicks, D 227
historical fiction 174, 194–8, 201–5
historical figures and real people 26, 185, 176, 190–1, 201–2, 218, 221
historical literacy 174, 194–5, 202
historical perspective 173–80, 186
history mysteries 203–4
Holub, J 6, 134–6, 141–51
home 32–3, 71–84, 211–16, 223, 227–29, 242–7
humour 133–35, 143–6, 160, 164, 270–3

identity texts 123, 128
illustration 26–9, 39, 42–7, 88, 148,
image 14–50, 67–71, 89–90, 147, 211, 258
imagination 17, 25–46, 73, 83–91, 99, 120, 163
improvisation 103, 164, 182, 193, 250
independent reading and writing 5
informal learning 139
inner lives 109, 114
inquiry based learning 5, 60, 83
intergenerational stories 79, 128
interiority 100, 109, 120
intermodal 16, 19, 21, 39, 41, 47, 49
interpretation 19–35, 90–1, 117, 140, 186
intertextuality 28, 71
inter-thinking 138–9
intervention 178–9, 222, 227, 231
intramodal 19–21, 39, 41–9
invention 32, 41, 68, 188

Jewitt, C 18–23

Kress, G 15, 18–24, 63
Kirkland, D 100–5
Kucirkova, A 103–5, 121–2, 136–8

landscapes for learning 36, 49, 74–5, 106, 178
Lankshear, C 142, 163
learning intentions 6, 211
learning trajectories 104
list making 8, 73, 100, 113–15, 194
lived experience 7–9, 78, 136–8, 230, 253, 262–7
lives as storied works of art 76, 85
local histories and stories 151

make a book 50, 67
making text 79
mantle of the expert pedagogy 193
mapping 13, 17, 23–4, 33, 41, 83, 181
Markel, M 6, 175, 182, 187
materiality 20–1, 31–2, 39, 42
mental health literacy 237–8, 240, 264, 274–6
method writing 183, 186
multidimensional texts and resources 107
multiliteracy approaches 19, 22
multimodality 13, 17–8, 21–3, 39, 48
multimodal memoir project 89
multimodal pedagogical approaches 32
multiple perspective inquiry approaches to reading 5, 22, 56, 70, 90, 151, 162, 195, 240
music 5, 27–8, 38, 56–74, 88–9, 118–24, 144, 165
myth 66, 88, 144–6, 151–2, 162, 219–21

narrative non fiction 6
narration 38–9, 47, 82, 100, 105, 112–6, 127–8, 247, 268–71
narrator 30, 99–100, 109–16, 122, 128, 183, 246–52
natural inquiry 75
negotiated Integrated Curriculum 6, 210–12, 224, 228–34
new literacies 16, 63–4, 106, 163
non linear narrative 128
non traditional texts 98, 104, 127–9

objects 14, 28, 35–41, 75, 86, 120, 127–8, 146–51
observation based pedagogies 62
oral storytelling 73

parody 127, 143–7, 155–65
people study 202
performance 59, 99, 106, 119–25, 203, 213
peritext 40–2
personal histories 103
personal literacy 76–7, 103–4, 124
personal resonance 5, 98, 103, 113
philosophy for children (P4C) 243
photography 14, 18
picture books 14, 41–50, 67–8, 82, 147
plot 80, 103, 127, 144–9, 223–6, 262–9
podcasts 165, 193
poetry 49, 80–2, 119–22, 135, 155–65

popular culture 193, 211–2, 223–34
positionality 174, 181, 231
primary sources 117, 175, 183–6, 191, 203
project based learning 117, 126
psychology 195, 265

questioning 30–1, 50, 62–4, 77, 140, 186, 260

read aloud 5–6, 73, 99–101, 121–2, 137–8, 153–62
reader response criticism 108
reader's theatre 119, 122
reader writer relationship 82
reading for pleasure 136–38, 152–4
reciprocity 136, 210, 216, 234
reflection 31–3, 62, 115–29, 177–81, 242–52
remembrance and memory 46, 60, 98, 103, 119–23, 152
remix 141–64, 201
representation 4, 14–21, 85, 141
research based approaches 232
restorative justice 274
rhyme 144, 155–63

sculpture 14, 18, 26, 39, 61, 127
self inquiry 77
self portraiture 74–5, 90, 185
sensuous knowing 57, 63
Serafini, F 19, 35, 41–2, 52
setting 38, 74, 164, 185–8, 227, 262
Shapiro, KJ 135, 155–61
shared histories of reading 64
Short, K 3–7, 101, 133, 176
situated learning 63
skills 17–21, 134–43, 160–3, 256
soap opera 67–8, 76, 223
social change 180–6
social literacy 107, 126
sociopolitical 3
sound 38–9, 71–2, 82, 99, 119–24, 156–64, 223–6
storyboards 38–9
story fragments 24–40

talking 50, 97, 118, 218
Tan, S 24–41
technology 135–6, 163–5
theatre 26–7, 119, 122–6, 202–3
threshold concepts 241
time capsule writing 117

283

Index

top down approaches to reading 70
translation 100, 117, 123

upside down stories 85–7

values 2–8, 25, 63–71, 143, 185–6, 212–17, 237–42
verse novel 45, 49, 58, 77–89
video 50, 89, 120, 154, 164, 199, 232
virtual spaces 141, 152
vocabulary 4, 7, 17, 72–6, 109, 122

ways of knowing 21, 193–1, 230, 237–45, 253–4
Wenger, E 104, 121, 193, 216, 221
Wild, M 41–51
workshop based approaches 85–6, 126, 154, 225, 268
world building 145, 151

Zepf, M 58, 76–90
Zipes, J 152
Zipin, L 237–45, 253–4

For Product Safety Concerns and Information please contact our EU
representative GPSR@taylorandfrancis.com
Taylor & Francis Verlag GmbH, Kaufingerstraße 24, 80331 München, Germany